Bubba Haupt:

Since the first day of his first grade in elementary school in Savannah, Georgia, the author has been called 'Bubba'. For the past nine years, Bubba has been busy assisting attorneys with complex litigation in state and federal courts in Georgia. He is an avid fan of the University of Georgia Bulldogs and Benedictine Military School. Haupt's history, legacy, and heart are deeply embedded among the oak trees and moss of Savannah and Wilmington Island.

Teresa Ward:

Teresa Ward, a retired university researcher, is a world traveler who has settled in the beautiful mountains of North Georgia, where she is an avid runner and hiker. Dr. Ward is the author of numerous journal publications and is currently working on another book.

Haupt:

To the late Caroline and Ted Ridlehuber, whose constant encouragement inspired me to finish the manuscript. To my family, whose patience and love endured the events of this book. To my brother in faith, Rev. Bobby Gale, and his family, whose ministry (Unto the Least of His), serving the poor in under-developed countries, inspires me daily. To Matthew Washington, who has been serving time in prison since 1976 for a crime he did not commit. Hopefully, the publishing of this book will help get him pardoned during his lifetime.

Ward:

To my daughters, Wendy, Molly, and Christy. They are my heart.

Bubba Haupt and
Teresa E. Ward, Ph.D.

MOB ISLAND

AUSTIN MACAULEY PUBLISHERS™

LONDON ∗ CAMBRIDGE ∗ NEW YORK ∗ SHARJAH

A CIP catalogue record for this title is available from the British Library.

ISBN 9781398494596 (Paperback)
ISBN 9781398494602 (Hardback)
ISBN 9781398494619 (ePub e-book)

www.austinmacauley.com

First Published 2023
Austin Macauley Publishers Ltd®
1 Canada Square
Canary Wharf
London
E14 5AA

My son, Chris Haupt, worked hard and long hours assisting in getting this book to publication. His unwavering support and active promotion of the book resulted in numerous opportunities to advance the project forward. Dennis Barr, Clifford Meads, and the HOA of the Wilmington Plantation, formerly, the Savannah Inn and Country Club, for their unlimited access to the properties and support in compiling historical facts that are displayed in the book. Thanks to my co-author for making me prove everything I wrote and told her. Our research into the archives in Savannah brought it all back to me. Dr. Ward is a jewel.

Writing a book is never a solitary endeavor. So many people have contributed to the successful completion of this project. I am especially grateful to my daughter, Wendy Ward, who read through iteration after iteration of the manuscript and offered valuable advice on all aspects of writing. I cannot overstate how much I have benefited from her degree in English. Many thanks to Jer Anderson for his helpful comments on the manuscript and his enthusiastic support. I, too, would like to thank Chris Haupt for all his help and support.

We thank Jameson Campaign for his support and for introducing us to Dara Ekanger, who helped in editing the manuscript. We also thank the editors we worked with at Austin Macauley Publishers.

Table of Contents

Foreword

When I first met Bubba Haupt, he told me he was writing a book on his experiences as a lawyer for the Mob. It wasn't that he was *writing* about the Mob that startled me, but that his name was Bubba, and that he had been a lawyer for the Chicago Mob. Really? The Mob had a lawyer named Bubba? I was intrigued.

Bubba asked me to read his manuscript and I found his stories to be remarkable, but I wanted to know more. As an anthropologist, I wanted to know who he was, how he felt and what he knew. I wanted to know *his* story. And boy, does he have a story.

Bubba takes us into the private dealings between the Teamsters and the Chicago Mob—better known as the 'Outfit.' No longer under Omerta (a code of silence and honor), he gives us an accounting of his close friendship with Outfit member Louis Rosanova (pronounced 'Louie') and meetings with such significant figures as 'Uncle Sam' Giancana, 'Big Tuna' Accardo, Allen Dorfman, Johnny Roselli, Santo Trafficante, and Frank Fitzsimmons. He also relates an explosive confrontation between Lou Rosanova and Dean Martin. Bubba contributes to the growing body of evidence suggesting that there was a second shooter in the Kennedy assassination, gleaned from his conversations with actual participants. The most explosive revelation, though, concerns the contents of a mysterious package that arrived by plane on Mob Island. Bubba eventually learned what the package contained and discloses the final resting place of Jimmy Hoffa.

More importantly, Bubba gives us stories that resonate today. Bubba was one of only two trial attorneys in South Georgia qualified, under the rules of the US Supreme Court, to defend death penalty cases back in the seventies and eighties. There was no public defender system at that time. Through the depiction of a number of defendants and their trials, this book takes an unflinching look at the injustices and carnage perpetrated by a profoundly uncaring justice system, where money and power determined one's fate. It looks at the underbelly of a judicial system that eats its young. Such was also the fate of Haupt. It eventually destroyed his family and career.

Bubba was an intellectual and spiritually progressive visionary who cared deeply about the economic disparities in his community. He was also an utterly brilliant attorney. Over time, however, the cases he was asked to take—compounded with his work for the Teamsters and the Outfit—took its toll. His life reflects the way many of us operate in the world: we have strong principles, yet harbor weaknesses that make us who we are—epitomizing the human condition of strength, frailty, and redemption.

Enjoy his stories because they will make you laugh and they will make you cry. You'll shake your head and say these events could not have happened, but they did.

Teresa Ward, Ph.D.

Prologue

The Beechcraft King Air set down on the grass runway of a small island three miles southeast of Savannah, Georgia, just before sunset. Using most of the 3,400-foot runway, the plane came to a bouncing stop just short of the trees that bordered the airfield. Turning, it taxied several hundred feet towards a dark-colored Ford van waiting with its rear doors open. The van's two occupants waited at the rear of the vehicle. They wore colored polo shirts and beltless slacks, the golfing attire of the day in the coastal south.

The twin-engine plane had flown from a private airfield near Detroit, Michigan, with a pilot, one passenger, and a large package. The door swung open and the steps unfolded down. The men on the ground quickly ascended the stairway, retrieved the package, and carried it out to the waiting van. They shook hands with the pilot and passenger, then quickly drove away. Minutes later the plane sped down the grass runway of Saffold Field, disappearing into the moonlit night. The package had been delivered to this insignificant island under the cover of darkness, where it remained. It held the key to solving one of the more enduring mysteries in American culture: where is Jimmy Hoffa buried?

Now that all the major participants in this story are deceased, and attorney/client privilege is no longer a consideration, it is time to tell the story, the real story, about the package and how a young and ambitious Savannah lawyer became a top attorney for the International Brotherhood of Teamsters and the Chicago Mob.

Saffold Field, Wilmington Island, Savannah, Georgia

Photograph courtesy of Paul Freeman: www.airfieldsfree

1. Growing Up in Savannah

As the baby boy of Milly and Reginald Haupt Sr., I had every opportunity to turn out right; to be the dentist or Baptist preacher my mother wanted, or the All-American football player my father considered my destiny. Instead, I became one of the top lawyers for the International Brotherhood of Teamsters and the Chicago Cosa Nostra. This is my story and the story of how a shadowy group of men changed American history, Savannah, and me.

Considering my background, it was more likely that I would become governor of Georgia than one of the top lawyers for the Chicago Mob. I was born into a religious family. My mother was a Sunday school teacher at Calvary Baptist Church, the largest Baptist church in Savannah. She believed in the biblical instruction that if you teach a child in the way he should go, he will never depart from it. Whenever the church doors opened, our family was there. As Milly watched proudly, I recited the entire first chapter of Genesis before the church congregation one Sunday morning, the first indication that I had a photographic memory that would serve me well the rest of my life.

After skipping the seventh grade, I attended Benedictine, a small military Catholic school where my father had become a football legend in the early thirties. My father was 'Bubber' and I was called 'Bubba.' I was expected to follow in his footsteps but could never score enough touchdowns to live up to his legend. Yet, I became the first non-Catholic student to be named Brigade Commander in the school's fifty-year history. As the star quarterback and the captain of the baseball and basketball teams, being Baptist didn't matter; I became the Irish and Catholic communities' high school hero. This experience shaped the rest of my life. The concept of inclusion became a cornerstone in the way I would practice law.

It was during high school that I had my first introduction into Savannah high society. I was asked to escort Barbara Pinckney to the Savannah Junior Debutante Ball. I don't think my mother knew that there would be dancing at the ball, otherwise she would never have let me go. Barbara was beautiful. She became my first love and the first girl I ever kissed. She came from a good, solid Catholic family, but she was a wild child. As first loves go, Barbara and I broke up, and I met Jean, who would eventually become my wife. But you never really forget that first love. Barbara graduated from high school, hopped a freighter to Europe, and eventually came back to Savannah as the renowned author and fitness expert Callan Pinckney. I stayed close to home.

In my junior and senior years at Benedictine, my father enrolled me in the American Legion National Youth Baseball Program. The program was headed by Lou Brissie, a former major-league player who selected outstanding high school players from across the country to participate. I played for the American Legion Post 36 team out of Savannah. I made my father proud when I was selected to the All-American Legion Team that would tour South America the following summer, but that didn't last long.

We were playing in Macon, Georgia, for the Georgia state title. Each time I came to the plate a crowd of Macon fans heckled me because of the publicity connected to my All-American status. After constant harassment for six innings, my father had had enough. He and a pastor from Savannah (whose son was pitching) went into the stands with baseball bats and threatened the people who questioned my heritage and my mother's chastity. While my father and the pastor accomplished their goals by silencing the hecklers, their behavior disqualified me from participating in the tour.

I forgave him for costing me my position on the tour. In fact, I was a bit proud of how he had handled the situation. Maybe that says something about my own notions around honor and revenge; notions that would inform my future. Although I didn't get the opportunity to travel with the team to South America, I was invited to a Cincinnati Reds baseball camp in Greenville, South Carolina, where I was offered a minor league baseball contract. After considering the offer, I decided not to report to the minor league team.

I received a nomination to West Point, but my father encouraged me to turn it down and accept a football scholarship to Wofford College in Spartanburg, South Carolina. He expected me to become a football star. At that time, Wofford was used by the University of Georgia (UGA) to develop young athletes who were not quite ready for UGA. I had the talent, but I was only sixteen and weighed 150 pounds.

Within a week, I had injured my knee. No longer able to play football, I left Wofford and returned home where I enrolled at Armstrong College in Savannah and captained the basketball team in my second year there. It was at Armstrong that I became the student body president and received the award for Outstanding Graduate. My mother's expectations were coming to fruition. I had become, not just an over-achiever, but a super-achiever and the blessing that God had promised her. I would become the professional she wanted, an accomplished dentist in Savannah.

After completing an associate degree at Armstrong, I enrolled as an undergraduate at the University of Georgia with the sincere intent to become a dentist and make mama proud. During my junior year, I took the dental program entrance exam at Emory University in a dismal dental lab room. The smell in the room—over the course of several exam hours—was awful and lingered long after I had left. I was accepted into the program, but the thought of smelling that odor for another four years and then having to look into the mouths of people who had just finished breakfast was enough to give me the strength to go against my mother's wishes. She was not pleased, to say the least.

A couple of days later, I drove over to Athens and saw some of my fraternity brothers sitting on the porch of the Pi Kappa Alpha house. They were filling out entrance forms for law school, and I could see how excited they were. It was at that moment that I decided to become a lawyer. To my mother's chagrin, I was accepted into the Lumpkin School of Law program at the University of Georgia. After earning a bachelor of science, I remained at UGA and began my legal studies. I had never wanted to be a lawyer, but I had really never wanted to be a dentist either, so I took the road less troublesome at the time.

Regardless, I was required to achieve no matter the odds. I never questioned whether I would win or lose; I would win. This attitude informed not just my personal life but also formed the basis of my accelerated success as a criminal trial lawyer. I passed the state bar exam at the age of twenty-one and was appointed to my first murder case at the age of twenty-three. I won it. The race to the top was on. Little did I know what it would ultimately cost me to cross the finish line.

Bubba's mother, Milly Willis Haupt

Bubba's father, Reginald C. Haupt Sr., "Bubber" Haupt

Bubba on the Island

Bubba as Brigade Commander at Benedictine

2. The Savannah Inn and Country Club

General Sherman did not burn Savannah in his fiery march through Georgia. Instead, he burned Atlanta. He gave us as a Christmas gift to President Lincoln. Some have said over the years that Sherman burned the wrong city, but I disagree. Savannah had unique historical associations that Atlanta did not have at that time. For example, the State of Georgia had its birthplace on the Savannah bluff in 1732, and Savannah became Georgia's first capital city. Savannah sits on the shores of the Atlantic Ocean as far east as one can go in Georgia and not get wet. No other city in the South can boast of thousands of beautiful ancient live oak trees festooned with cool scarves of grey Spanish moss ravished by centuries of oceanic storms, looming over the many town squares surrounded by unburned antebellum mansions and old-South customs.

At the heart of the historic city sits Forsyth Park and its famous fountain and monuments. This was the center of Savannah life, where parades began and ended and where families gathered at Easter to hunt eggs. Couples got engaged and married at the fountain. Sunday strolls were a way of life. And there were pigeons, thousands of pigeons; more pigeons than Baptists. Children and adults came to the park with bags of peanuts to feed the pigeons. They were as much a part of Savannah as the inhabitants. So Lincoln would receive the right gift at Christmas if he wanted an aristocratic, European-inspired Southern city, replete with the air of condescension that would eventually attract millions of tourists to worship at the feet of the many monuments glorifying historical battles of the past. He also received a city that seldom permitted an outsider to gain hold of any significant authority or distinction until a hundred years later when the largest labor union in the United States took root under the beautiful oaks of one of the many islands surrounding Savannah, while the protectors of the revered past slept.

In 1926, Henry Walthour constructed a beautiful Spanish-style hotel on the banks of the Wilmington River, a short distance from the Atlantic Ocean and nine miles from the city center. By 1972, the stucco hotel was eight stories tall and contained an elaborate ballroom with great chandeliers not seen in this day and age. Everything was elegant and fashionably large, from the marble foyer and lobby to the penthouse suites. The grounds were vast, containing a finely manicured eighteen-hole golf course, several tennis courts, and an Olympic-sized pool with platform high dives overlooking the beautiful Wilmington River. Spanish and royal palms, along with great and ancient moss-covered royal oaks, adorned the grounds and provided a sight unseen anywhere on the Eastern Seaboard, or in the South. Its original name was The General Oglethorpe Hotel, named after General James Oglethorpe, the founder of Savannah.[1]

In the late sixties, the International Brotherhood of Teamsters, through its Central States' Pension Fund, quietly acquired the hotel and property through foreclosure and set out remodeling the entire complex, renaming it the Savannah Inn and Country Club. To the general public and the US Department of Justice at the time, the intent of the developers was to provide one of the best golf vacation venues on the East Coast. To those involved, it also was an elaborate scheme for money laundering and a safe method for providing cash benefits as kickbacks to prominent union officials, the Chicago Mob family, and their friends.

They succeeded in making the complex a unique destination golf venue by hosting major golf tournaments during the late sixties and early seventies until 1972 when Jimmy Carter, as governor of Georgia, established a crime commission to investigate the activities of the 'Mafia' at the complex and its ties to the Teamsters.[2] Needless to say, this event quickly woke up the slumbering fathers of this historic aristocratic city, and the city was never the same again.

Sometime during 1969 or 1970, a Chicago native known as Lou Rosanova was sent to the inn to be the executive director and general manager. Rosanova's arrival brought mixed reviews. The elite leaders and politicians thought that his 'Mafia' influence would hurt the reputation of their sacred city, while the middle-class golfers and 'regular people' were excited and flocked to the newly refurbished golf course.

Lou Rosanova was an imposing man. He stood around six foot two and weighed at least 250 pounds. His hands were large and his fingers thick, and when he shook your hand, it was as if he were holding onto a five iron; your hand would disappear into his only to re-emerge somewhat crushed, if he liked you. His broad shoulders and muscular arms bespoke of his alleged time as a linebacker for the Chicago Bears.[3] His thick black hair and dark complexion denoted his Sicilian background. He resembled Dean Martin—the prevailing heartthrob of the time—if Martin had played football without a facemask. Like Martin, Lou had a good singing voice, which I only heard on rare occasions when he had had too much vodka or made a difficult putt on the golf course. He was an impeccable dresser, never seen without his dark-blue blazer with brass buttons, an open silk shirt, and gold chain with a gold nugget around his bull-like neck. He looked just like how we thought a Mafia member would look. Strangely enough, Rosanova became a local celebrity.

Contrary to Governor Carter's crime commission, Lou Rosanova was not a Chicago Mob boss hiding from the federal government. Indeed, he was well qualified to run the inn because of his expertise in golf course design and maintenance. Furthermore, he had a history of turning other Teamster properties from losing propositions into profitable ventures. He was a 'scratch' golfer, and he eventually set the course record from the championship tees (blue tees) with a score of sixty-four. However, his greatest asset to the Teamsters and the other related organizations was his close relationships with major celebrities such as Dean Martin, Frank Sinatra, Vic Damone, the Broadway star John Raitte, and Buddy Hackett, just to name a few. I remember when John Raitte would visit the inn, his daughter, Bonnie, often would join him. Of course, she became as famous as her father as a singer and songwriter.

It was also helpful that Lou was friends with some of the top professional golfers at the time. Raymond Floyd, World Golf Hall of Fame inductee, spent time at the Savannah Inn and considered Lou to be a decent fellow, smart, and fun to be with.[4] Lou's purpose was to attract major golf tournaments and vacation packages from major cities in the Midwest and East using his known connections and celebrity power. I discuss his other unique qualifications later.

From my personal observation beginning in 1971, Lou accomplished his goals because of the many golf tournaments hosted at the complex. Although I had heard many rumors of the 'Mob' owning the Savannah Inn and being run by a guy named Rosanova, I did not meet Lou until 1972 when one of my best friends, the mayor of Savannah, John Rousakis, invited me to a round of golf with him and Lou. I accepted because I was curious whether the rumors were true about the Mafia, and I loved playing golf with my buddy the mayor. So, on that bright Saturday morning, I became one of the many friends of Lou Rosanova, and my life took a new and unexpected turn at the age of thirty-three.

I would eventually lose my naiveté and the bliss of being just a simple Southern trial lawyer who enjoyed defending impossible cases that would often irritate the self-absorbed fellow blue-bloods in my sleepy historical hometown.

The famous fountain in Forsyth Park, Savannah

The Old Chatham County Courthouse, Savannah

3. The Young Southern Lawyer

Until the first round of golf I had with Lou, and even long after, my time was mostly taken up with murder trials and politics. The murder trials were the worst you could imagine. From a man throwing a two-year-old little girl off the 136-foot high Talmadge Bridge; to a couple of marines on wild mushrooms kidnapping, raping, and shooting two nurses in the head; to a jealous crazed ex-husband who killed his wife and two innocent bystanders in a downtown bar. At that time in my life, I handled more murder cases in Georgia than any other attorney, and that record probably still stands.

On the political side, I was active in the Georgia Jaycees, served as president of the Savannah Jaycees, and was a national director of the United States Jaycees. This organization of men under the age of thirty-six was one of the most powerful political activist organizations in Georgia. I was named the Most Outstanding Young Man in Savannah (The Desbuillion Cup). In 1972, I ran for the Georgia senate opposing a six-term incumbent, losing by only 134 votes. I was popular, respected, and well-connected in local and state politics, as well as being considered one of the best trial lawyers in Georgia. Thus, I became attractive to the Teamsters in order to counter the Georgia State Crime Commission's interest in the Savannah Inn and Country Club. The Teamsters needed local flavor, a local 'star on the rise' with a 'can't miss' brand; I was the one chosen. I guess I gave them a new and unexpected fresh look.

On the morning of the state senate race election, I was given a handwritten note by one of my campaign workers. The note was on a plain white sheet of paper, and read, 'Good luck, [signed] Big Lou.' I only knew of one 'Big Lou,' and that was Lou Rosanova. On the night of my senate race defeat, Mayor Rousakis and Lou met with me late in the evening after my supporters had gone home. Lou offered to cover any campaign debt I had, which was none, and he assured me that he would make certain that I had the funds to take another run at the seat in 1974. I told both of them that I was no longer interested in seeking

23

political office and would concentrate on my law practice. This is when Lou asked me to represent the International Brotherhood of Teamsters. Without giving it much thought, I accepted, and we set a date for me to meet with the Teamster officials at their complex at the Savannah Inn and Country Club.

1972 state senate campaign flyer

4. The International Brotherhood of Teamsters

During the seventies, the single most powerful labor union in the United States was the International Brotherhood of Teamsters, headquartered in the 'Marble Palace' in Washington, DC. Understanding who they were when I began representing their interests in the Deep South, and their significance in American politics, is important to my story.

Until I started representing them, I never knew what the term 'teamster' meant. I don't credit this to ignorance, but rather to my lack of interest. When I asked Lou about the term after they had hired me, he looked at me in amazement and told me that a teamster was a truck driver or a person who drove a team of draft horses. So, teamsters meant 'truck drivers.' However, not meaning to correct my friend Lou, I did some homework a few days later and soon learned that not all Teamsters were truck drivers. By the seventies, the rank and file numbered 1.5 million and consisted of truckers, airline workers, maintenance workers, hotel employees, and many public- and private-sector workers. It was by far the largest labor union in America and Canada.[5]

Needless to say, the power they wielded controlled the economy of the greatest nation on earth. Without the approval of the Teamsters, no trucks moved and no airlines flew. No oil or gas could be transported from the refineries to the pumps, and that automatically would shut down automobiles, garbage trucks, and most jobs in America. That was real POWER! And, they had it at their disposal.

Because of the power and influence the Teamsters had in major industries, they became a major player in politics in Washington, DC. They spent more and lobbied more than any other single organization in the country. Getting the Teamsters support in money and the voting power of 1.5 million families was very significant in getting elected—locally or nationally. Savannah, however, was not a 'union' city and had very little labor union clout in its local elections. Otherwise, I might have considered another run in a state race.

Unfortunately, with power and unimaginable wealth came corruption. And the Teamsters, since the early fifties, has had their share. When they came to Savannah to play or for meetings, the men that I met with, played golf with, and partied with, did not maintain their silence regarding power, politics, and kickbacks. Neither were they silent on the private unsecured loans they made to prominent people within the union ranks, as well as the well-connected people who helped their causes. For example, on many occasions, I was privy to conversations Lou Rosanova had with Teamster officials regarding the worthiness of 'off-the-books' loans. Lou told me that the Mafia never made loans with their money; it was always Teamster money. My understanding was that loans to various people or entities affiliated with the Mob were made by the Teamsters' pension fund. The Mob did not maintain large bank accounts due to the risk of leaving money trails that federal officials could follow.

One of these officials was Allen Dorfman, the titular head of the Teamsters' health fund. Dorfman was a former marine who had been awarded a Silver Star for heroism at the Battle of Iwo Jima in World War II. He had returned from the war and earned a college degree from the University of Illinois. He became an attorney and a very close friend of Jimmy Hoffa in the early days of the rise of the Teamsters.

In 1949, Dorfman had formed the Union Insurance Agency, and with the help of Jimmy Hoffa, then president of the Teamsters, he gained an exclusive contract to provide health and welfare insurance for the Teamsters Central States' union members. By the mid-fifties, Dorfman had become involved in approving real estate and unsecured loans from the Teamsters Central States' Pension Fund for high-ranking union officials, and eventually for organized crime figures and their friends. In this position, Dorfman acquired vast wealth and influence that he frequently used on behalf of himself and his close friend, Hoffa.[6]

When I came on the scene in 1972, Dorfman had just been convicted for jury tampering and was serving his one-year sentence in federal prison. On his release in April 1973, I was introduced to Dorfman by Lou on the practice tee at the Savannah Inn. My first impression of Dorfman was not a good one. On introduction, he did not smile, which was not acceptable in the South in that day and age. His handshake was weak, and he withdrew his hand quickly. His eyes gave me a cold, hard stare. All the instincts I had cultivated growing up were activated; I knew that I should not trust or turn my back on this man.

Within minutes, the three of us left the tee area and went to the clubhouse where Lou explained to me why the meeting was taking place.

"Allen's down here to play golf and get some advice. He just got outta the joint, but the government ain't satisfied. He got word they're looking at embezzlement. I wanted him to talk to you. He can't trust the Chicago lawyers. I told him you'd take a look at it."

Still looking at Dorfman's steely eyes and knowing full well that I would not believe anything this man said, I agreed to review the file he placed on the table—not because I wanted to, but only out of respect for my friend Lou.

We met several times that week and the subject matter broadened to Jimmy Hoffa. Hoffa had been convicted of jury tampering, bribery, and fraud. He was sent to federal prison. President Nixon pardoned Hoffa in 1971 under the condition that Hoffa would not seek to regain his position as president of the Teamsters. In defiance of the pardon condition, Hoffa was pressuring union officials to support him at the next convention to oust Frank Fitzsimmons, the current president and a close friend of Lou's.[7]

Since Dorfman was a loyal Hoffa supporter, he was suggesting that Lou switch his support to Hoffa. Lou was in a bad situation because he was an employee of the Central States' Pension Fund and ultimately his friend, Fitzsimmons. To make matters worse, Dorfman had control of the private lending of the fund, and he offered, while I was present, to give an unsecured loan to Lou to purchase a golf course in South Miami for his (Lou's) retirement.

One afternoon, after many discussions with Dorfman, both on and off the golf course, Lou asked me to ride nine miles to Savannah Beach to pick up a friend. When we were finally alone riding to the beach, Lou said, "Cracker, we're not picking anyone up. I had to take a break. Do you understand what Dorfman is asking me to do for a lousy golf course for me to die on? Frank Fitzsimmons has been my friend for years and asking me to betray him is like asking me to betray my mother. I can't do that. It was Frank that got Hoffa out of prison on the pardon. How come Hoffa can't just keep his word to Nixon and the Teamsters? Where's his honor? I never liked him to start with. He's never had any loyalty."

Then he paused, "Cracker, Hoffa is messin' with fire. And, Dorfman, he's fanning the flame!"

Lou wanted me to say something, I thought, but he didn't ask. My thoughts were on my new nickname and I was amused: 'Cracker.' The name references rural Southern mule-drivers who, in order to make a mule move, cracked a whip. I wasn't offended. To me, it was another example of Lou wanting to talk 'Southern'. Finally, after blowing off some more steam, Lou changed the subject. "What do you think of the new investigation? He got trouble?"

"Lou, the fact that they are still investigating Dorfman means that he has trouble. They'll keep at it until they get him again. Apparently, they were not satisfied with him getting only one year to serve."

"The ghost of Bobby Kennedy is still after him. They hated each other and I'm on Dorfman's side on that," continued Lou. "Maybe I'll talk with Accardo and get him to cool this thing down. What do you think?" Lou was referring to Tony 'Big Tuna' Accardo who was the head of the Chicago Mob (better known as the Outfit). With one phone call, Accardo could control Dorfman because of Dorfman's reliance on the Outfit's protection.

Without knowing what I was talking about, I quickly responded, "That's a good idea."

We pulled back into the inn's parking lot, and I told Lou that I had something that I had to do. He looked at me with questioning eyes and said he would see me at dinner with Dorfman.

The next time I saw Dorfman, however, was in Chicago during a trip to take the depositions of the *Playboy* magazine editor in a libel suit I had filed in federal court on behalf of Lou, and I'll get to that soon. That was in late 1975, a couple of months after Hoffa disappeared from the parking lot of a restaurant in Bloomfield Township, Michigan, just outside of Detroit. We had arrived in Chicago a day early just to meet with Dorfman. On the plane, Lou told me that Dorfman was mad and scared. Knowing better, I did not ask why.

Lou was in a good mood, unlike the last time I'd been with him and Dorfman in Savannah. At this meeting, Lou knew that he was in charge instead of Dorfman. As Lou sipped his vodka and played gin with me on the plane, he opened up.

"Cracker, Dorfman is scared shitless. He knows why Hoffa bought the farm. He broke the deal with Nixon and disrespected everyone that had a part. If we'd let him get away with it, who would've dealt with any of us in the future? Dorfman wants to know if it's over and he can't get anything from Big Tuna.

Big Tuna's silence is deafening to him. The sucker thinks he's next." Which, in fact, he was.

As usual, I let Lou talk without my responding except with my eyes. Besides, Lou didn't want me to respond or get involved, plus, he would have never taken my advice on such personal matters like killing someone. Legal advice was my expertise and what I was around for, thank God! To both of us, my silence was golden.

I sat outside Dorfman's office talking with his pretty young receptionist while Lou met with him. After two hours of endless conversation with the woman, Lou finally came out with Dorfman. Unlike before, Dorfman smiled at me as he shook my hand and apologized for the length of time I had had to wait outside. He told me that he was looking forward to seeing me in the spring when the pension fund trustees met in Savannah. I smiled back as chills ran up and down my spine. I didn't trust the man. I didn't like Dorfman's smile any more than I had liked his steely stare when we'd first met.

Going down to the main floor in the elevator, Lou summed up the meeting: "He approved my loan to get the golf course in South Miami and told me that I didn't have to pay it back. He said he would lose the paperwork as long as he lived." Lou chuckled and said, "That means that I'll have to pay it back pretty soon."

He reached into his inside coat pocket and took a check out of an envelope. "Cracker, he wants me to buy a new Mercedes when we get home."

I saw Dorfman the next spring on the golf course at Dino's, the popular nightclub on the premises of the Savannah Inn, and again a couple of months later. In 1981, Dorfman was indicted for embezzlement and eventually convicted. Just prior to his sentencing he was shot eight times and died in a Hyatt Hilton parking lot in Lincoln, Illinois, on January 23, 1983. Newspapers speculated that Dorfman was killed because he was planning to give the government information on the death and burial of Hoffa.[8]

I never had the chance to ask Lou about such speculations because Lou retired to his golf course retreat in South Miami Beach the year before Dorfman was killed. However, I did get the chance to see and meet with Accardo many times in the coming years at the Savannah Inn and Country Club before and after Lou retired. Those meetings concerned Hoffa and other hidden matters that are the subject of later chapters. But forgive me for getting ahead of my story.

Jimmy Hoffa (Photograph from Wikimedia)

5. The Chicago Outfit

Most people in the seventies knew the Mafia as the mobsters from 'up north.' But I found out that the Mafia was much more complex than that. *The Godfather* movies tried to educate us, but most Americans considered them as entertainment only.

Organized crime in America was basically divided into two factions in 1972. There were the five New York Mafia families that were separate and distinct from the Chicago family. The Chicago family was known as the Chicago Mafia, the Chicago Mob, or simply, the Chicago Outfit.

The Chicago Outfit was at its peak in the seventies with satellite families in the western states (especially the cities of San Diego, Los Angeles, and Las Vegas), as well as Florida and New Orleans, Louisiana. It was the Chicago Outfit that infiltrated the Teamsters and took control of the lucrative casinos in Vegas, Havana, Iran, and Central America. So, when most people talk about the Mafia— including me in this accounting—it is the Chicago Outfit that takes center stage.

With its origin in Sicily, the Chicago Outfit grew from the Prohibition years under the rule of Al Capone and George 'Bugs' Moran to its glory days of great power and wealth under Tony Accardo. Born Antonio Joseph Accardo in 1906, Accardo rose from a small-time hoodlum and driver for Al Capone to the head of the Chicago Outfit. He became the day-to-day boss as early as 1947 and assumed ultimate authority in 1972. In 1992, he died at the ripe old age of eighty-six of natural causes.[9]

Known by two nicknames, 'Joe Batters' and 'Big Tuna,' Accardo stepped back from public scrutiny in 1957 because of income tax investigations, and handed the day-to-day operations over to Sam Giancana, known to me and the employees and members of the Savannah Inn and Country Club as 'Uncle Sam.' Eventually, and for reasons we will discuss later, Giancana stepped down in 1966 to voluntarily exile himself to Mexico until his return in 1974 and his ultimate demise on June 19, 1975.[10]

When I met Accardo at the inn in 1973, I was confused as to what his real name was. Lou referred to him as 'Big Tuna,' while other guests of the hotel from Chicago and Las Vegas referred to him as 'Joe Batters.' Naturally, I asked Lou why the Godfather had two nicknames.

"Simple. Capone told him to whack two snitches. He beat 'em to death with a baseball bat at a dinner in their honor. That impressed Capone so much he named him Joe Batters," Lou explained.

"What about 'Big Tuna'?"

"Simple. He's on a fishing trip in Bimini and he lands a tuna that he says weighs over two hundred pounds. That's a world's record if you believe it. So we started calling him Big Tuna."

"What do you call him?"

Lou gave me a stern look and said, "Cracker, when I'm with him I call him 'Don Accardo.' When I'm talking about him, I call him the Big Tuna. If you're asking me what you oughta call him: Don Accardo. Nobody—and I say nobody—ever calls him anything but Don Accardo to his face."

Then Lou paused a moment and said, "I'm glad we had this talk, or you'd be lying alongside a lot of my old buddies. Cracker, you don't want that."

6. The First Case

Unbeknownst to me, Lou had done his homework before I was retained. He had gathered newspaper clippings on several of my high-profile criminal cases. He knew that my talent was in the courtroom and that I didn't yield to public opinion, because every case I handled offended the normal Southern-bred native, especially in Savannah, Georgia. He saw that the vast majority of accused killers I represented were black and that I fought to the end for each of them and ignored the personal ramifications that would follow.

One morning in mid-January of 1975, Lou invited me to the inn for lunch to discuss a legal matter. When I arrived at the clubhouse, Lou was sitting alone with a magazine lying in front of him. It didn't take me long to recognize the magazine as a *Playboy* edition. I could also see that Lou was not happy. He didn't stand up to shake my hand as he usually did, and he had a look on his face that I had never seen. He had his hands on the table and both were in tight fists. I sat down and nodded to Lou. Lou said nothing as he pushed the magazine over in front of me. He told me to turn to a certain page and read the featured article. I did, and it didn't take me long to understand why Lou was upset.

Playboy had a featured article about organized crime's part in the presidential pardoning of former Teamsters President Jimmy Hoffa in 1971. Specifically, the article referred to Lou as a member of the 'Chicago mob' who met with Teamsters President Frank Fitzsimmons and other known Mafia bosses secretly at the La Costa Health Spa in San Diego, California, that led to a deal with President Nixon to pardon Hoffa. The article claimed that Lou was quietly residing in Savannah, Georgia, at the Savannah Inn and Country Club securing the interests of the Teamsters and their connection with the Mob.[11]

His first words were, "I want to sue the bastards for libel!"

I was confused because truth was always an ironclad defense to libel. Still looking at the article, I replied, "Lou, truth is a defense to libel. If they can prove that you are a member of the Chicago family, you can't win."

With a stern look on his face, he replied, "They can't prove it! Who they gonna ask? How can they prove that I am? Besides, I'm just a Teamster, and I got a lot of friends in Chicago. What's wrong with that?"

"Lou, did you attend the meetings they are talking about in San Diego?"

"No, I was there playing golf with a couple of those guys and relaxing," he replied. "Besides, how would they know what we talked about over coffee or while we were on the golf course? None of my friends would ever give anyone the information they are writing about. Cracker, they've ruined my reputation. I can't let 'em get away with this."

Lou lifted another magazine from a chair next to him and put a *Penthouse* edition on the table. He opened it to a similar featured article about him, his buddies, the Teamsters, the Chicago family and the Savannah Inn. "I want to sue them, too!"

I knew then that his 'Cracker' lawyer was going to file two libel suits in federal court in the coming weeks on behalf of a well-known Teamster/Chicago family member that would claim that he was not a mobster and that no such meetings took place. Needless to say, I had a difficult task ahead. But that was not new to me.

At the end of our meeting, Lou said he would walk me to my car. As we got to the car Lou said, "Cracker, what upsets me more than the words they used is the fact that they put me in their porn magazines. That is an insult that I can't let 'em get away with! They've embarrassed me with my friends and family. I want to sue them for everything they're worth."

"Lou, in order to have a good libel suit, you have to show significant damages. Because of this article what have you lost? As an example, did you lose your job? Your wife? Property?"

Lou stood there silently thinking and then said, "What if the Teamsters were to meet with me and tell me I'm bringing too much heat on them and they want me to resign as the executive director?"

"Lou, that would be perfect. There would be significant damages."

I drove back to Savannah in somewhat of a confused state. I thought it would be an easy task for the magazines to prove Lou's connection to the Mafia from what little information that I had accumulated by reading newspaper accounts published by the Carter Commission. However, I had agreed to be his advocate and that was my life. Tough cases energized me, and this one would be no different. Besides, this was a case that no one would think that I could win and that was compelling. In other words, this was a case that I couldn't lose, regardless of the outcome.

The next day Lou delivered to my office a box containing $25,000 in colorful Bahamian bills that looked like monopoly money. I had no idea what the value was in US currency, so I called a friend at the largest local bank in Savannah. When he told me the value was approximately $24,900, I quickly dispatched one of my secretaries to the bank to deposit the money. So that this amount can be put in proper perspective, a new Chevy automobile cost about $7,000 in 1975. That means that this amount was equivalent to about $120,000 today. That was not a bad retainer, and it shifted his libel suits up to the top of my priorities.

The suits were filed the following week in the United States District Court in Savannah. Not only did we go after *Playboy* and *Penthouse*, we filed a suit against the American Broadcasting Company alleging $30 million in damages resulting from his forced resignation from his position as executive director of the Savannah Inn and Country Club.[12]

The local newspaper and television news outlets loved the notoriety Lou was bringing to the inn. For them, it was proof that Lou was a member of the Mob. This infuriated Lou that much more. Soon Ray Lukban arrived to take over the position of executive director, but Lou was still the man in charge, as far as I could see.

7. Getting to Know 'Louie the Tailor'

"It was not perhaps the warmest friendship in the world, they would not send each other Christmas gift greetings, but they would not murder each other."

Mario Puzo, *The Godfather*

With the filing of the lawsuits, I started spending more time with Lou. In addition to playing more golf with him, I was getting invitations to special events and meeting some people that I had only heard or read about. On many occasions, Lou brought me gifts from LA, Vegas, New York, and Chicago of nice sport shirts, watches, and golf shoes. I also became a VIP at the hotel, a member of the golf club, and a frequent visitor to the Savannah Inn's nightclub called 'Dino's Den.' You could say that we were becoming good friends.

Dino's Den was the watering hole for many famous and infamous characters. From its expansive rear windows, one could enjoy the beautiful sunsets over the Wilmington River that flowed in front of the hotel. The walls were dark wood and as you entered the large double doors, there was a striking thirty-foot mahogany bar to the left. If you were a friend of Lou's, you would be seated in the VIP area of the bar. Locals and guests of the hotel were seated in the dining and dancing area. Dino's was designed to reflect the historic look of the old Savannah riverfront. Models of old sailing ships decorated the walls. The bar was named Dino's in honor of Dean Martin, a good friend of Lou's.

Martin, along with a small entourage from Las Vegas and Hollywood, spent several of his birthdays with Lou at private parties that I attended, along with a few select friends whom Lou trusted. During these special occasions, Dino's would be closed to the general public and hotel guests.

I started noticing that Lou had a lot of personal friends who frequently took vacations at the inn. These guys could have easily been stand-ins for the actors in *The Godfather* movies and *The Sopranos* TV series. There was 'Lefty' from Miami who showed me and the rest of the bar customers at Dino's the six healed

36

gunshot wounds to his stomach. Although I became friendly with Lefty, I never knew or asked what his last name was, although the rumor was that he was a 'torpedo' (gangster hired as a bodyguard or hit man) from Miami. After about four or five weeks of Lefty's stay at the inn, he departed one night under cover of darkness after an angry Lou Rosanova told him to leave because he was drinking and talking too much. I never saw or heard of Lefty again.

Then there was the visit of Lucky Luciano's thirty-eight-year-old son who came to the inn for a week of golf and relaxation. Historians claim that Luciano had no children, but I prefer to believe Lou who personally knew Luciano and other children that he had sired. So that you will appreciate my desire to cooperate with Lou, and his request for me to entertain Lucky's son while he was at the inn, I want you to know who Lucky Luciano was and his place in history. He was one of the few members of the Chicago Outfit that I had actually heard of prior to meeting Lou.

Charles 'Lucky' Luciano was born in Sicily in 1897. He began his life of crime as a bootlegger during Prohibition in New York and Philadelphia. His first employer was the infamous Al Capone. Although he eventually climbed the ranks in organized crime and was instrumental in dividing the New York Syndicate into five families, I choose to remember him for what he did for this country during World War II.

On June 7, 1936, Luciano was convicted on sixty-two counts of pandering and was sentenced to a term of not less than thirty years and no more than fifty years in prison. In 1942, the United States Office of Navy Intelligence contacted Meyer Lansky, a long-time friend of Luciano, about making a deal with the New York Families. At that time during the Second Great War, the New York harbor was under serious threats of sabotage from German and Italian spies, along with the constant threat of union strikes.

A deal was brokered with the help of the New York crime family to secure the harbor and a promise that there would be no union strikes at the harbor during the war. Because of Luciano's influence in his native country of Sicily, Luciano agreed to aid the United States in securing cooperation in the towns of Sicily when and if an invasion occurred. Eventually, the invasion did occur and many towns cooperated with the American forces because of the Mafia friends of Luciano. This apparently saved many American lives.

Luciano was rewarded by the government commuting his sentence on January 3, 1946. The condition for the commutation was that Luciano be deported to Italy and not return to the United States. He died in Naples, Italy, of natural causes on January 26, 1962.[13] Because of Luciano's contribution to the war effort, he was highly respected by the Mafia.

Unfortunately, I was with Lou when Lucky Jr. arrived at the inn on a Saturday morning. I first saw him as he approached Lou in the golf shop. He was a slender medium-height man in what I thought to be his mid-thirties. He wore glasses and had features that put him on the ugly side. His large nose was surrounded by a pimply face with teeth that needed a lot of work. But you can't judge—or shouldn't judge—a man by his looks.

We were introduced, and Lou asked me later that day to take Junior out on the town and show him Savannah. Lou told me that he personally didn't care for the guy, but as a favor to a friend in Chicago, he would take care of him for the next week. So, that night Junior accompanied me to the Plantation Club in Savannah. What a mistake that was! The guy bullied several guys at the bar for no reason other than he was Lucky's son. He insulted their women and wouldn't take 'no' for an answer when he approached a few women to dance with him.

Eventually, I determined that the night had to come to an early end for my safety as well as Lou's friend. I made a call to Lou and told him of my intentions and why, and Lou agreed. He offered to send a car for Junior, but I told Lou that wasn't necessary. Shortly after hanging up with Lou, I gave the news to Junior that we had to go. Junior didn't agree with me and disappeared into the crowd near the bar. I said my goodbyes to several friends I had mingled with and went out the door to my car. When I approached my new Lincoln Continental in the parking lot, I noticed that it was sitting much lower than I had left it. Someone had slashed all the tires, and it wasn't hard figuring out the offender.

Junior was standing near the entrance to the club. He walked over to me and said with a smirk, "Looks like someone don't like you." Then he turned and walked back into the club. Livid, I found a phone and called Lou.

Within the hour a silver Mercedes sedan arrived with two of Lou's friends: Billy Kidd and a big guy in his fifties who looked like he had won a lot more barroom brawls than he had lost. As I found out later, 'Billy Kidd' was an alias used by Chicago mobster William Jahoda, who made millions over the years for the Outfit as a bookmaker. He would eventually turn on the Outfit and become a government witness.[14] But now he was here to rescue me. He and his friend found me standing near my crippled car. Billy was the first to speak.

"Bubba, we'll take care of this. Lou wants you to use another car to get home. It'll be here in a few minutes. We'll have your car in front of your house by dawn. Lou said he's sorry and that he owes you a favor for what happened."

With that said, Billy and his sidekick entered the club as another Mercedes pulled up and I got in. The next morning my car was in my driveway. I never saw or heard from Lucky Luciano's son again, and I was never asked to entertain another friend of Lou's. He had been embarrassed while granting a favor to a friend.

A few days after this weird event, Lou called and asked me to meet him at his cottage at the inn. As I approached the front door, Lou called out, "Come on in, Cracker!" When I stepped into the front foyer I saw Lou at a sewing machine sewing on what appeared to be one of his sport coats. Now, that was a strange sight. Can you imagine seeing the man that you and everyone in the world believed to be a top Chicago mobster sitting at a sewing machine sewing on a coat? I could never have imagined it, but it happened. Needless to say, I had a lot of questions concerning Lou's ability to sew and the fact that he was sewing. So, Lou let me in on one of his secrets.

Lou told me that as a kid growing up on the streets of Chicago, he had to have a job to help his family put his older brother, Frankie, though Notre Dame. He got his first job with Hart, Schaffner, and Marx where he learned to be a tailor, just like his father. As he got older and became a process server and an enforcer for the Chicago Family, he kept his part-time job as a tailor. He said that he loved it, and when he got mad, or very mad, he would take one of his coats and rip the sleeves or pockets off, and then ease his anger by carefully sewing it back together. He said it was mental therapy for him. Then he told me for the first time that on the streets of Chicago, and to his close friends, he had always been known as 'Louie the Tailor.'

"Cracker, I don't care to be called 'Louie the Tailor' down here in the South. I don't think they'll understand that I was a real tailor one time. So, let's keep this between you and me and Chicago, okay."

Of course, I had no problem with that and I assured him I would forget it. But I couldn't! From that time on, whenever I saw my client from Chicago, I saw 'Louie the Tailor.'

Lou Rosanova (Photo courtesy of *Savannah Morning News*[15])

8. The Police Are Banished

The Savannah Inn and Country Club was located within the corporate limits of Chatham County, Georgia. As such, the law enforcement agency in charge of keeping the peace and enforcing the laws of Georgia on the property of the inn was the Chatham County Police Department and the various departmental supervisors.

When Lou and the Teamsters arrived to take control of the property, the presence of the county police, and in particular its drug squad, was a common occurrence at Dino's Den. Knowing the rumors that were prevalent and swirling around the courthouse, I did not doubt that drugs were being distributed and minors were being served alcohol at the popular nightclub.

When I began representing Lou, I noticed from the outset that he did not like the frequent visits of the county police or the perks they were demanding when they were off-duty and enjoying themselves with their girlfriends or wives at Dino's Den. To these officers, it was normal to expect unlimited free drinks and sometimes dinners. After all, these were perks that the other clubs rendered, so why not Dino's?

It didn't take long for the county police supervisors to discover that Dino's Den was not just another nightclub. Neither did it take long for them to get the word that they were not welcome on property owned by the Teamsters and run by Louie the Tailor. While I don't know how the police initially learned they were not welcome, I do know the real reason they decided to stay away from the nightclub.

I received a call one morning from Lou approximately a week after my initial employment by him and the Teamsters. He asked if he could come down to my office around lunchtime. He told me that the county police had raided Dino's Den the night before and had arrested his favorite server. She was charged with serving alcohol to three minors. He sounded upset and refused to say anything further on an open-line telephone that he knew was tapped. Within an hour Lou was sitting in my office looking perplexed.

"Are you eating rotten peanuts?" he asked me.

I pulled another peanut out of the brown bag sitting on my desktop, put it in my mouth popping out the nut with my teeth and spitting the shell into my waste basket. "Lou, this is how we eat peanuts down here. There was never a week where my dad didn't boil a big pot of green peanuts. And he always told me that the more peanuts I ate, the smarter I would get. So, I eat these boiled peanuts whenever I'm working on a case. It opens my mind. Here, have some."

"Cracker, I ain't Southern enough to eat that shit. But if eating rotten peanuts helps increase your smarts, then have some more because I got cops trying to shut down Dino's. I want you to defend the girl and get her off, okay. If she's found guilty she can't serve alcohol again and Dino's will lose its license. That's a big hit."

He handed me the arrest tickets and invited me to lunch. I looked at the papers and noticed that the preliminary hearing was set two days away. I followed Lou out of my office and onto the street. As we walked, Lou began talking again.

"Cracker, they say you're the best. That's why we hired you. Win this and you'll get an extra bonus. We really need to beat 'em and Johnny [Mayor Rousakis] said you can do it."

Two days later, Lou brought the girl the county police had charged with the alcohol violation to my office. Ozella was a twenty-year-old dark-haired beauty. She was clearly Lou's favorite server. Lou told me every time the guys from Vegas and Hollywood came into town, they asked for her. Because of her beauty and Southern charm, she made a ton of money as Lou's best server. Ozella confided in Lou that when she'd been arrested, they had handcuffed her and placed her in a police car, driving her around the island while repeatedly offering to tear the tickets up if she would admit to being a hooker for Lou. Lou was livid when she'd told him about her ride with the officers. I could see that this was personal for him.

We went over the facts and then Lou and I accompanied her to the courthouse for the hearing. I told her to say nothing and that I would do all the talking. She seemed relieved. Lou was unsure if this was the best way to defend her since she looked like she would be a good witness.

An assistant district attorney called the case and quickly placed the arresting officer on the witness stand. The officer happened to be the head of the Chatham County Drug Squad and second in command of the Chatham County Police. His name was Billy Freeman. They had sent their top gun undercover to go after Lou's favorite. In fact, it appeared as a setup the longer the major testified.

When the witness was turned over to me for cross-examination, the county had established that three seventeen-year-old girls had each ordered a gin and tonic; that the major, seated at an adjacent table, had witnessed the order and Ozella bringing the drinks to them.

Before the girls could take a sip, the major had moved in and arrested Ozella. He'd handcuffed her, marched her out of Dino's in front of a packed Saturday night crowd, and hauled her off to jail in a waiting police unit.

I was convinced that it was no coincidence that Freeman had been seated next to the three young girls. To me, this was an obvious sting. Freeman had brought those girls into the club on a crowded night since the servers would be very busy and distracted. It was a perfect setup: except for one thing.

Then I began my cross-examination and it was easy pickings.

"Major, you said that the drinks contained alcohol. Is that correct?"

"Yes. The drinks contained gin."

"Major, did you take a sip of the so-called gin and tonics after they were served to the minors?"

"No. That's not allowed. An officer on duty can't drink any alcohol."

"Then, how can you swear that the drinks contained gin?"

"Because that is what they ordered. I heard them order."

"Did you see the bartender pour the gin into the glasses?"

"No. I didn't. I didn't have to."

"Who told you that?"

"No judge ever required us to taste the drink or test the substance," he angrily replied.

I turned from the witness and approached the judge's bench. "Your Honor, I move for the dismissal of the charges on the ground that there is no evidence that the beverages served to the minors contained alcohol."

The judge looked at the assistant DA and said, "Do you have any evidence that the beverages contained alcohol other than the major guessing at it?"

The assistant DA looked at the major and then back to the judge. "No sir. That's all I have."

The judge slammed his gavel and declared, "Case dismissed!"

Walking back to my office, Louie the Tailor had a smile on his face that sandpaper couldn't erase. "Cracker, you made a fool of that cop. I'm glad I was there to see it."

"Lou, the word will circulate through the courtrooms today that in the future, police will have to taste the liquor to make this type of charge. I know that the chief is not going to let his officers take sips all evening if they're staking out a bar. It's going to aggravate him and Freeman to no end. This hearing changed the rules because they messed with you and the Teamsters."

Lou chuckled at the thought that the cops had screwed themselves up by messing with him.

When we got back to the office and out of the hearing of the young server, Lou spoke softly and said, "Cracker, it ain't gonna stop here. They're gonna come at us in a different way. They're gonna try to plant drugs on the property."

"Lou, let me take care of some business and I'll meet you down at your cottage at six o'clock this afternoon, and I'll give you some information that will put you in control of the situation."

"Cracker, you give me good information, and I'll grill you the best steaks you ever ate." He turned and headed to his car where the delighted server was waiting.

Lou was standing near the bar, fixing drinks as I entered his cottage that evening, he handed me a Johnny Walker Red on the rocks. To those of you who don't know, this scotch is what made the Kennedys rich since they owned the rights to the US franchise. If Lou had known this, Dino's would have banned all Johnny Walker brands. I was not about to tell him, but I had to smile at the irony.

"Lou, not too long ago a county police lieutenant came to my office to ask me to represent him before the civil service board for wrongful firing. He had been fired by the police chief because he'd gone to a local bar after hours and demanded the bar owner serve him some drinks. When the owner refused, the lieutenant, whose name was Billy Fields, promised him that he would come back during the coming week and charge him with an alcohol violation. When the owner complained the next day, Fields was fired."

I continued my story as Lou brought the steaks to the table. "The same day he was fired, Fields came to my office to retain me. He had quite a story to tell."

Lou squinted and said, "Cracker, this place is full of bad cops." He took a sip of his scotch and waited for me to continue.

"Lou, Fields had something on the chief and the same Major Freeman we just whipped. He told me that the chief and Freeman ordered a lieutenant named Freddie DuBois to tap the phones of two county commissioners. He told me the reason for the taps was that these commissioners suspected there was missing money in the county police department. The taps were done and the tapes were saved. Fields told me that the chief and Freeman didn't know that he had copies of the tapes. Lou, if the commissioners found out about the tapes, the chief and Freeman would be fired on the spot and taken to federal court."

Lou listened intently as I continued, "Lou, there was no doubt in my mind that if Fields could back up his claim, he would quietly and quickly get his job back. I wanted to see and hear the tapes. I called the chief the next day and told him that Fields had a copy of some tapes and he wanted his job back. I told the chief that I didn't know what was on the tapes, but Fields said the chief would know. Lou, the chief told me he would rehire Fields and I should forget about the tapes."

Lou, after taking a few more sips of his vodka and lemon twist, smiled and expressed concern that it may not help him. Then he asked, "Cracker, is Fields still around?"

"Yep. He's still on the force and is now un-fireable. You know he got a new county car and doesn't have to come into the office because he has no assignments."

"Can I talk to him and maybe buy the tapes?"

"Lou, that's not necessary. I didn't charge him a fee. But I did get a copy of one of the tapes."

"Cracker, you got a copy?"

"Yep, and here is one for you!" I handed him the tape.

We had a few more drinks while we ate our 'Steak Rosanovas.' As he served me, I asked for some ketchup, which got a sharp glare and a shake of his head.

How Louie the Tailor handled the matter was never known to me. But what was clearly obvious was that I never saw the county police on the property of the Savannah Inn and Country Club again. They had been banished.

9. The LA Encounter with Dino

The *Playboy* and *Penthouse* articles mentioned that the source of the information concerning the secret meetings in San Diego was a retired federal Drug Enforcement Administration agent who lived in LA. We sought and obtained his name through the discovery procedure in federal court. Within days of obtaining the information, we scheduled to take his testimony in LA. Several days later, Louie the Tailor and I flew on Delta to California.

On the flight, I noticed that Lou was not in a good mood and was greatly disturbed about something. I asked him if he wanted to play gin, hoping to change the atmosphere and his attitude. Gin was the golf club's card game of choice back in that day and both of us were good at it, and both of us were intently competitive at winning. But after a few silent games, we gave it up. Lou kept his attitude, and since there was no sewing machine handy, I had to live with it until we landed. Hopefully, getting a chance to interrogate this 'lying' drug enforcement agent would perk my client up.

Once on the ground in LA, we headed to the baggage claim area, and to my surprise, I saw Dean Martin and an older black guy heading towards us. Martin was not as tall as he was depicted on TV and in the movies. He looked much older, and he was wearing a wrinkled sport shirt that was not tucked in like in the movies. I expected Lou and his buddy to give each other a big hug of greeting that included a good Dean Martin hug for Lou's lawyer, since this was a significant moment in my life (I had not attended any of Martin's parties at Dino's yet). But nothing of the kind happened. Instead, Lou told Martin's black friend not to touch our luggage or he'd "make cufflinks out of his eyeballs!" Then he turned to Martin and peeking through squinting eyes that could kill, Louie the Tailor, with an edge to his voice, said, "And you, if I knew where your mother's grave was, I would stomp on it!" I stepped back, not believing what I was seeing and hearing. I was stunned! But I wisely said nothing.

Martin was equally shocked at his old friend's demeanor and words. He replied, "Louie, what's going on? What's the problem?"

Lou gave no reply and handed me my baggage as he took his off the rotating conveyor belt. Lou waved down an airport aid and motioned for him to carry our luggage to the taxi area.

Martin, still puzzled, said, "Louie, it's me, your buddy, you got to tell me what I did to deserve this. We've stood up for each other for years."

Looking down on him, Lou stood inches from Martin's face and said, "You, my friend, are a fucking rat, and I suggest that you shut up and go home and never mention my name again."

Still stunned, I handed my luggage to the baggage carrier and headed with Lou towards a taxi, leaving a confused Dean Martin watching his old friend and his cracker lawyer walk away. We got into the taxi and Lou told the driver to take us to the Beverly Hilton Hotel. Louie the Tailor said nothing during the trip. He did nothing but scowl. I said nothing, believing that if I did my eyes would eventually be cuff links, and I didn't want that to happen to my kids' father.

When we arrived at the Beverly Hilton the bell hop knew Lou and welcomed him back to LA. Then he promptly carried our bags to an area next to the front desk. Lou motioned for me to follow him to the VIP lounge adjacent to the marbled lobby.

"I need a drink. Let's have a couple before we check in. I got to cool off. I can't let that jerk get under my skin. We got a case to win, right, Cracker?"

I welcomed his invitation and his desire to talk to me again. But I wanted to know what had set Lou off on Martin, and I hoped that he would eventually tell me after a few drinks. I had never been more curious in my life. Little did I know that all the answers would come before he'd finished his first drink.

Within minutes, I heard a very familiar voice coming from the entrance to the lounge. It was the voice of the jovial driver of "Herbie," the magical number 53 Volkswagen.[16] I turned as I heard him say, "Louie, did you bring me some new balls? I drowned the others!" Yes, the short chubby man walking towards where we were sitting in a corner booth was Buddy Hackett. His hair was disheveled, his polo shirt was hanging almost to his knees and he really looked in disarray. His face was one big grin as he approached Lou.

Lou got up, gave him a big hug, turned towards me, and introduced me as his 'cracker' lawyer from the South. Hackett shook my hand and with a big smile said, "Welcome to LA." He sat down and motioned for his 'usual', whatever that was.

Lou and Hackett chitchatted for a few moments and Hackett revealed why he had suddenly appeared at the VIP Lounge at the Beverly Hilton Hotel on a Sunday afternoon to see his old friend. Obviously, Dean Martin had called him and asked him to intervene, or at least find out why Lou no longer wanted a friendship with an old friend.

"Lou, Dean called and said you were upset with him, and he asked me to find out why."

Lou replied, "He knows why."

"Lou, he honestly ain't got a clue," Hackett replied.

Lou stared at Hackett and said, "Dean hung an old friend out to dry. That friend was me. He made me a liar in front of my guys in Savannah. He's got me ashamed to go to my own joint." Hackett got a serious look on his face and asked Lou to tell him about it so that he could be mad at Martin himself. I then heard the whole story, and here it is:

A few months before, a member of the golf club at the inn had told Lou that he was going to Las Vegas for a few days to play the tables and hopefully get a seat at one of Frank Sinatra's shows at Caesar's Palace. The guy had told this to Lou while several other local members had been sitting in the clubroom playing gin. Lou then told the guy that he didn't have to worry about that because he, 'Big Lou,' would set him up. Lou said that he would see to it that a limo would pick the guy up at the airport to take him to the MGM Hotel where his room would be comped and tickets to Sinatra's late show would be waiting for him. Lou told him to let him know what week he was going. The guy called Lou the next day and told Lou he wanted to go within the next two weeks on his birthday. Lou called a guy named Bobby Freeman, who was the CEO at the MGM, and told him of the local guy coming and told Freeman to take care of the limo, the room, and the tickets. Freeman told Lou he would handle it.

Where did Dean Martin fit in? Freeman worked for Martin, who owned the majority interest in the MGM. Freeman was Martin's guy like the local member was Lou's guy. It was also a man-thing with Lou because Lou often bragged of the clout he had in Vegas and this was the perfect occasion to show it to the members of the local club.

Unfortunately, for Dean Martin and for Lou's image, when the local member had arrived at the airport in Vegas there'd been no limo, no comped room at the

MGM, and no tickets to see Sinatra. So, when the member got back to Savannah after his trip failed, he came into the clubhouse where Lou saw him and made the mistake of asking the guy out loud if his guys had taken care of him in Vegas. Expecting the member to tell all the other members gathered that day that Lou's name was magic in Vegas, Lou instead received the news that no one had helped his guy at all.

Lou told Hackett that his guy couldn't stay on the Strip; everything had been booked, including all of Sinatra's shows for the week. "My guy had to stay at the Silver Dollar or something like that." Seeing Lou's face as he was telling of 'his guy's' plight, Hackett could see Lou's anger and embarrassment.

After a few moments, Hackett spoke. "Lou, did you call Freeman?" Lou was angered more, and said, "Why should I have to? He's Martin's guy. Martin should have taken care of it! Not me."

Hackett thought a moment and asked Lou if he could tell Martin, who happened to be waiting outside. Lou said, "Do what you want. I'm through with it and the jerk outside!" Lou motioned for another round for him and his cracker lawyer, who happened to be entranced over the whole scenario. Hackett got up and left the room to talk with Dean Martin.

After about twenty minutes, Hackett came back with Martin in tow. Before Hackett approached the booth, he asked the bartender to send a telephone to the booth where we were sitting. The bartender complied and sat a telephone on the booth table. Hackett approached and told Lou that Dean Martin had been in Europe when Lou had called Freeman. Lou quickly responded, "That don't matter. His guy should've taken care of it! You know the rules. Martin's responsible for his guys just as I am for mine. Don't give me 'I didn't know' shit!"

Martin, still standing near the booth, and hearing Lou's reply, spoke for the first time in the lounge, and said, "Lou, I want to fix this. I'm going to call Freeman and fire him."

That statement got Lou's attention, but he said nothing. Hackett adjusted the phone so that Martin could make the call while he was still standing. As Martin was making the call, I could see the beginning of a smile on Hackett's face. Then I saw Hackett pat Lou on the shoulder.

When Martin got Freeman on the phone, the conversation was short and straight to the point. "Why didn't you handle Lou Rosanova's call to comp one of his guys a few weeks ago? I'm in LA with Lou and he's hot, and I don't blame him. Get your shit together and get out!" With that said, he hung up the phone.

Lou looked up at Martin, who was still standing and smiled in agreement. Lou stood up and hugged Martin while Hackett and I looked on in relief. The crisis was apparently over, and Lou motioned for Martin to sit down. Martin motioned for another round for everyone, and his 'usual.' Lou, Martin, and Hackett started bringing each other up to speed as to what was happening in their lives as if they hadn't seen each other in years. After about an hour of many drinks, casual talk, and renewing old lies, Hackett went back to the subject of Freeman. I could see that Hackett knew what he was doing and had everything under control.

"Lou, what Freeman did was terrible and what Dean did was right. But I feel sorry for Freeman's oldest son at Notre Dame." The mention of Notre Dame (intentional on Hackett's part) caught Lou's attention.

"What about Notre Dame?" asked Lou.

"His son is a junior at Notre Dame and he'll have to come home. Ain't no way Freeman can afford to keep him there without a job. But that's not your problem. That's his. Dean did the right thing. The son has to pay for the sins of the father. That's the rule. Right?"

It was obvious to all that Hackett had struck a sensitive chord with Lou. I could tell Lou was disturbed with the thought of any kid having to leave Notre Dame because of the stupidity of the father. (Remember, Lou had helped put his brother through Notre Dame and Notre Dame was Lou's favorite school.)

As another round was being served to us, Lou asked for the phone. He told Martin to get Freeman on the line for him. Martin did and Lou began speaking to Freeman in a soft, fatherly tone, "Hey, they tell me you have a son at Notre Dame. That's a great school, and I admire you for paying the bill. I'm gonna tell Dean to give you a pass on the very serious embarrassment you caused me. I'm gonna send my guy back and I expect you to give him the house." Lou looked at me, then at Martin and Hackett. "The problem is handled and I'm satisfied. Let's have another drink to old Notre Dame."

With World War III over, Lou and I eventually checked in and the next day I took the testimony of the drug agent who denied under the oath that he had ever told *Playboy*, *Penthouse*, or anyone else that Lou Rosanova had been present at the meeting at La Costa. Then, we went home happy and content. Lou knew that I would tell everyone at the inn what I had witnessed in the VIP lounge at the

Beverly Hilton, and he knew that they would know how much clout he had in Vegas, and in particular, with Martin and Hackett. Lou was again the ego-driven 'Louie the Tailor.'

I also came to the conclusion that Buddy Hackett was much smarter than he looked. He knew what had to be done with the firing of Freeman and he also knew how to undo it. He knew that Lou would never approve a solution that required a kid to leave his favorite school, Notre Dame. He knew exactly how to reconcile his two friends and bring LA back to normal.

When we got back home, as expected, I told everyone who would listen about the incident in LA and the 'clout' that Lou had with the movie stars and the CEO of the MGM. However, I and many other members of the club couldn't understand why Lou had done this for the particular member who went to Vegas. That member was a guy no one would play golf with because he was notorious for dropping golf balls illegally and cheating in card games. We also knew that Lou didn't like him. But we all finally agreed that it was only a matter of pride and respect that the Mafia required of each other. Being a man of your word was foremost in their relationships.

Dean Martin (Photograph from Wikimedia)
Buddy Hackett (Photograph from Wikimedia)

10. OMERTA

One day in 1975, while I was embroiled in the libel suits against *Playboy* and *Penthouse*, I drove to the inn for lunch and a few games of gin. As I drove to an area where I usually parked, I noticed that there were very few automobiles in sight. For a midday Friday that was very strange. I looked at the golf course and saw no one. The place seemed deserted. I had never seen the Savannah Inn and Country Club deserted. Never!

I went into the clubhouse and the usual employees were working as if they didn't notice that they had no customers, or should I say members. I walked over to the clubhouse manager and asked her, "Where's everyone? Is the golf course closed? Where's Lou?"

She answered none of my questions. She just said, "Uncle Sam is coming!"

I had no idea who she was talking about because, at that time, I had never heard of 'Uncle Sam' except in reference to our beloved country. Furthermore, her response did not answer any of my questions and made no sense to me. I sat down and ordered a chili burger. While waiting for my food, Lou came in and motioned for something to drink. He sat down and knew exactly what I was about to ask.

"Uncle Sam will be here tonight. We've cleared out the hotel. The golf course is closed to everyone, including members." That told me nothing since I still didn't know who 'Uncle Sam' was.

I responded with the obvious question: "Who is Uncle Sam?"

Lou hesitated and quietly said, "You'll know tomorrow morning. You're going to meet him. Be here at 7:00 sharp. Don't be late."

Lou excused himself and said he had a lot of things he had to do. As he was leaving, I asked him one more question. "Lou, where are the guests in the hotel?"

He turned and said, "They all checked out this morning and the joint will be empty for the next five days." Becoming irritated with my inquiries, he left with these words, "Cracker, leave it alone until tomorrow morning."

I agreed, ate, and left, noticing that the staff appeared to be relieved.

Because of my unbridled curiosity, I could not leave it alone, so I drove from the inn to my most informative Italian source at a little restaurant named Anna's Little Napoli. This was the place where Lou ate when he did not dine at his own restaurants on the premises of the inn. This was also the place where he brought his 'special' guests from Chicago. To Louie the Tailor, Anna's Little Napoli was the closest to being good Italian food cooked the way food was supposed to be cooked.

The owner was Anna. Although I had eaten there many times before I knew Lou, and many times with Lou, I never knew her last name. But in the South that's not unusual. First-name basis was all that was required in good friendly relationships, and Anna was no exception.

Anna saw me as I walked in the front entrance. She was a small little lady, about fifty years old, dark complexion, and beautiful dark hair neatly arranged in a bun on the back of her head. And her personality matched her beauty. I had never heard anyone say a bad thing about her or her food. Lou swore by her.

As I walked over to where she was standing at the hostess station, she spoke first: "Hey, Bubba. What brings my lawyer to this humble establishment without your usual friends and Lou?"

"Business, I guess." This reply surprised her.

"Business? What kind of business? Monkey business?" she replied with her usual smile.

I motioned towards a door that had the word, 'Office' on it. She quickly walked over to it and we entered her office. "What's up?"

"Anna, who is Uncle Sam? Lou just told me he was coming to the inn tonight and that I was to meet him tomorrow morning. Who is he? Tell me something about him."

"Bubba, he's a Don. His name is Sam Giancana and he's the one that called all the attention to the family when he had a mutual mistress with President Kennedy. He ran the Chicago family until he went to Mexico a few years ago to escape the heat—and the bottom of Lake Michigan," she paused and then continued: "He's never been down here, as far as I know. Why would you have to meet him?"

"I have no idea, but Lou has made the appointment for the morning, early," I replied.

"There are hundreds of family members who are well connected who can't meet privately with him. That's an honor not extended to many. But be careful and speak only when spoken to. And, you don't want to know anything," she cautioned.

"Anna, I know the procedure. I just wanted to know what I was walking into. Thanks," I replied, just before she gave me a goodbye hug in her usual fashion.

She walked me to the door and once again told me to be careful. Then she said, "Bubba, don't get so deep that you can't get out. I don't want to lose my mouthpiece," she paused, then added, "and a good friend."

I nodded affirmatively and left.

'Uncle Sam' was the former Godfather of the Chicago family who had recently returned from Mexico where he had been self-exiled since 1966. Although he was not currently in power on this visit to Savannah, he was still a 'Godfather' and was respected as such until he was shot and killed in his kitchen on June 19, 1975.[17] Why he was coming, I had no idea, and I certainly was not going to ask anyone—including Lou—out of fear they would tell me. Remembering Anna's warning, I was nervous about the meeting. What did Uncle Sam have to do with me?

As I drove onto the inn property the next morning at a few minutes before 7:00, I noticed several Lincolns parked in front of the hotel. I drove past them to my parking area and stopped. I got out with my briefcase and was met by two oversized Italians. One frisked me while the other put my briefcase back into my car. They motioned for me to enter the side door to the hotel. Upon entering I saw Lou standing next to a door marked 'Conference Room.' I felt naked. I was now a lawyer who had been stripped of his briefcase. Such inhumanity and disrespect to a Southern trial lawyer!

Lou shook my hand and whispered, "Say nothing until you're asked." I quickly agreed as he led me into the room. There were several overweight older men sitting around a huge table smoking cigars and cigarettes. However, the guy that sat at the head of the table was older, much thinner, and looked sickly. This man was Sam Giancana.

After a few minutes, Uncle Sam spoke in a voice that was so soft I could hardly make out his words. I thought he said, "Louie, is this the young lawyer handling the magazine cases?" Lou nodded affirmatively. Then he looked at me and I think he said, "I've heard some good things about you. They say that you're a fighter. I like that."

Then Uncle Sam began telling me why he wanted to meet with me. He wanted me to update him and his companions on the status of the litigations. I acquiesced and nervously gave them an off-the-cuff analysis that lasted about an hour. They asked many questions that focused on getting the names and locations of people who had given the magazines information that formed the basis of the articles. They were delighted with my handling of the drug agent in LA who had testified that he had not given Lou's name as one of the participants in the La Costa Health Spa meeting.

I thought the meeting went fine. That belief was confirmed when Uncle Sam ended the meeting by telling me he had some matters he wanted me to handle in the coming months. I said okay, and Lou ushered me out and asked me to wait for him in the clubhouse. Two hours later Lou came in and asked me to walk with him on the golf course. As we slowly walked, Lou said, "Uncle Sam likes you and you can expect a call from him in a few weeks. He wanted me to tell you that you are now under the rules of Omerta." I had no idea what that meant.

"What is Omerta?"

"Omerta is the unspoken law of Sicily that means 'silence.'[18] From here on out you can't repeat anything told you when it concerns Uncle Sam's business. That means that you'll be willing to die before you tell anything that concerns Uncle Sam and what he wants you to know. Cracker, there was no meeting this morning." I nodded in agreement.

I kept the conversation going by asking, "Does that involve the Teamsters?"

Lou quickly responded, "No. Uncle Sam has nothing to do with the Teamsters."

Relieved, I acknowledged my understanding as it applied to Omerta and Uncle Sam's business, which I knew absolutely nothing about, and I vowed silently to myself, would never know anything about.

As we walked back to the clubhouse, Lou invited me to stay and play a round of golf with him and a couple of Uncle Sam's companions. Who were the companions? I have no idea except to say that I never asked. I dodged the golf invitation telling Lou that I had a function to go to involving my young daughter. There was no way that I was going to spend any unnecessary time with those guys who might give me more information than I could handle under the rules of Omerta.

Unfortunately, even though I was made aware of Omerta, it did not diminish my curiosity on matters that Louie the Tailor needed to discuss with me under the influence of too much vodka, such as Uncle Sam's involvement with the assassination of John F. Kennedy and Lou's knowledge of the disappearance of Jimmy Hoffa and his burial place.

Don't get me wrong. I have never forgotten the doctrine of Omerta; however, I was still curious and kept hoping all the while that my curiosity wouldn't kill the cat.

Sam Giancana (Photograph from Wikimedia)

11. Bailout—Citizens and Southern National Bank

In the seventies, the largest bank in Savannah and the state of Georgia was the Citizens and Southern National Bank, one of the predecessors of the Bank of America. During this time, this once-prominent bank hit the rocks and had no future without a cash bailout. As strange and unbelievable as it may seem, Louie the Tailor bailed them out. This is how it happened.

Early in my representation of Lou and the Teamsters, Lou was successful in bringing to Savannah a PGA-sanctioned golf tournament. In doing so, Louie the Tailor had to overcome a lot of barriers. The first one was the lack of airline flights in and out of the Savannah Airport. At the time of the announcement of the tournament, there were only three daily flights and all of them were to and from Atlanta through Delta Airlines. Lou needed at least nine with several direct flights to Midwestern cities without touching down in Atlanta. He especially wanted golf packages from Chicago in addition to flights servicing the tournament.

Lou called me one morning and asked if I was going to be in my office. I told him that I would make a point to be there whenever he came. I had just opened a fresh bag of boiled peanuts when he arrived. Ignoring the sight of his alleged high-power attorney spitting out peanut shells into a waste basket, Lou told me he needed to use my telephone because he couldn't take the chance of his phones being bugged by the Justice Department. He needed to call his friend with Delta Airlines in Chicago. His friend's name was Sandy Miller, and according to Lou, Miller was a vice president of Delta.

Apparently, Lou had had previous conversations with Delta officials concerning the additional daily flights he needed in Savannah and had received a negative response. So, he told me he needed to 'muscle' Delta to get the flights, and he didn't want the government listening in. Threatening and/or blackmailing a vice president of a major airline was even then a serious crime in America.

I asked one of my secretaries to get coffee as Lou walked into my office and over to the phone. I always felt uncomfortable when Lou used my office phone to make his untapped calls. Lou was able to get Miller on the phone within minutes. They exchanged niceties and Lou got down to the business at hand. He explained to Miller the necessity of having nine daily flights to serve the Teamsters' need to make the Savannah Inn and Country Club a major golfing venue.

He explained that the Midwestern cities were being targeted with advertising attempting to lure golfing vacations away from Florida and the Carolina coast. He told Miller that the Teamsters were counting on him to get the deal done. He stressed that they were tired of losing money at the Savannah property.

I couldn't hear what Miller was saying, but I could tell Lou didn't like Miller's answers. After about thirty minutes, Lou told Miller that if the request was not granted within the next few hours, he would make the necessary calls to shut down the trucks servicing the Delta hub at Atlanta. Lou's final comment was, "Sandy, call me back within an hour at my lawyer's office and tell me that you want Delta to be flying out of Savannah tomorrow." After giving him my number, he hung up.

Lou turned to me and winked. He was confident he would have the nine daily flights before the day was over. I understood what he was doing. The International Brotherhood of Teamsters totally controlled the trucking industry in America. Every truck that backed up to a Delta flight to either refuel or load food and supplies was driven by a Teamster union member. In other words, without the Teamsters, Delta could not fly. Period. And if the Teamsters' hierarchy backed Lou up, Louie the Tailor had the kind of clout that made Vegas clout look very small in comparison.

Thinking we would be waiting a few hours before Miller called back, I asked Lou if he would like some peanuts or to have lunch sent to us. He responded, "Cracker, I ain't eating rotten peanuts and lunch can wait until after you go with me to the C&S Bank for a meeting I've set up with Dick Katell. I need a favor from him and thought I'd use your clout."

I replied, "I know him as a casual friend, and his bank was one of the largest contributors to my senate campaign. So, I guess I could help. What do you need from him?"

Lou explained to me that in order to meet the requirements of the Professional Golfers Association (PGA) the tournament host had to verify that a trust account had been set up with a bank that would guarantee the winning purses, regardless of the outcome of the financial aspects of the event. This fund was set aside solely to pay off the winnings of the players. Lou told me that he wanted the account in a separate bank not associated with the inn's business account. At that time, the operational account of the inn was located at the Savannah Bank and Trust Company. I understood and thought that the C&S Bank would enjoy participating in an event that would bring golfers and enthusiasts from all over the country to spend their money in Savannah. I was wrong.

We walked from my office to the bank's main office at the corner of Liberty and Bull Streets in the heart of Savannah. We took the elevator upstairs to Katell's office. His receptionist recognized me and asked if I had an appointment. I told her that I had accompanied Lou Rosanova for his appointment with her boss. She invited us to sit down and asked if we would like a cup of coffee. She picked up the office phone and told someone we were there.

After sitting there for about thirty minutes, I began thinking of accepting the lady's offer of coffee. I could tell that the receptionist was getting a little antsy. She probably thought that it was unusual for Katell to keep an appointment waiting so long. My opinion of Katell, from what I had heard and witnessed, was that he was very organized and courteous in his dealings with local people. I always thought that since he was from the Atlanta area, he found it necessary to treat the local gentry very politely because of their long-standing distrust of people from Atlanta. After another fifteen minutes, I began to worry. Something was wrong, and I noticed that Lou was of the same opinion. It was obvious to all three of us that Lou was being disrespected.

A few more minutes elapsed and a young man came into the reception area and introduced himself to Lou. They shook hands and he said hello to me and asked how I was doing. I said fine and expected him to lead us into Katell's office. However, that didn't happen. Instead, he told Lou that his boss was unable to meet with him and that the bank was unable to help him create the trust account. Lou's face turned red and he asked if his (expletive) boss was in his office. Lou told the fellow that he wanted Katell, not someone else, to tell him why the bank wouldn't do the account.

The surrogate began stuttering and said that Katell had left the office for lunch and that because of Lou's reputation and the involvement of organized crime at the inn, C&S could not be a participant. To say that I was shocked would be putting it too mildly. I was stunned! I knew that if Katell was in and Lou could get to him, Lou would do something that he would regret later that would not serve the interest of the Teamsters. Luckily, Katell was not in, and we left. Needless to say, we did not stop for lunch and went straight to my office where there was a message from Miller advising that Delta would grant the additional flights. He had asked that Lou call him back for the details. Lou thanked my secretary and told me that he had to go back to his cottage and sew. He said that he would call Miller later that night after he'd cooled off. Lou left with his fists clenched and fuming about the way he'd been disrespected in front of the receptionist, and in particular, his cracker lawyer.

After Lou left, I called Katell's office and asked his receptionist to have him call me when he returned. After personally apologizing to me, she said she would. Katell never returned the call. I was sure Lou would find a way to pay Katell back for his disrespect and the decision not to handle the account. How? I had no idea.

A few weeks passed and the planning for the tournament went according to schedule. Lou didn't talk about Katell again and I never mentioned it. I hoped, for Katell's sake, that the matter was over. Again, I was wrong!

Lou showed up at my office early one morning with a broad grin on his face. He stopped in the lobby to tell one of my secretaries, Lucy, to bring her boss a good cup of coffee and include one for him. I knew immediately that Lou was in one of his best moods and that he had some good news to tell his cracker lawyer.

When Lucy brought the coffee in, he hugged her and told her how good she looked and winked at her. I could tell Lucy was surprised at Lou's hug and compliment, and pushing aside her vanity, she also knew that Lou was up to something. Knowing that she shared my curiosity addiction, I could see that she wanted to stay and find out what was up. Had it been any other client, she would have stayed and learned all she could, but because it was Lou—whom she believed was actually *the* Godfather—she knew that she had to go back to her desk and try to listen through the walls, which I'm sure she did as she had done many times before.

I took a sip of my coffee and asked, "What's up, Lou?"

He took a sip and with a broad smile on his face replied, "The C&S Bank in Atlanta applied for a loan from the pension fund for $92 million. They need it now. They're in deep trouble. The trustee handling the application wants my recommendation since I'm the man in Georgia. He wants me to find out what I can and get back to him. Cracker, they don't get the money unless I recommend it. Katell has to go through Big Lou."

Katell's disrespect for Lou and the Savannah Inn was a blunder of $92 million. In today's currency market that is about $1 billion! Can you possibly imagine what Katell was thinking and how much he would have loved to turn back time and graciously offer to help Lou by opening a simple trust account for the golf tournament? Well, he couldn't turn back the clock, and I knew that he would finally have to meet Louie the Tailor on Lou's home turf and on Big Lou's own terms.

"How are you going to handle it, Lou?" I asked.

He responded, "I want you to write a letter and hand-deliver it today. As my attorney, I want you to advise him that the loan is denied, but I'll be glad to discuss the matter further if he's interested. When he calls you this afternoon, don't take the call. Tell Lucy to say you're out and you'll get back to him. But wait two days. Invite him to lunch at the inn on Thursday at noon. Tell him that I'll be glad to hear what he has to say."

He continued, "Cracker, don't let anyone pressure you. You're in the driver's seat and I own the car. Remember, if any of your best friends call and ask you to help Katell or the bank, tell them that they need to talk to me. And they won't! I want the jerk to squirm. I want him to sweat blood, because when the bank's board finds out that they'll not get bailed out because of the way he treated me, he's gonna lose his job and I'll take you and Jean to Las Vegas to celebrate, okay."

Between the time that the letter was hand-delivered to Katell, and the lunch on Thursday, I received several calls from old friends whom I had not heard from in months, some for years. One call came from a man for whom I had a lot of affection and esteem. He was a balcony person to me. A 'balcony' person is a person that someone looks up to and one that serves as a model and mentor in one's life. In other words, I had always looked up to him since my football days as the quarterback for the best high school in Savannah, Benedictine Military School. He was the head of the athletic association, and he was always there to give me a bear hug after each game and to lift me up if we lost (which was seldom). After I became a trial lawyer, he would come and cheer for me during the trials. Mike Finocarrio was always a special person to me. Mike called me the next day and told me to help out Katell, whom he had just met at an athletic banquet through a banker friend of his. Apparently, Katell was told that if anyone had any influence over me, it would be Finocarrio. And he was right. After Mike had given the request he added, "But only if you want to. Either way, I'm with you!"

That single message affected me. Katell had no business getting my balcony friend involved. That to me was personal, and I had no problem telling the others who called that they should talk to Lou, not me.

Lou had me come early for lunch that Thursday at the inn. We went to the cottage and waited for Katell's arrival. I didn't inquire as to what Lou's plan was because I thought that he was going to play it by ear. Promptly at noon Lou's phone rang and the lady at the clubhouse advised Lou that Mr. Katell was there for a meeting. I heard Lou ask her if all the guys (members) he had invited for lunch were there, and she said they were. Lou looked at me and said, "Okay, Cracker, let's go to the clubhouse and take this jerk down."

We walked briskly to the clubhouse and entered the main room where about twenty club members were seated eating lunch, courtesy of Louie the Tailor. Katell was sitting alone at the table where Lou had prearranged for him to be seated. As we approached, Katell stood up and greeted me and Lou with his hand out. Lou ignored his attempt to shake his hand and told Katell in a voice loud enough for all to hear that he didn't really care to sit at the same table with a man of Katell's reputation. Everyone turned as they heard these words, and you could hear a pin drop.

Katell was visibly shaken by Lou's remarks but said nothing. Lou spoke again, "Before you and I talk, I wanna hear you apologize for refusing to meet with me three weeks ago and I want you to do it with a few of my Savannah friends present."

Katell responded, "Lou, I am deeply sorry for the treatment you received in my office." Lou stopped him from going further and said, "My name is Mr. Rosanova to you." Katell, still shaken said, "Mr. Rosanova, I want to make things right with you and the Savannah Inn."

Lou responded, "How about my friends sitting here? You insulted them too." Katell, with a humble look that had probably never adorned his face before, looked around the room and said, "I apologize to each of you on behalf of myself and the C&S Bank. We want to support the golf tournament and do anything to help make it a success." He looked back at Lou and said, "Mr. Rosanova, we truly want to participate with you and your members in any way you see fit."

I was moved by the moment and started to say something that would get these two guys together, but wisely decided I better keep silent. I was hoping that Lou would accept the apology, and we all could be friends again. But Lou had something else on his mind that he had obviously put a lot of thought into.

"You will have to do more than just give me and my friends a bunch of words. My lawyer will deliver a letter to you this afternoon outlining the terms and conditions that are acceptable to me, and if you comply, I'll see that you and your lousy bank get the loan you want. Personally, I don't give a damn if your bank goes under or if you get fired, but I see a way you can help us with the golf tournament."

He motioned to me, and we left. As I walked by the other members, I could see that they were proud of Lou and how he stood down and humbled an arrogant banker who had probably stuck his nose up at all of them sometime in their banking lives.

As we walked to my car, Lou handed me a sheet of paper that contained a proposed letter to Katell, and he told me to get Lucy to type it on my letterhead and deliver it to the jerk before five. Then he asked, "Did I do good?"

I replied, "You got your point over and you totally humbled the guy. I almost felt sorry for him. You made him beg."

Lou looked at me with a big grin on his face, and said, "I got him!"

I took Lou's note and went back to my office where I promptly dictated a letter to Katell that set the terms out. The terms were simple: Lou wanted a written apology to both him and the Teamsters sent to him within twenty-four hours. He wanted the C&S Bank to issue a press release that the bank was joining the golf tournament as a sponsor and would service the trust account. He wanted the bank to donate $25,000 to the tournament to cover costs.

After it was delivered, Katell and the bank complied with all the terms and Lou kept his part of the agreement; he notified the Trustees that he was satisfied, and the loan was made within a few days. Hence, Louie the Tailor bailed out the largest bank in Georgia in the early seventies. Richard Katell was shortly thereafter reassigned back to Atlanta. He died a few years later. I understand it was from natural causes.

12. Two Million in Funny Money

Lou called me one Saturday afternoon and asked me to come down to Dino's and meet a friend of his from New York. I arrived at about seven and walked over to Lou's favorite table in the back of the bar area where he was seated with two men somewhere in their thirties. All three stood up to greet me as I approached the table.

The shorter of the two was introduced as a dentist from New York and a long-time friend of Lou's. The other was introduced by the dentist as his personal friend from North Carolina. Although I can't recall the dentist's name, I can never forget the name of his buddy, David Crawford.

Crawford was a white man with a dark brown afro hairstyle. He was about six feet tall and appeared to be slender under his double-breasted dark blue sport coat that he wore over a red pull-over sport shirt with a big collar. He wore an expensive gold chain around his neck, which was in fashion in that day and age. However, what separated him from all of the other men in the room were the dark blue sunglasses that prevented me from seeing his eyes.

As far as the dentist was concerned, I can only remember him as a short, dumpy white guy with a balding head, and he too was wearing a dark blue sport coat. I cannot remember his shirt, but I do recall that he had the fashionable gold chain around his neck with a large gold medallion hanging from it.

The dentist spoke first. "Lou said that you were the man we should talk to about a legal problem that David has in South Carolina. He said that you represent him and the Teamsters, and I can't think of a better recommendation than that."

Lou quickly interceded and said, "Cracker, my friend from New York came down here to get my advice. After he told me the problem, I thought you might be interested in representing David over in Carolina. Hear them out as a favor to me. Then if you don't want to mess with it, that's your decision."

With that said, Lou told Crawford to tell me the problem and not to leave out anything. I listened intently as he told me that he was under indictment in federal court in Columbia, South Carolina, on eighteen counts of counterfeiting money. He told me that the feds were contending that he headed a group that put out approximately $2 million in a three-week span in the Myrtle Beach area a few months prior. He reached into a briefcase sitting on the floor under the table and pulled out the indictment. I asked him to let me read it before he continued on with his story.

If I took the case, it would be my first counterfeiting case. I did not tell him this fact, mainly because I thought it insignificant. When I had tried my first murder case, it had been my best effort, and I'd won it. My ego always welcomed new and difficult cases that I had no experience in. That applied to all lawyers who wanted a career in the courtroom. If you don't try the first one, you can't be a trial lawyer.

The indictment was very specific and outlined dates and places that $20 counterfeit bills had been distributed in the Myrtle Beach area, and by whom. In each count, the government charged David with conspiracy as the leader of the scheme to defraud the federal government. Each count included a separate distributor and the specific transactions. Practically all involved supermarket sales transactions.

When I finished, I asked Crawford, "Is there anything in here that is not true?"

"I don't know because I never heard of these people. I have no idea who distributed the bills," he answered.

"Did you have anything to do with the making of the bills or selling the bills to someone else?" I asked as Crawford glanced over at Lou and the dentist as if to say, "Should I answer?"

Lou spoke up and stared at Crawford, "Whatever you tell him stays here. But you gotta tell him the truth if you want him to help you." That advice coming from Louie the Tailor seemed comical to me as I recalled how Lou had insisted that he was not a mobster who'd met with Frank Fitzsimmons in San Diego as alleged in the porn magazines.

Actually, my question to Crawford was against my normal procedure in representing criminal defendants. I never asked defendants if they'd committed the crime. There were many reasons why I did not. The first and foremost was that I was their advocate, not their judge. My job was to give the defendant the best defense possible and make sure that any conviction was error free. The second reason was that in most of my cases the crimes were horrendous. If I'd known for sure that my client had committed the act, I was afraid that I might not defend him or her the way I should. The third reason was that I never wanted to put my client on the stand to testify and be cross-examined by the prosecution. In all of the approximately four hundred trials I participated in, I can count on my right hand the defendants who testified for themselves. And out of those, none helped themselves.

Another significant reason was that the truth, in any case, was a matter of perception. Let me give you a great example. Very early in my career, I attended a trial lawyer's seminar in Atlanta featuring a well-known trial lawyer out of Houston, Texas. To kick off his first speech and to put the seminar in proper perspective, he gave us a 'learning moment'. As the more than fifty lawyers sat there, the double doors to the room burst open and a man came running in with a pistol and told us all to get on the floor and put our wallets next to us. He also told us not to look up at him while we were complying with his command. Of course, since we were all lawyers and curious beyond reason, we all looked at him during the process. Just as quickly as he appeared, he exited. We lay there a few minutes until the speaker broke the silence and said, "Okay, guys, you can get up and take your seats."

The speaker was not upset nor was he excited as he should have been. Then he told us that he had set the incident up to teach us the meaning of the truth in criminal and civil trials. He had his assistant pass out sheets of paper with several questions to answer. As I read mine, I realized what he was doing. The questions were directed at obtaining our individual accounts of the incident, such as the color of the intruder's hair; what type of pistol he had pointed at us; the color of his shirt, pants, and shoes. It also asked our version of his statements and how long he had stayed in the room. The speaker told us that in the afternoon session he would reveal our answers and what each of us perceived to be the truth.

That afternoon my entire perception of the 'truth' was changed. The results were shocking. Out of the approximately fifty lawyers, the 'truth' was that the man had five different colors of shirts and pants, and two colors of shoes. We were split about fifty-fifty as to the color of his hair, and the type of weapon he displayed was all over the board. When the speaker brought the 'felon' back out on the stage, we all saw the differences in our identification. However, the most shocking revelation was that he pulled his weapon out and we saw that it was a dark water hose spray nozzle.

To make matters worse, the speaker told us that no one had an accurate description, yet each of us would have insisted that we knew the truth. Then he told us what the truth was: "Every witness that testifies at trial believes that what he saw was accurate. However, when another witness is presented giving testimony that differs in just about every aspect from the former witnesses of the same incident, it doesn't mean that either of them is lying. Both are actually telling the truth in giving different accounts of the same crime. They are testifying as to what they saw and each had a different perception of the incident." Then he said, "If I was to hold each of you to what you described on the information sheet, I would have to say that all of you were liars because no two of you described him the same."

What this taught me was that in each case the 'truth' was a matter of perception and that it comes in many forms. This was important in the trial of a criminal case because I could get more mileage out of the facts of a case to benefit my client if he did not testify. If he did, then my closing argument would be restricted to my client's perception of the truth. In jury trials, the closing argument is the most effective way to convince a jury to free your client. It is ninety percent of your defense. It is the last voice the jury hears about the case, other than the dull instructions the judge gives them. Hence, in all criminal cases, I wanted to be in a position to be able to combine all of the witnesses' perceptions of the truth in a way that demonstrated my client's innocence.

Crawford was different. What I knew of counterfeiting cases—which was very little—was that technical details of the crime were very important. I would want to know everything Crawford knew so that I could find a flaw in the prosecution's burden to prove a counterfeit crime. Judging from what Crawford was telling me, I would never put him on the stand because I didn't believe everything he was telling me. I could only win for him by looking for technicalities that would legally dismiss the indictments.

After Crawford gave me his rendition of the issues presented in the indictments, I told him that I would get back in touch with him the next morning. He didn't like that. He wanted an answer much sooner than that. With that said, he asked Lou and me to walk outside with him because he wanted to show me something.

As we entered the parking area, he pointed to a four-door blue Cadillac Deville that appeared to be brand new. He handed me the key and asked me if this was enough for a retainer. I looked at Lou and nodded in agreement. The following morning, along with my investigator, Fred Dubois, a retired county police detective, I met for several hours with David Crawford in the conference room at my office. The battle was on!

We arranged to meet Crawford in Myrtle Beach two days later so that he could be of whatever assistance Dubois needed at each of the stores where the bills had been passed. At each of the stores, the person who had passed counterfeit bills as named in each indictment lived in the immediate area. In other words, the person was a frequent shopper. To me, it didn't make sense. It was like robbing a liquor store where you always purchased your beer.

After interviewing a few of the government's witnesses, I found that all of them were in their early twenties and looked like hippies. They had purchased the twenty-dollar bills for five dollars each, and then had gone to stores in their areas and bought a pack of cigarettes for two dollars; for each bill circulated, the person made thirteen dollars. All of them said that they had never seen or talked to Crawford when Fred showed them a current photograph of him. Each had purchased phony bills from a different person and not from Crawford.

After the first day of investigating, we met Crawford in the bar of the hotel where we were staying in Myrtle Beach. We had a few drinks and I decided to go up to my room for an early end to a very busy day. I left Fred and Crawford at the bar. After about two hours, I decided to go back to the bar and make sure Fred didn't drink too much, so that he could get an early start the next day.

As I entered the bar, I saw Crawford playing pool while Fred was standing close by. I walked up to Fred and asked how things were going. He said that Crawford was pretty good at pool. I watched the match he had going on with a local pool shark and noticed that Crawford was cashing the guy's one-hundred-dollar bill. Crawford gave him five twenty-dollar bills, and the guy thanked him and paid Crawford with a new twenty-dollar bill for losing a game of eight-ball. Crawford then went to his drink server and asked the lady to break the twenty he had in his hand. She gave him a ten and two fives. He thanked her and ordered another drink. I turned to Fred and told him to get out and head to the car. I walked over to Crawford and told him that I was checking out of the hotel and heading back to Savannah. He put the pool stick down and wanted to know why. I asked him to walk outside with me.

"David, I just saw you pass five counterfeit twenties when you changed that guy's one-hundred-dollar bill. Then I saw you get change from the server for another phony twenty. I'm not going to be present when you're passing this crap and neither is my investigator. We're leaving. And I don't want to be around you again until trial. I'll call you next week and bring you up to date. My advice to you is to retrieve your twenties as quickly as you can and go back to North Carolina tonight."

Whether he did or not, I never knew. However, Fred and I checked out and drove back to Savannah that night in my newly acquired Cadillac. The following night I met Lou at Dino's and told him about the incident. Lou motioned the bartender for a telephone, and he called his dentist friend in New York. The message was clear, stern, and simple. Crawford was never to bring the funny money near Savannah again and never around Lou's cracker lawyer.

Approximately three months later, Crawford's trial in Columbia, South Carolina, began. Publicity of the trial packed the opening day. The prosecutor for the federal government was a young guy named Rickenbacker. He was polite and confident, and we began a friendship that would last beyond the Crawford prosecution.

The judge was the senior jurist of the district court division and had a 'hang 'em high' reputation that struck fear in the hearts of the local trial lawyers. To me, he was typical of many judges I had faced in South Georgia over the years. He did not like criminals, and he didn't care for lawyers who made their living getting them off. However, he also was known for making sure the prosecutors presented the cases before him in a fair manner. In this regard, he insisted that the government make available to the defense attorneys all the evidence they had against the accused prior to trial. Rickenbacker complied with this rule and made sure I had all the statements of every witness he had, including his expert witnesses on currency.

The trial did not start well. Prior to empaneling a jury, I made a motion that the judge could have no conversation related to this case with the prosecuting attorney or anyone connected to the district attorney's office without me and a court reporter being present. When I completed the motion, the judge stared at me and asked why I needed such a motion. I replied, "Because I don't want you to obtain any evidence or information other than what is presented in the courtroom. In other words, I don't want there to be any instances of ex parte." (That meant prejudiced by private meetings between the judge and the prosecutor. This was a normal activity in some courts, especially when an out-of-town defense attorney was involved.)

He turned to his law clerk and told him to find out if I could do this. He turned to Rickenbacker and me and announced that he was recessing for lunch. He said nothing further and left the courtroom, disappearing into his office door immediately behind his bench. The scowl on his face told me that he was not happy. But that had never mattered to me in other trials, so why should this one be different?

News of the out-of-town lawyer making the restricting motion on the judge spread rapidly throughout the courthouse and the judicial community in Columbia. When I returned after lunch, every lawyer in Columbia was crammed into the courtroom while the courthouse employees stood at the doors to see if the judge was going to hold me in contempt and order me to spend the night in jail. But they received a big surprise. The judge came in after the US marshal gave his regular announcement alerting the spectators to stand.

The judge took his seat, looked over the courtroom and told me to stand. "I have looked at your motion and considered the law. From what I could gather, you are entitled to have it granted. Frankly, no one has ever made such a motion in this court, and this was all new to me. Mr. Haupt, I assure you and your client that there will be no contact with the prosecutor without you being present along with a court reporter. Let the record show that the motion is granted."

We empaneled a jury and the trial began. At the end of the first day, Rickenbacker came over to me and invited me to have coffee with him at a cafe next to the courthouse. I met him twenty minutes later at a table in the back of the cafe. When I sat down, he asked the obvious question: "Why did you think you had to make that motion?"

I replied, "Because I did my homework on him. I found out that he normally has lunch with your boss, the DA. They're big buddies and I don't want to lose my case without me being present. This happens a lot in Savannah as well."

Rickenbacker laughed and said, "You're right, he does have lunch with my boss several times a week. I don't blame you, but he'll pay you back for not trusting him to be fair."

I replied, "Good. Then I can build error in the record."

Sometimes by infuriating the trial judge, a good trial attorney facing a serious criminal case can lead the judge into making a reversible error. It was called 'building a good record for your client.' I believed that Crawford was going to need an error to eventually win his case.

Unfortunately, the judge did not take my bait. The jurist conducted a very fair trial and allowed me great latitude in defending my client. I couldn't get him mad, although I gave him many opportunities. I even pulled the 'Oliver No Smoking' violation. This was a way to distract the jury from hearing the most incriminating evidence from the government's witnesses. I first did this in Savannah before Judge George Oliver, and it was very effective in making the judge mad and building a good record on appeal. It went like this:

In most courtrooms, there are 'No Smoking' signs posted in obvious places. Several signs were posted in Oliver's courtroom. When the local DA put his primary witness on the stand in a murder case, I would begin the scenario. As the DA asked the witness to describe the murder scene or some other necessary element of the case, I would take a big cigar out of my inside coat pocket. The jury's attention would be diverted immediately to me. They would watch as I slowly unwrapped the cigar, wondering if I really was going to smoke it. Then I would slowly lick it, which all cigar smokers did before lighting up. (I also made sure in selecting a jury that I had a few cigar smokers on the jury.)

While this was going on, Oliver could see what was happening and he would stop the DA in the middle of a question and tell me that I could not smoke in his courtroom. He would ask me to read the signs. Then he would tell the DA to continue his interrogation of the witness. Sometimes the witness would be watching and wondering if I were going to light up, and he/she would be distracted from the question. And remember, the DA had his back to me and wasn't normally aware of what was going on.

But I wouldn't stop. I would continue on by pulling a pack of matches out of my pocket and placing them on the table in front of me. Then I would put the cigar in my mouth. Without exception, Oliver would interrupt the DA again and tell me that I could not smoke in the courtroom. Then I would reply that I was not smoking. I was only licking it and what was the difference between having snuff and chewing tobacco in my mouth like many lawyers were always allowed to do?

Now, what was going on was silly and was not in violation of any courtroom rule. However, it would shift the attention of the witness, jury, and trial judge away from the issues and damning effect of the evidence against my clients. It would always make Oliver furious and cause him to make more errors than I needed to reverse the case, if necessary. At the end of each trial, Judge Oliver would shake his head saying, "You're one of a kind, Haupt. I'll figure you out eventually if I live that long." Then he surprised me one time by ending the refrain with, "Keep it up."

Did it help me in the Crawford case? No, because the old judge was smarter and fairer than Oliver. When I pulled out my cigar while the expert from the US Treasury Department was on the stand, the judge immediately announced a recess to allow "Mr. Haupt to smoke his cigar outside the courtroom." That took me by surprise. He knew that I couldn't keep this up because all juries want to go home as soon as possible, so if I did this again that day, they would blame me for delaying the trial proceedings and ultimately that anger would hurt my client. Hence, he wouldn't take the bait. He wanted to accommodate the visiting out-of-town lawyer. Frankly, I think he did his homework on me after I made that motion the day before. Perhaps he knew Judge Oliver.

The trial lasted for five days. Crawford was found 'not guilty' on all but one count. The judge sentenced him to twelve months in prison and allowed him to file an appeal bond so that he would be free while the appeal was being heard in the next ten to twelve months. I considered this to be a great victory since the lowest plea offer from Rickenbacker had been a twenty-year sentence with ten years of the sentence to be served in prison.

Before I left Columbia, Crawford had told me he wanted me to handle the appeal and would pay me an additional ten thousand. He said he would be in touch with me within the month. I agreed and came back to Savannah and began his appeal.

Two months later I received a call from Rickenbacker. "Bubba, you know the Cadillac that Crawford gave you and you took me to lunch in a few times? Well, it was stolen out of New York."

I replied, "You're kidding!"

"No, it was a Hertz vehicle and was rented with a phony credit card and disappeared about six months ago. When you got your Georgia tag, it was flagged. It came to me because you listed Crawford as the seller and he is considered in custody in my district even though he's out on bond. I'm going to need a statement from you and then I'll send the file to New York. Is that all right with you?"

My answer was obvious. "I'll cooperate in any manner you see fit. I appreciate the call and I will make sure the car is delivered to you tomorrow. Where do you want me to deliver it?"

He replied, "Send it to my Charleston office and leave the key."

I thanked him, hung up, and called Lou. You guessed it! Lou was furious. He called his buddy the dentist in New York and told him of the stolen Cadillac and abruptly told him to never call him for a favor again. Then he apologized to me and said he would make it up to me in some fashion. I hung up and told Lucy to get me the Crawford file. She did, and I started calling all the numbers Crawford had given to me if I needed to contact him on the appeal. No one knew where he was.

Three months later, I received a call from a US marshal in Columbia inquiring about the location of Crawford. The marshal told me that Crawford did not check in with him as he was required to once a month under his bond terms and conditions. It had been two months without contact. The marshal told me that his office would have to notify the court of appeals that Crawford had absconded. That meant that the appeal would be dismissed and Crawford would have to start serving his time. I wasn't surprised. The case was now over, and it sickened me that I had put so much time into defending Crawford and getting seventeen counts dismissed for no fee. The guy had robbed me.

I heard nothing from Crawford for a few months, and I purposely avoided any conversation about Crawford with Lou until one Friday evening when I received a call from my former client. It was about seven o'clock and I was the last one remaining in my office. I was about to leave when my phone rang. I answered and my long-lost client was the caller.

"Bubba, it's David. How's the appeal going?"

"It's not going at all, David. It can't go further until you report to the US Marshal's Office in Columbia."

There was a pause: "I'm not gonna do that. I don't trust them and I'm gonna wait till we win."

"That's not how it works. Your appeal is on hold until you report to Columbia. There's nothing I can do to change that."

Another pause, "The judge liked you and if you go to him, you can get it done without me showing up."

"David, that's not the way it works. I'm not going to go and see the judge. He'd throw me out. They've already revoked your bond and they're looking for you."

"You're gonna give me your word tonight that you're gonna take care of it or I'll have to do something."

There was a moment of silence as I stood by the window trying to make sense of what was going on. "David, what do you mean by 'something'?"

"Bubba, right now you're wearing a dark blue blazer with a white polo shirt and grey pants."

At that moment, I knew he was looking at me and I quickly stepped away from the window.

David continued, "Your daughter is in Bluffton at a party."

I was shocked. How did he know that? It was a question that wouldn't be answered; the dial tone told me he had hung up. I stood motionless, my heart racing, trying to consider my options. There was only one, I had to call Lou.

Nervously, I dialed Dino's knowing that Lou was waiting for me at his table. "Lou, I just got off the phone with your buddy Crawford. He threatened Caron and knows where she is tonight!"

"Slow down. Why is he threatening her?"

"Because I told him I can't continue with the appeal until he turns himself in. Lou, there's nothing I can do and he didn't believe me. He was watching me. He had his eyes on me while we were talking. Lou, this is about my family. I need your help."

"Where is Caron?"

"She's with one of her classmates in Bluffton, the daughter of an attorney friend of mine. She's at an oyster-roast and staying overnight," I rapidly replied. "Lou, I'm heading over there now and bringing Caron home."

"No. Let her have fun at the party. Don't say anything to Jean about this. I'll take care of it. I'll send my guys, just give me the address."

I hadn't planned on telling my wife about Crawford's call anyway. I knew it would scare her to death. I always tried to keep my family out of the fray.

As Lou and I talked, I anxiously thumbed through my Rolodex looking for the address of my attorney friend's house in Bluffton and gave it to Lou. After I had hung up, I went back to the window that overlooked the DeSoto Hilton Hotel. I looked to see if I could spot Crawford. I wondered if he would be dumb enough to follow me to Dino's.

When I got to Lou's, he was on the phone engaged in a conversation with someone who was on their way to Bluffton.

"Cracker, sit down." He motioned for the server to bring me my usual Johnny Walker.

"I've sent my guys to Bluffton. I hope the rat shows his face. I sent a guy over to the Hilton to look for Crawford."

Lou squinted his eyes and without blinking said, "Cracker, trust me. This is what I do."

Lou did not locate Crawford that night nor did his guys see Crawford fly out of the Savannah Airport the next day. Ironically, after getting Delta to increase flights in and out of Savannah, Lou was now complaining that there were too many flights. It was getting too hard to track people coming in and out of the airport.

Caron came home safely the next afternoon from Bluffton. Lou called me and told me that he would always have someone watching my daughter and for me to tell no one. I agreed, and everything calmed down and life became normal again.

About three weeks later, I went to the inn for a round of golf with a guy named Irving, one of Lou's friends from Miami who lived at the inn. When I entered the clubhouse, I saw Lou sitting with Ken Harrelson, better known as 'The Hawk.' The Hawk had been a schoolmate of mine. We had played baseball together at Benedictine. Ken had just retired from the Red Sox and was trying to get on the PGA golf circuit. As I sat down with them, Ken brought up Crawford. Ken had been at Dino's the night Lou had introduced me to Crawford.

"Bubba, you remember the counterfeit guy from North Carolina, Crawford?" he asked. I looked at him surprised that he would suddenly bring up Crawford's name. Before I could respond, he continued, "I was in Miami Beach last week, and I read in the newspaper where they found a David Crawford floating in the pool at the Fontainebleau. You reckon that was the same guy?"

All I could do was look at Lou, who grinned and said, "He must not have been able to swim. What a shame."

I said nothing in response, ordered some breakfast and went on to enjoy a good day on the golf course. Whether the non-swimmer in Miami Beach was my former client, I never knew because I never inquired. I never heard from Crawford again nor did I hear from the federal marshals who had been looking for him. The appeal lapsed and I went on to other pressing cases. But over the coming weeks, I began to understand the seriousness and consequences of asking Lou for help. While I had never expected Crawford to be found floating in a pool, I wasn't sorry.

I revisited my feelings about Crawford and more importantly, my feelings about Lou. I had never realized that asking Lou for help with Crawford might go beyond protecting my family, but now I had to be cautious and consider the consequences. Was I sorry that Crawford had disappeared from my life? No.

13. The Tidal Wave

One Saturday afternoon I was playing golf with Lou and Ken the Hawk when I saw Lou's driver, B. Days, coming towards us in a golf cart running full speed, frantically waving at Lou. When he got to us, he jumped out and began telling Lou that the front lobby needed his help in a hurry. He said that the lady desk clerk was having trouble with some guys on dope. Before he could finish explaining, Lou jumped into the driver's seat of the golf cart and took off with Days back to the hotel.

Not wanting to miss this, Ken and I hurriedly followed them to the main lobby area of the Savannah Inn and Country Club. Lou ran through the side door into the marble lobby with me, Ken, and B. Days following. It was the only time that I had seen Lou run. As I entered the lobby, I saw Lou enter the area behind the front desk where a very frightened lady was pressing herself against the wall while a man in his late twenties was going through the reservation cards. Lou grabbed him and literally threw the man over the counter onto the floor of the lobby. There were two other young men watching as their friend was being tossed like a rag doll. They didn't help him because they were too busy running out the door towards the dock where their boats were moored. Lou's rag doll got to his feet and ran out behind them.

Lou saw that the three guys had left their luggage on the floor in front of the check-in counter. He told B. Days to put the luggage in his golf cart and to follow him. B. Days complied, and he and Lou headed to where the three boats were pulling off. Ken and I followed suit and witnessed the guys giving Lou the 'bird' with their middle fingers. We also saw that there were other people on each of the boats. The boats were easily forty-footers; they were headed upstream, towards Savannah and the vicinity of Savannah Yacht Club.

As Lou saw the men giving him the finger, he went over to the golf cart and grabbed a couple of suitcases and yelled at the fleeing men, "You forgot something!" Then he lifted each piece of luggage and tossed it into the

Wilmington River. Ken and I stood watching to see if the luggage floated. It didn't. As I watched the boats disappear around the bend in the river, I knew for certain that Lou wouldn't let the 'finger' issue go. To him, that was the ultimate sign of disrespect.

When we returned to the lobby, Lou made sure the desk lady was okay. We all went into an office behind the desk area, and Lou began getting the facts as to what had happened. The men had arrived in the lobby after mooring their yachts to the Savannah Inn docks. When they had approached the desk, they'd told the lady they wanted three suites overlooking the river and pool. The lady had told them that she had no vacancies at the inn, but she could get them reservations at Savannah Beach.

The men had said no, they were staying here. One of them had jumped over the counter and pushed the desk lady out of the way. He'd taken the card reservation box she had just looked through and pulled three cards out and torn them up. He then told her that they wanted the three rooms he had just pulled out. While this was going on, B. Days had come into the lobby and seen the trouble the lady was having; he'd also thought that the guys were drugged out. He'd immediately left to get Lou.

Lou wanted to know their names and where they were from. The lady showed Lou the reservation request each of them had completed before they'd been told that the inn was full. Lou took all three of the sheets and put them in a file. He turned to us and said, "Those rats are from Augusta, Georgia. And I'll bet you this hotel that all three of their boats are full of dope. The reservation request said they wanted to stay here all week."

He stared at the information a while longer and asked us if we wanted a drink at his cottage. We thought that was a good idea and followed Lou to his abode. The next morning, I met Ken and Lou in the clubhouse to finish the golf match that had been interrupted the day before.

Lou and I were sitting drinking coffee when Ken walked in with a newspaper in his hand. He sat down and smiled at me. He handed me the paper and told me to look at a certain page and article. I read where three yachts had sunk the night before while moored at the Savannah Yacht Club a couple of miles up the river from the inn.

I gave the paper to Lou and showed him the article. He read it and looked up at us and said, "Must have been a tidal wave." Ken and I said nothing and left it alone.

About five days later Lou received a call from a physician in Augusta, Georgia. He told Lou that his son had been involved in the incident at Savannah Inn and that one of the boats that had sunk was his. He wasn't angry. He just wanted to apologize and assure Lou that his son would never cause him a problem again, and he hoped that everything was over. He also confided in Lou that his son had a drug problem. Lou told me that he and the doctor had a good, long conversation and that he'd invited the doctor to be his guest for a week of golf. Whether the doctor took Lou up on this, I don't know. But I knew that it was over. The tidal wave had receded!

Bubba Days (B. Days) 2018 (Photo courtesy of Bubba Days)

14. The Helicopter Celebration

Ever since I can remember, Savannah has been the home of the Hunter Army Airfield. Within a few minutes of Savannah and the Hunter Field complex is Fort Stewart, an army helicopter training base. The presence of military personnel was commonplace and no more so than at popular entertainment establishments. It was no different at Dino's.

Lou and I were enjoying a few drinks one evening in the bar area at Dino's watching a celebration of some sort by about fourteen helicopter pilots and their wives or dates from either Hunter or Fort Stewart. They were dancing, eating, and drinking, and appeared to be having a great time. I saw Grady Braddock, a close friend of mine who was the chief of police in Thunderbolt, maneuvering his way through the crowd towards our table. He was in his civilian clothes.

Midway through the evening, we heard a commotion in the hallway near the restrooms. All three of us took our drinks in hand and walked towards the hallway with Lou leading the way. Several of the pilots and their companions were standing outside of the women's restroom as if guarding it against one of the pilots who was demanding that his girl come out. They were resisting his efforts to enter the women's restroom.

Lou stepped into the middle of the crowd in an attempt to calm everyone down and send them all back into the main room where they had been having their party. But a couple of the women—who were friends of the woman who wouldn't come out—insisted on telling Lou the problem and why she was afraid. They told Lou that the couple had had an argument over her dancing with someone who was not a part of the party and not military. Then they told Lou something that infuriated Louie the Tailor. They told him that the woman's husband had bit her on the face and she was bleeding and scared to death. Lou went into the restroom and looked at her and saw the blood and bite mark on her right cheek. His face turned red and the veins in his neck bulged. He came out and looked around.

As Grady and I watched, Lou asked the women to point out the 'face-biter' to him. They did and Lou grabbed the guy who was standing nearby. As he held the guy's shirt by the collar and drove him against the wall, Lou shouted, "You fucking scumbag, how can you bite a woman's face. You've scarred her for life!"

He turned the pilot around and grabbed hold of the back of his pants at the waist and led the man to the front door of Dino's to throw him out. As this was occurring, Grady and I noticed that several of the other pilots were heading towards Lou in defense of their buddy. Grady motioned to me to follow him and we jumped in.

I was holding on to a guy who was trying to choke Grady with another guy on my back when suddenly the guy on my back disappeared. I turned and saw him flying through the air and hitting the wall with his feet off the ground. Lou had hit him so hard that the pilot never knew what hit him, and for him, the fight was over.

To say it was a brawl is putting it mildly. It was a slaughter. Grady held his own, and I hung on. It was obvious to me—and probably Grady—that Lou was in his element and had a lot of experience with barroom brawls. It was over when there were no more pilots standing. Half were on the floor of the bar and the dance floor while the other half were lying outside on the grass. With the war zone subdued, and the women nursing the wounds of their men, Lou made a polite announcement to his employees and friends, who had just witnessed the greatest fight ever at Dino's, that Lou wanted them to help the women get 'these guys' to their cars. He also told the women and those pilots who were able to hear, not to come back to Dino's. They were no longer welcome.

After the pilots had been cleared out and order restored at Dino's, Grady, Lou, and I sat down to finish the drinks we had started before the man bit his wife on her face. Grady and I had suffered some bruises. If Lou had been hit, I couldn't tell it, but I did learn a few lessons that night. One, if you get in a fight, you want Lou on your side. Two, never bite a woman on her face. (I knew that one.) And three, do not, and I repeat, do not get involved or interfere with other people's arguments amongst their friends. Lou should have been the bitten-woman's hero, but when the fight broke out, she was calling Lou every filthy name in the book. She had no gratitude at all.

15. Roses from Ol' Blue Eyes

Back in the seventies, my wife, Jean, was in love with 'Ol' Blue Eyes,' Frank Sinatra. It didn't upset me because all the wives back in that day felt the same way. However, I am one of the very few men who can say that his wife met Sinatra and he gave her roses. I would venture to say that she was the only woman in Savannah who can boast of this experience, even after the passing of forty years.

One of the perks that I enjoyed as Louie the Tailor's attorney was the opportunity to go to Vegas anytime I wanted. And I don't mean just 'going' to Vegas. Prior to becoming Lou's cracker attorney, I had been just once. Although I'd enjoyed it, it was nothing like going to Vegas as Louie the Tailor's lawyer.

When I went with Lou, everyone who had anything to do with running hotels, shows, or gambling knew Lou as 'Louie the Tailor'—so much for keeping Lou's nickname a secret between Chicago and me. Apparently, everyone in Vegas was from Chicago, or so I thought.

From the time we were met at the airport by a stretch limo until we were shown to our suites in the MGM without checking in at the desk, we were given VIP treatment because of Lou's presence and influence. Even when I went without Lou, which was seldom, Lou's prior call that I was coming did the trick. But there was one trip that I will never forget and that I will always thank Louie the Tailor for.

One evening, Jean and I were with another couple enjoying a night out at Dino's when Lou came in and immediately joined us. Jean and her friend Theresa were talking about going to Vegas and seeing some shows. In the discussion, Jean mentioned that meeting 'Ol' Blue Eyes' would be the highlight of her life. Both of them were tipsy and neither Dwayne, Theresa's husband, nor I took them seriously and generally ignored them. However, Lou was listening and was impressed. Lou liked Jean and the kids and whenever Lou was around, Jean usually got what she wanted.

The next day on the golf course Lou recounted to me the conversation the girls had had the night before. "Does Jean really wanna meet Sinatra or was that just woman talk?" he asked in the middle of one of my many bad swings that morning.

"Lou, she's always been a Sinatra fan, and I think that she was giving me a big hint that we should go to Vegas," I responded.

Lou stepped up to the tee and stroked his ball three hundred yards down the middle of the fairway. He turned to me and, as he was walking to the cart to put up his club, asked me if I wanted to take her in the next two weeks because Sinatra was going to be in Vegas. I thought a moment and took a wild dash through my trial schedule and realized that I could take a few days off two weeks away. I told Lou yes and he said he would set it up. Two nights later he told Jean that he was giving us a trip to Vegas and "maybe you'll see Sinatra, if he's in town."

Two weeks later Jean and I landed in Las Vegas where a limo was waiting to take us to the MGM Hotel. On the way in from the airport, I noticed several large fifty-foot billboards that were solid light blue with nothing on them except 'He's in town!' Both Jean and I knew what that meant.

When we arrived at the MGM, our luggage was taken to the huge front desk where the mention of my name was met with the desk manager being alerted. He came over to where we were standing and quickly offered a kind handshake. He introduced himself and said that he was personally taking charge of our visit. He summoned the bell captain and instructed him to show us to our suite and to make sure that he took care of us. Minutes later I found out what 'taking care of us' meant.

As the captain ushered us into a suite that had a living room and bedroom luxuriously decorated in baby blue furnishings (that was popular in those days), he asked if we would like our champagne iced. I nodded with a large smile, and he quickly left and brought back a standing bucket of ice with a bottle of champagne in the center. Behind him, a lady stepped in with fresh flowers and frosted champagne glasses. We both thanked them as I dug deep into my pocket for a tip. He held up his hand and said, "No. It is our pleasure to show a friend of Louie the Tailor the best of Vegas. If there is anything else you and your lovely wife need, just call my desk." He handed me an expensive engraved card and told me to keep it with me. Before he left, he told me that a car would be picking us up at eight o'clock to take us to Caesar's Palace for a Sinatra show. That statement pleased my wife to no end.

At eight o'clock sharp, we were standing at the front door beside the bell captain as the long black limo arrived. The driver came around the limo and opened the door for Jean; I followed her in and we were driven a short distance to Caesar's Palace. Before the driver opened the door for us to exit the limo, he met briefly with the doorman and gave him a small white card. The doorman read the card and with a smile assisted the driver in helping us out of the limo. He welcomed us to Caesar's Palace and escorted us inside where he promptly motioned another uniformed man to escort us to where Sinatra's show was to begin at nine o'clock.

We were handed off to another gentleman in a light tan suit and a blue tie. He introduced himself and asked me how Louie was doing. I told him that Lou was doing fine. He escorted us down to the front of a large theatre where there was a table for two next to the stage. On the table were a dozen red roses. Standing next to the table was a champagne stand with a covered bottle iced down. Another person, this time a beautiful young woman, approached us with champagne glasses and asked us if she could get us another type of drink. We told her that the champagne was okay with us. She removed the top and poured us our first glass for the evening and told us to motion to her if we needed anything, and she disappeared.

Jean and I felt very special and knew that everyone else in the full theatre was impressed with our seats and the attention given to us. But before we got too deep in our self-adulation, the curtain opened on the stage and a band was revealed playing the popular music of that era. After a few moments, a comedian came out and entertained everyone for about thirty minutes or so. We listened, laughed, and drank champagne.

When he finished, lights were turned off, and the music died. After about five minutes of silence and no movement in the theatre, different lights came on, primarily aimed at the curtain where the comedian's band had been located.

We looked on with excitement as the bandstand started turning around and new music from an obviously large orchestra began playing. Then we heard the voice of Frank Sinatra singing, 'I Did It My Way.' In moments, Frank himself came into view as the bandstand rotated around. When he was directly in front of us, he stepped off the rotating stage and finished his song with everyone clapping, whistling, and standing in admiration, including Louie the Tailor's lawyer and his wife.

I believe that he did one more song before he stepped over to where the Haupts were sitting. As he approached us, he motioned for someone on the side of the stage and another beautiful woman brought him a red rose. He took the rose then turned to the orchestra and they began playing 'I Dream of Jeannie With the Light Brown Hair.' He walked over to where Jean was sitting, bent down, and handed her the rose. He told her she was a special lady and for us to give Lou his best regards. He stood again and sang the song to Jean. Needless to say, everyone in the theatre was impressed with the special attention given to Jean and me, and I actually thought that Jean was going to faint, but she didn't. She was caught up in the moment, along with her husband.

We drank the bottle of champagne and enjoyed the show that lasted about an hour. When it was over, the gentleman who had seated us came to retrieve us. He told us to follow him as he led us into a private secured area where a couple of roulette wheels were operating. There were only a few well-dressed couples in the area and around the wheels. He told us that Sinatra would be with us shortly. He motioned for a beautiful woman to come serve us and left us with the host of the roulette tables. He, too, asked how Louie the Tailor was doing.

Within the hour, Frank Sinatra entered the area with his wife; he immediately walked over to where Jean and I were standing and greeted us warmly. He asked Jean if she was enjoying her trip to Vegas. Stuttering somewhat, I think Jean said yes, or so I believe. I know that he spent more time with us at the tables, but for the life of me, I cannot remember the exact conversation other than him telling me that he and Lou had been close friends for a long time. He said he knew Lou from their Chicago days and more recently in Vegas. He said that he was impressed that such a young lawyer was representing the Teamsters. He told me that Lou said I was sharp and 'scared of nothin'.'

'Ol' Blue Eyes' made his exit after a couple of hours, and then we were escorted to our waiting limo with the same driver who drove us back to the MGM. Two days later we flew back to Savannah. All of Jean's girlfriends knew of the details before the week was out and I told a few people myself. But one thing was for sure, in Jean's eyes and mind, Lou Rosanova could do no wrong ever again. If you had something negative to say about Louie the Tailor, then you were no longer a friend of Jean's. I couldn't have agreed with her more.

And, for what it is worth, Frank Sinatra was not the arrogant man I had read about. We found him to be a cordial host and a loyal friend of our friend at the Savannah Inn and Country Club.

16. The Pirates

While growing up in the wetlands of coastal Georgia, the greatest enemy of kids were 'stickers.' I learned later in life that the proper name of stickers was 'cockspurs.' Whatever you may want to call them, they hurt. They hurt going into your flesh and they hurt worse being pulled out.

To a kid living near the ocean in a city such as Savannah, you would always encounter stickers if you played barefooted in the grass or a field. To my knowledge, every kid I knew growing up had fought ongoing battles with stickers and assumed that the wounds incurred were a part of life.

It was no different in the seventies when I coached the Wilmington Island Pirates' twelve-and-under football team. Our home field was at the May Howard Elementary school located less than a mile from the inn and its vast golf course. To bring this location into perspective, the Savannah Inn and Country Club was located on Wilmington Island nine miles east of Savannah.

When I began representing the Teamsters and Lou, I had coached for three years on the island. My credentials were impressive because of my background as a star quarterback in high school and my participation in youth sports. It didn't take long for Lou to inquire as to why I was not available for meetings from five to seven each weekday afternoon leading up to the first season of my coaching the twelve-and-under Pirates. He raised the issue on a Saturday morning at the clubhouse. I told him that I coached the Pirates and where we practiced.

The following Monday afternoon, Lou's silver Mercedes, driven by B. Days, pulled into the parking area at the football field. Lou got out and came over to the bleachers and sat there and watched us practice. At the end of practice, he came over to me and asked, "Is this where y'all play your games?" I nodded in the affirmative.

I want you to note that I often quote Lou as using the Southern term, 'y'all,' in a lot of his conversations with me and other local Savannahians. I do that because he took great pride in adopting our language and he always spoke it with a smile. I guess he thought that it made him one of us, and in a way, it did.

"You got some good players," he said smiling. "What are the colors of the uniforms?"

"The color of the Florida Marlins."

He pondered a moment and asked, "Why don't you change them to Notre Dame's?"

"Lou, we can't. Some of these kids are using their uniforms from last year." Lou thought a moment and said, "How 'bout I buy their uniforms?"

Two weeks later the kids received Notre Dame gold pants, helmets, and dark blue jerseys with gold numbers. We looked like miniature 'Fighting Irish of Notre Dame' thanks to Louie the Tailor.

The opening day of the season arrived within two weeks after we had received the uniform transformation. The Friday afternoon before the Saturday morning kick-off, the Chatham County Youth Athletic Commission sent grass cutters and a maintenance crew to cut the grass and line off the field. They completed their task in time for the Pirates to get in their last practice.

As we were practicing, Lou drove up to check on the team and to see if they were ready to kick butt the next morning. While he was standing on the sidelines with me, he observed the kids picking painful stickers from their hands, arms, and legs. Lou asked me what they were doing. I told him about the stickers and that when the county cut the grass, they didn't vacuum the stickers that were now lying loose on the field.

Lou, with a scowl on his face, told me to get the kids off the field and he would take care of it. "Ain't no way my kids gonna play on that field with those stickers." He turned and left in his silver Mercedes.

Thirty minutes later as the last kid was picked up by a parent, I heard a rumbling sound coming up the road from the direction of the Savannah Inn. I looked down the road and saw a line of machinery heading my way. The tractors and related machinery turned onto the field with a silver Mercedes following them. I watched as the units re-cut the football field and vacuumed the cut grass and stickers from the field.

By the time they had finished, it was dark. Lou came over to me and told me that they would line the field in the morning at least two hours before game time. He proudly boasted to me, "Cracker, now that's how you get a football field ready for our kids. Now they can hit the ground without worrying about stickers. Now, we're ready to kick ass!"

One hour before kick-off the next morning, Lou arrived with several guests he had invited to attend the game with him. Two of them were from Chicago and one from Miami. One of them had allegedly attended the secret meeting at the La Costa Health Spa with Frank Fitzsimmons, according to the articles in *Playboy* and *Penthouse*. His name was Charlie Greller. I knew Charlie because he was a regular at the inn, and I knew him to be an avid Notre Dame fan like Lou. Charlie had a Pirate jersey on and was seen chanting along with the cheerleaders. (It's a shame *Playboy* wasn't covering these guys that morning.)

As we got close to the 10:00 a.m. game time, a county vehicle drove into the parking area that was rapidly filling up. It was Don Golden, the head of the Recreation Department, who had sent the county units to mow the grass and leave the stickers on the field. He walked over to me and shook my hand and asked how I was doing. I told him we were ready to play. He said a couple of other unimportant things that I no longer remember. Lou was standing nearby with Greller and seemed interested in Golden's conversation. I saw Lou's interest and invited Lou to meet him. That was a mistake!

After being told who Golden was and what his position was with the county, Lou's face and neck muscles tightened. He stepped closer to Golden to privatize their conversation more, and said, "You the guy who mowed this field last night and left my kids to battle with the stickers this morning?" Without waiting for an answer, he continued, "Don't bring your equipment down here anymore. We'll take care of the field. Remove this field from your memory. Am I making myself clear enough for you?"

Apparently, Golden had read some of the articles about Lou and his Chicago ties. Perhaps he had even read one of the magazine articles. I don't know. But Golden didn't reply and offered no counter conversation. He understood exactly what Lou meant. He nodded to me and walked to his car and left. Golden never came back to the Pirate field again that year, and more importantly, never sent the county maintenance crew back to prepare the field. It was Lou's pleasure to take care of the field for the remaining weeks of that first season. We won the county championship with Lou and his many pals from Chicago on the sidelines rooting for little Notre Dame.

It wasn't just the youth football program that benefited from Lou's sponsorship and generosity. Young golfers benefited as well. Dale Lundquist (now Dale Eggeling) won the National Junior College title in 1974 and won her first LPGA title in 1980. In her LPGA biography, she credits Lou with refining her game.[19] When I would see Hollis Stacy, a World Golf Hall of Fame member, at the golf course, Lou would tell me that he was working with her on various parts of her game. Lou was a well-respected golf pro and before the big golf tournament held at Hilton Head Island, the PGA Heritage Classic, many of the golf pros playing in the tournament would come by the club and ask Lou to take a look at their golf swing or putting. Lou enjoyed helping kids and up-and-coming young golf pros.

17. Steak Rosanova

Louie the Tailor frequently invited Jean and me to dine in the Grand Ballroom of the Savannah Inn and Country Club. It was a special occasion for a young Southern couple to have dinner with the head of such a nationally publicized hotel and to meet celebrity guests who might appear at our table at any moment.

The room was decorated in dark green or emerald drapes that made the green drapes at the Tara Plantation in *Gone with the Wind* look inadequate. From the tall (at least fifty-foot) ceiling hung gigantic crystal chandeliers. Plush deep-green carpet covered the dining area and stopped at the brilliant hardwood dance floor and bandstand. A pianist entertained each evening from a baby grand centered on the edge of the bandstand. Everything was immaculate and Lou was a very proud CEO.

On this particular evening, Lou had invited Jean and me for dinner at the hotel and then drinks at Dino's where a very popular band was playing for the week. Jean wore a beautiful dress and her favorite diamond jewelry; I wore my favorite blue blazer. Lou met us in the lobby on arrival and we entered the ballroom under the eyes of everyone. The hostess guided us to Lou's private table and Dottie joined us.

Everyone was aware that Dottie was Lou's long-time mistress. In her late thirties, Dottie was a strikingly beautiful woman. Her American Indian heritage was clearly visible; she had long black hair, dark brown eyes, and high cheekbones. She was from Arizona. Lou had met her there at a celebrity golf tournament. She always wore some form of turquoise jewelry. Jean and I liked her, and she was a favorite with the club members. It's interesting that while Dottie was a frequent visitor to Savannah, no one, including me, ever met Lou's wife. Indeed, we were so used to being with Dottie and Lou that Jean made a major blunder when the four of us were dining at Tony Romo's in New York one time. This is what happened: Near the end of dinner, and after we had all had several drinks, Dottie excused herself and went to the ladies' room.

It was then that Jean leaned over towards Lou and said in a low voice, "Lou, when are you going to make Dottie an honest woman?" Back then, this meant, "When are you going to marry her?" It was one of those 'Oh, crap' moments. Lou looked sternly at Jean and scolded her.

"Jean, I'm a married man and a devout Catholic. We don't believe in divorce and don't mention it again, especially to Dottie. Leave it alone." I didn't say a word, but I could see that Jean realized she had made a great mistake and began apologizing to Lou as Dottie was approaching the table. Lou raised his hand indicating that Jean needed to shut up. I got the message and told Jean she needed to go to the ladies' room pretty quickly. Lou never mentioned it again, except to tell me that I needed to have better control over my wife when she's drinking. I agreed.

Back to our night in the Grand Ballroom: The ballroom was not only known as the most elegant place to dine in the Savannah area, but it was known for its food. First, it served only aged beef that was shipped from Chicago almost daily, and second, the menu was unique. Lou had hired a man named Estrada as the executive chef. To us members, he was known as Chef Estrada. Every item from seafood to beef was the personal recipe of Chef Estrada, who supervised every order so that the food was cooked and prepared exactly as Chef Estrada intended.

As we were reviewing the menu to order, Lou called our attention to an item known as 'Steak Rosanova.' It was right above the 'Steak Diane.'

"Y'all gonna love my steak. Chef Estrada created it and it's the best in America." Since we were his personal guests, we made no objection. Besides, Lou had great taste in food and was a wonderful cook in his own right. Don't get me wrong; he had to be a better tailor, otherwise, he would have been known as 'Louie the Chef.'

At the same time we were ordering, a couple at the next table was being served a Steak Rosanova. Lou noticed it as each plate was put in front of the guests. Lou winked at us and nodded towards the couple. Expecting them to sigh in admiration as each took their first bite, Lou kept our attention on them. But it didn't go the way Lou had expected. Instead, the man (who looked to be in his fifties and was on the big side at about 250 pounds on a six-foot frame) asked his server to bring him a bottle of ketchup. Lou didn't hear the order since we were in a deep conversation. However, Lou did see the lady server place the ketchup bottle on the couple's table. He also saw, as we did, Chef Estrada heading towards the table. Lou let Chef Estrada handle the problem and directed our attention to what was about to take place.

"I want to apologize for my server bringing the ketchup to your table. She is new and is still training. We have a strict rule that no ketchup can be used on any of our steaks. If you would like a child's order of cottage fries, then you may retain the bottle," explained Chef Estrada in a very polite tone.

The man did not quite understand what the chef was telling him. He told Chef Estrada that they were guests at the hotel and he didn't order cottage fries, but he needed the ketchup to put on his steak. His wife looked at the chef in agreement. Estrada explained it to them again, but in plainer words: "You cannot put ketchup on your Steak Rosanova. It is our finest steak and ketchup will not only ruin the taste, but it will show disrespect to the man it was named after and who happens to be sitting at the next table."

Unfortunately, the 'plainer' words did not help. Instead, it made the man angrier. He took his napkin from his lap, placed it on the table and replied, "I bought this steak. It's mine and I will put anything I want on it. As a matter of fact, I can throw it on the floor if I want to."

Lou heard that and his face reddened and neck muscles tensed. From personal knowledge, I knew exactly what that meant. I had seen the raging-bull look before during the brawl with the helicopter pilots. Lou motioned Chef Estrada away and he called a server over to the table. Jean and I watched, expecting anything to happen. But I can honestly say, I'd never seen a man get killed because he'd put ketchup on his steak, so I removed that thought from the list of options and choices. Jean, however, did not!

When the server arrived, Lou got up and walked to the couple's table with the server and told her to remove the bottle of ketchup. When she went to reach for it, the man told her to leave it alone and wanted to know who Lou was. Sizing Lou up, he asked to see the manager before matters got out of hand.

"I'm the head guy and I own this joint. I'm the guy that steak you ordered was named for. That steak is not yours until you pay for it. As far as I know, you ain't paid for it yet. So, it's not your steak; it's mine. No ketchup will be poured on it. You understand?"

The man's wife, I guess, spoke up and asked her companion to not argue with 'this fool.' Right away I knew that the magic words were finally spoken, and I was right!

Lou reached over them, picked up the bottle and handed it to the frightened server. He then motioned for Chef Estrada to call a busboy over to remove the plates and glasses from the table. Before the busboy could get there, Lou told the couple to leave, immediately.

The couple got up from their table and the guy turned to Lou and said, "I'll leave, but I'll never eat here again."

Lou responded, "I'll go you one better. You'll never stay here again and that includes tonight. Get your stuff together and be outta' here by ten tonight. If you're not, my guys will throw both of you off my property. Understood?"

Realizing the mess they were in, the couple, without another word or another look in Lou's direction, left the Grand Ballroom. Lou came back to our table, sat down and apologized for the interruption. We all enjoyed the rest of dinner and our nightcaps at Dino's.

However, I want you to know that I couldn't let it go when we were at Dino's. While we were sitting and having a drink, most of Dino's guests were having dinner and enjoying the music of Deep South, a band from Oklahoma. After a few drinks, I saw that Lou was now in a good mood fueled by several vodkas on the rocks.

"Lou, can I order a steak in here and put ketchup on it?" I asked. Jean looked at me in amazement.

Lou looked at me and gave me a very simple answer as he glanced out the window overlooking the large Wilmington River, "Cracker, you know that river out there is probably full of Southern lawyers that people didn't want. So, you need to stay off ketchup when you're near it." Then he laughed and asked Jean, "Does he always take everyone to the edge?"

She quickly replied, "He sure does and it drives me crazy."

I replied, "No, honey, it makes you crazier."

18. Deep South

Dino's had become very popular in the Savannah area as a great nightclub attracting the upper crust of Savannah society. It was THE place of choice for the young movers and shakers, and far enough removed from traditional Savannah behavior expectations that they could let their hair down. The reasons for this popularity were threefold: first, it had a great view of the river; second, it had great food; and third, it had great entertainment.

Lou showed his expertise and business savvy by spending money on good bands brought in from all parts of the country. One of these bands that became very popular and created overflow crowds was a band called Deep South.

I believe there were six members—all men sporting bushy hairdos and wearing hippie clothes. To my surprise, the members of the club enjoyed mingling with them in the daytime around the golf course and clubhouse. This was not the norm. Very seldom had other entertainers from Dino's been seen with Inn members.

I recall the many times I had lunch with one or more of the band members. They seemed to fit right in. They were polite, respectful, and charismatic, and soon they became part of the family. And this applied to Louie the Tailor. He liked them to such an extent that he began giving a couple of them golf lessons.

One of the problems entertainment venues faced with bringing in out-of-town bands was drugs. In the seventies, marijuana reigned among the hippie bands and groups. And contrary to public opinion, the Teamsters and the Chicago Outfit did not tolerate the presence or the use of drugs on their properties, especially at the Savannah Inn and Country Club.

I had personally witnessed guests being ushered out of the hotel when maids reported finding evidence of drug use. I was summoned many times to review incident reports where people had been kicked out of Dino's and other areas of the property, to determine if Lou was legally protected in doing so. In every incident, Lou was adamant about not permitting drugs on the premises. So much so, that I thought Lou was overreacting in some cases, and I told him so.

His attitude in the seventies also reflected the policy of his friends in Chicago. Unlike the Five Families of New York, the Chicago Outfit did not deal in drugs and would not associate with those who did. Their reasoning centered on the welfare of their children. In Chicago, they did not want to risk the chance that their own children would be exposed to drug use and addiction. However, on Mob Island, the close scrutiny of the Teamsters by the feds made it essential that drugs not be on the island, especially at the inn.

At several of the meetings I attended in Savannah, the issue was raised when there was a discussion on loan requests by friends of the Teamsters and others. A reputation or report that the person used illegal drugs of any nature, or permitted drug use at his business, brought a prompt rejection. Unfortunately, Deep South did not know just how obsessed Lou and his associates were about this issue, but they soon found out.

When I left Dino's this particular night, everyone was happy and enjoying the show that Deep South was putting on. Lou and a close friend from Arizona were getting tipsy on vodka. Lou had been singing a couple of Dean Martin songs and everything appeared okay at the nightclub on the beautiful Wilmington River.

The next morning, I drove to the club for breakfast and maybe a round of golf if my old friend the Hawk (Ken Harrelson) was willing. When I arrived, I was met by the club manager, Ray Lukban, and he asked me to step outside with him. Ray's voice had a higher pitch than normal.

"Bubba, you have got to try to calm Lou down. He's going crazy."

I quickly interrupted him and said, "Crazy in what way? What do you mean? Where is he?"

"He's at the Deep South cottage. A maid found some marijuana residue or pipes this morning when she was cleaning up. Instead of calling me, she called Lou. All hell broke loose," Ray responded as I turned and headed towards the cottage.

The sight of Lou smashing and breaking expensive musical instruments on the lawn in front of the cottage was unexpected. My first observation was that he had just about finished because I could see a lot of smashed metal, broken guitars, and busted drums. I had never witnessed such a sight.

As Lou saw me walking towards him, he let out some words that would embarrass the filthiest speaking sailor that I had ever heard. I said nothing. I watched as he continued breaking more instruments. B. Days was standing in the doorway handing him other things to break. B. Days finished and held up his empty hands to indicate to Lou he had nothing else to destroy. Lou looked disappointed and turned to me. "Why are you here?" he asked.

"I happened to be walking by. Have you seen the Hawk? I thought we could get a threesome together," I lied.

Lou was cooling down. He wiped his hands on the sides of his pants. He motioned to B. Days to come away from the door. Then he told B. Days to go get some maids to clean the room. B. Days pointed at the smashed instruments and asked Lou if he should get someone to clean up the mess. Lou nodded in the affirmative.

Lou walked over to his golf cart and told me to get in. We drove off towards the clubhouse. He finally broke the silence. "The jerks smoked some joints last night. There ain't no telling how long they been smoking the shit. They knew the rules. They're gone and they ain't coming back."

"What happened to them?" I asked, not really wanting to hear the answer.

Lou looked at me and smiled, "They're still alive, Cracker. I ain't that crazy. But they better be heading back to Oklahoma."

I silently hoped for the same thing.

Later that day I spoke with B. Days and found out how everything had gone down. B. Days said that he and Lou had been at the driving range when Lou had been called back to the front desk. They had driven to the hotel and a maid had been waiting at the side door. She'd said something to Lou and then he had run towards the cottage area where the band was staying. B. Days had followed in the cart.

Lou hadn't knocked on the door; he'd kicked it in and disappeared inside the cottage. B. Days said he'd walked close to the cottage and seen the band members running out, some of them in their underwear. The last one Lou had put in a headlock and as he'd gotten to the grass area, Lou had thrown him on the lawn. The band member had hustled to his feet and run. B. Days said he didn't know where the band members had run, but it had been in the direction of the Wilmington Island main road.

B. Days said he found out later that one of the employees, whom he wished not to name, drove a van down the road and picked them up. How they got clothes and their personal belongings, he didn't know, and he didn't want to ask. But he said, "Bubba, they are on their way back to Oklahoma. I don't think they will ever come back to Georgia."

I agreed.

A week later I was given a telephone number by Lou that purported to be a lawyer friend of the band. He was a local and I knew him well. Apparently, he had enjoyed their music and become friends with them during their stint at Dino's.

The conversation was short. He told me that they were considering suing Lou and the Teamsters for the value of the instruments Lou had destroyed, along with assault and battery charges. He said the instruments were very expensive, which I didn't doubt, but I let him finish, and then I briefly told him that they could certainly sue Lou and bring charges, but that would be a bad move for all concerned. He asked me to explain.

"Henry, do you understand who my clients are? Do you know that these guys were lucky to have escaped? Have you any idea how long the owners' memories are? Personally, if you really want to help them, then tell them to thank the Lord they are still alive," I responded.

"What about the instruments?" he asked.

"Henry, I'm your old buddy. I liked these guys. But they were stupid. They knew that they couldn't have dope on the premises. Tell them that I'll get whatever paycheck they're due and send it to you. That way they'll know you helped them out. And Henry, I'm not going to tell Lou you called because I know that you'll still want to come to Dino's or play golf someday." Henry thanked me and it was over. Henry continued to enjoy his access to the inn, and Lou never found out. As far as I know, Deep South never returned to Georgia.

19. Saving a Good Friend

I believe the meeting was in late 1974 or early 1975. The Central States' Pension Fund Trustees were in session for a full week at the inn. I was called in to listen to Lou and the trustees discuss renovations at the hotel and the golf cart shed. During the discussions, I never heard anyone mention what the cost would be. Neither did I hear why a renovation was needed. As far I was concerned, the hotel looked great in its present condition. Instead, all I heard were arguments concerning who would get kickbacks.

After the meeting, I asked Lou what the cost of the project would be. "Cracker, the cost don't matter. The higher the cost the higher the kickback." Because I had a bewildered look on my face, he went further and said, "Cracker, I couldn't afford to be here if I didn't renovate somethin' every two years. That way I get another hundred grand and it's tax-free! Each of my buddies in that room will get about fifty grand by the time the renovation is done."

"Why did you need me at the meeting?" I asked.

"To do the construction contracts."

"Do you know who the contractor will be?"

"Yep. Swiss." [Name changed.]

Swiss was a newcomer to Savannah. He was about the size of Lou and was a good golfer. I guess that is why Lou liked him. As far as I knew he was a member of the golf club and held himself out as a builder of some sort. The club rumor was that he came from the Miami area on the run. After giving Lou this information, I left it alone. Personally, I didn't care for Swiss, mainly because he had had an affair with the wife of a friend of mine; and eventually married her. I was very surprised that Lou kept him on.

After a week or so, Lou met with me and gave me the details of what he wanted the contract to include. Frankly, none of the provisions applied to the actual work that Swiss was commissioned to do. First, the total cost of the project was overestimated by at least forty percent. Off the record, Swiss was to increase every contractor bid by forty percent. For example, the contract called for new carpeting in every room of the hotel for $250,000. When Swiss submitted his bill for payment, Lou would cut him a check for $250,000. Swiss, in turn, would kick-back forty percent to Lou or $100,000. Lou would give his designated trustee $50,000 to be split with whomever he chose. Swiss would take ten percent of the $150,000 that was left for his profit. The subcontractor would receive the remaining $135,000, which was the actual cost of his labor and the carpeting.

Hence, while the contract said one thing, Lou had a different understanding with Swiss as to the actual cost and payments to everyone. I didn't know (or want to know) the details of any of this because it was illegal. I found out later that the renovation was a grand scheme to pay kickbacks to the Teamsters and their friends in Chicago. That is why they remodeled every two or three years and improved an already immaculate golf course every month or so. To play around the construction of a new green or hazard was commonplace at the Savannah Inn and Country Club.

After Lou had explained the terms of the contract to me, I asked him why he could trust Swiss to not make private deals with the local contractors he drank with. Lou replied, "I got that covered. I'm making him go through someone I trust who'll okay each bill."

Since I was heavily involved in trying major criminal cases, I could not be involved in overseeing a construction contract. I just didn't have the time.

"Who'd you get?" I asked.

"Your buddy Steve Harper," he answered.

Steve Harper [not his real name] was a member of the golf club and a former classmate of mine at the University of Georgia law school. Harper was a prominent lawyer in Savannah and was also a friend of Lou's and played golf with Lou frequently. Harper was a good choice and I told Lou as much. Harper would never let Swiss cheat Lou. But who in this world, with any sense at all, would make a conscious effort to cheat Louie the Tailor?

It didn't take long for me to get an answer to my question. One month into the project hell on earth broke loose. I found out through Tom Chancey, a visiting golfer. I was loading my clubs onto the golf cart when Tom came up to me and asked if I had seen Lou that morning. I told him that I had not and then asked if there was any reason that I should. Tom hesitated and said, "I'll ride with you to the practice green."

He got in and we slowly made our way to a deserted green.

He asked, "Are you and Steve still good friends?"

"Yep. Why you asking?"

Tom looked around to see if anyone had come up or was within hearing distance. "He ain't gonna live long. I was cleaning up the golf shack last night and heard Lou talking to Lukban. Lou told him that Steve had signed some phony invoices made by Swiss. He said that as soon as he found Swiss, he was gonna choke the truth out of him. If Steve is in on the scam, he's gonna make him disappear. Lukban was scared that Lou would act while he was mad, which ain't good. Lukban got Lou to promise him not to do anything yet until he thinks about it more. I think Lou's gonna wait."

I was surprised and asked Tom what he wanted me to do.

"Bubba, you need to find Lou and talk to him. He'll listen to you. You're the only person that can save Steve's life if what Lou says is true. For God's sake, don't mention I told you. You're better off if you act like you don't know what's happening. Let Lou tell you."

If Tom and Steve hadn't been good friends, I would have never known about Steve's predicament and would not have gotten involved. Because of rumors floating around the clubhouse, I already knew that Swiss was a scam artist. Yet, I couldn't believe that Steve would have been involved in any scam with Swiss, especially when the scam was directed at Lou. Steve couldn't be that crazy or that stupid!

I drove my golf cart back to the clubhouse alone, hoping to see Lou somewhere along the way. I spotted him walking towards his cottage. I drove towards him and yelled, "Do you want to play some golf?" He turned and did not answer, but he stood there with his hands on his hips, which was not a good sign.

I drove up alongside of him and grinned. "Well, you wanna' play? It's a nice day," I asked.

He looked at me with a scowl on his face. "Cracker, there's going to be one less lawyer in Savannah by tomorrow." He knew that would bring a response from me.

"What did I do?" I asked, still grinning.

"Nothing that I know of." Without changing his expression, he paused and said, "Yet."

"What lawyer you talking about?"

"Yo buddy," he responded, motioning me into his cottage.

"What's going on, Lou?" I asked as we entered his cottage.

"Sit down. I'll bring you some juice. This is gonna take a while."

He walked over to the refrigerator, took out a bottle of orange juice and poured me a glass. As he handed me the juice, he reached over and took a file from his desk next to the chair in which I was sitting. He opened the file and removed a couple of documents. He went over to the kitchen counter and picked up his reading glasses, put them on, and started reading the documents.

"These bums think I'm stupid. Can you imagine them thinkin' I don't know what a square yard of laid carpet costs in this Podunk town? All you gotta do is pick up the phone; these rug companies will tell you. Your buddy approves this bill for two times the cost. The deal was forty percent. They think they're gonna pocket the other sixty percent. Yeah, over my dead body!" Now he was getting hot again and the veins in his neck were bulging.

He showed me the invoice purporting to be from a local carpet store. The bill was for a portion of one floor at the hotel in an amount exceeding $60,000. The bill detailed the area in square yards. A few minutes after Swiss had dropped off the invoice, Lou had gone and measured the hotel floor and come up with a different figure.

"Those motherfuckers didn't know that I would check the space myself. I got eyes! And I got that yardstick over there," pointing to a yardstick leaning against the desk. Angry, he got up, walked over to the desk, and broke the yardstick in half.

"Well, they're dead!" he said, as his face was getting redder. "They tried to scam the wrong person. Your buddy was in on it."

"Lou, was this the first payment request they submitted?"

Waiving the invoice in the air, he said, "No, they got money last week for some stuff that checked out. But that ain't got nothin' to do with this."

"Lou, you're not out of any money yet, so why don't you just let it go and fire them."

"Cracker, you don't get it. Where I come from, you try to scam the family, you don't get another chance unless someone who holds a favor intervenes. That's where I come from. Scamming the boss is the biggest disrespect you can commit. If the boss don't make the scammers pay the price, he loses respect from everyone and he won't be the boss much longer. You understand?"

I did. I could not think how to reply at the moment. So, I nodded my head in agreement and told Lou that I needed to get back to my office. I said this already thinking of how quickly I could call Steve to tell him to get out of town.

I drove at breakneck speed to my home on Wilmington Island and called Steve's office. No one was in because it was Saturday afternoon, and in the South, no lawyers work after the noon hour on Saturdays.

I called Steve's home and his wife answered. "Judy, is Steve there?"

"Hey, Bubba. No, he's still in Atlanta. He took depositions last night. He'll be driving home sometime this afternoon."

"Judy, can you reach him?" I nervously asked.

"Yes, he said he would call me as he was leaving, and he hasn't called yet."

"Good, call him and tell him to call me at home. It's important!"

"Sure, I'll call now. Is there anything that I should know about?"

"No, it's a legal matter that concerns a case we have together. But please call him and tell him to call me. If you can't reach him, then call me back and let me know."

I hung up and waited for his call. About ten minutes later the phone rang and it was Steve. "What's up?" Steve asked in a cheerful voice.

"Steve don't come home. Lou's hot and he's going to do away with you very soon, like tonight. Now, don't ask me a lot of questions. The invoice you gave him a few days ago for carpet Swiss had laid was a hundred percent over the actual cost. Lou thinks y'all scammed him for sixty percent above the kickback cost of forty percent," I explained.

Steve was silent for a minute or two.

"Did you hear what I said?" I asked.

"Yes, but I don't know what to say."

"Steve, check into another hotel, and do not, I repeat, do not tell anyone which hotel you're in, not even Judy. Call me back and give me the information. Do not tell a living soul, and that includes your office and even your Rabbi. Stay in Atlanta until I call, no matter how many days or weeks it may take."

When I got his okay, I hung up and started thinking of a plan to save my friend's life. As far as Swiss was concerned, I thought he was a hopeless cause. I knew that whatever my plan was I would have to be careful not to push it too much or too quick. I had to turn it around so that it would be Lou's idea. That was the culture I was used to in the South in the circles I ran in. It also had to be a plan that would show respect towards Lou and his partners in Chicago and

Washington. My plan also would have to downplay my friendship with Steve in favor of my friendship with Louie the Tailor. The latter observation was the most important feature of whatever plan I could come up with, if any.

First, I had to wait for Steve to call me and let me know where his secret location was. When he did, I needed to get from him every known fact in order to devise a plan. Steve called me Sunday morning and told me where he was. I got a notepad and we talked for at least an hour. When he could think of nothing more to tell me, I told him that I would call him sometime Monday, and I hung up. I had emphasized the importance of not telling Judy where to find him, and I told him to tell her not to talk to anyone connected with the Savannah Inn and Country Club. As far as anyone was concerned, he would be out-of-pocket for at least a week. And believe me, he was!

According to Steve, he was responsible to Lou for keeping Swiss in check and verifying the invoices. His job was to check the prices from the subs and the cost of the material involved. For these tasks, Lou would pay him five percent of the invoices that were approved. When Swiss had brought the $60,000 invoice by his office, Steve had not been there, so Swiss had left it with a note attached: "Please approve as quick as you can, I need the funds."

When Steve had returned from wherever he'd been, he'd reviewed the invoice and seen that the rug company was owned by an old friend of his. He knew that his friend was honest and had taken his word as it appeared on the invoice. He had not thought that he had to check behind his longtime friend, therefore he'd felt safe in approving the bill. That was the biggest mistake of his life.

Swiss had taken the invoice to Lou and made a written request for the $60,000 payment with the check to be made out to Steve and him, jointly. Lou had looked at the invoice and the payment request and told Swiss that he would process it through the Teamsters' pension fund, and he should have a check within the next ten days. Based on the agreement Lou had with Swiss, Steve would pay Lou his percentage in cash or $24,000; he would pay Swiss his percentage, or $5,400; and he would pay himself 5 percent or $1,800. The carpet company would get the remaining $28,800. In Steve's own words, that was 'easy money.'

Steve told me that Swiss had harassed him every day for the $5,400, and he'd thought about giving Swiss an advance from his own account, but in the end, he'd removed that thought from his mind.

I thought all day Sunday and most of Monday about a plan that would fly. I knew that Lou would call me sometime Monday or Tuesday and would ask for me to meet with him to draw up another contract with another local contractor. My plan would be to start giving Lou some ideas that would eventually help get Steve off the hook.

Sure enough, Lou called Tuesday morning and wanted to meet with me about a new contract. When we sat down in his cottage, he told me he had another local contractor in mind to do the job who was a frequent guest at Dino's and a drinking buddy of our mutual friend, Chief Braddock. Before he could tell me the guy's name, I interrupted him and suggested that he not use a local contractor on this job. I suggested that he call in an out-of-towner.

Lou asked why, and I told him that he needed latitude in enforcing his agreement with the contractor. When he used a local like Swiss and a popular guy like Steve, he was limited in dishing out punishment if the new contractor attempted to scam him. I then mentioned to Lou how he wanted to do away with Steve for the disrespect he'd shown Lou, and that I understood how he couldn't because of his overall plan to gain respect in Savannah and build up the business at the inn.

"After all, Lou, your main task here is to make this losing proposition for the Teamsters a winner. That's why they sent you here. Punishing a local contractor and his attorney on a small remodeling job is a minor issue for you. I completely understand your reluctance in doing what you want to do with those crooks."

Lou sat back on his couch and after a few moments responded, "Cracker, I like the suggestion about an out-of-towner. I don't need to be dealing with a local on this project." Then he smiled, "Since your buddy and his pal didn't get any money and I lost nothing, I don't need to bother with it."

I smiled back and said, "Lou, that's good thinking. Can you imagine the rumors that would have flown out of here had Steve disappeared because you know that neither he nor Swiss kept this a secret? Steve is too well known. Your idea to bring in the out-of-towner is perfect, because if he tries to scam you, no one is watching and no one cares. You are a smart Italian."

He quickly corrected me, "You mean a smart Sicilian."

With the meeting over, I got up to leave when Lou stopped me and said, "Contact your buddy and tell him never to show his fucking face on the island again. If he does, I may change my mind."

"Sure, Lou, but he's no longer my good buddy out of respect for you." I left a smiling Louie the Tailor standing in his front door, went home and called Steve and told him that he could go home again. I also gave him the message from Lou.

As far as I know, Steve never graced the property of the Savannah Inn and Country Club again. I never saw Swiss again, and I've often wondered what happened to him; needless to say, I never asked my friend Louie the Tailor.

20. An Innocent Man

While I was involved in representing Lou and the Teamsters, I kept a full schedule of defending notorious characters for capital crimes in the state of Georgia. What I did not initially realize was that Louie the Tailor was an avid reader of the newspapers and that he was keeping abreast of those cases and the day-to-day media coverage.

I didn't realize this until one Saturday morning when he asked me about a black former marine named Matthew Washington and whether or not Washington was going to get the electric chair for killing a police officer and wounding three others. I was surprised. I'd thought Louie the Tailor's mind was on national concerns and matters in Chicago and Washington, DC. So, I welcomed his interest and began discussing the Washington case with him on a frequent basis. Eventually, Lou became involved in the preparation of Washington's defense. I guess you could say I had a new assistant, not only in the Washington case but also in several other murder trials.

Matthew Washington was a young ex-marine who'd taken a nosedive out of a window in a marine hospital in California and had been injured enough to be honorably discharged with a lifetime disability payment of about two thousand dollars a month. He'd been diagnosed as mentally incompetent suffering from paranoid schizophrenia, acute type. Upon discharge, he'd come back to his hometown of Savannah. Within a few weeks, he had shot and killed a man at a local car wash and then had been tried before a judge—not a jury—and found to be not guilty by reason of insanity. He had spent thirty days in the Georgia Regional Hospital that treated the mentally ill. He'd then been released back on the streets.

In March 1976, he'd showed up in Washington, DC, at the White House, with a pistol and had been arrested at the front gate for threatening to shoot President Ford because of all the 'wrongs' done to him. He'd been taken into custody, transported to St. Elizabeth's Hospital, and within a few days, had been released to his mother to take back to Savannah.

A few days after returning to Savannah, he'd gone to a local sporting goods store and purchased a twelve-gauge shotgun and tons of ammunition. He'd gone home to his mother's house in west Savannah and begun shooting from his front porch at nothing in particular. A neighbor had called the Chatham County Police and a dogcatcher unit had been dispatched approximately thirty minutes later. Upon arrival, the officer had observed Washington without a weapon, yelling obscenities from behind a car in the front yard.

When the second police unit had arrived, Washington had run onto the front porch where his mother was standing. As the two officers had approached the porch, the officer who was driving the dog catcher unit had challenged Washington to a fight. Both officers had then offered to remove their gun belts and fight Washington in hand-to-hand combat. His mother had pleaded with the officers to let her son go into the house and said she would take care of him because he was sick and had just been released from the hospital. The officers had not heeded the mother and had proceeded onto the porch where Washington at that point was hiding behind his mother.

At that moment, two other officers had arrived. Washington and his mother went inside the house as Washington continued yelling that he had done nothing wrong and that he was not a dog and why had they sent a dogcatcher to get him? As he'd disappeared into the house, he'd told the officers that he would shoot them if they came into his home. Ignoring him, the officers had drawn their weapons and proceeded into the home.

One of the officers had called his supervisor. More units had arrived and within minutes gunfire had begun from both the officers and Washington. In one of the thirty units that had arrived was a rookie officer named Alex Hodgson. Unlike the more than forty officers on the scene who had strapped on their protective vests before approaching the house they were now pelting with fire, Hodgson had secured his shotgun from the trunk of the unit he'd arrived in and had approached the side door to the house without a protective vest. When he'd approached to within thirty feet of the door, he'd been shot in the chest and had died on the scene within minutes.

After about a three-hour gunfight, Washington had surrendered because he had run out of ammunition. In the melee, three other officers had been wounded and transported to the hospital where the deceased Hodgson had been taken.

Needless to say, this was the most publicized event in media history at that time in Savannah, with live radio and television coverage during the standoff.

Within hours of the gunfight, my secretary received a call from the Chief Judge requesting that I go to the Chatham County Jail and notify Washington that I would represent him on a boatload of charges, along with the murder of a law enforcement officer, which by law demanded the death penalty. My first inclination was to refuse because I was already representing, at the request of the good judge, two men who had committed the most infamous crimes in the history of Savannah criminology. One of these men was Jerry Sprouse, who in 1974 had been charged with kidnapping, raping, and shooting in the head two hometown nurses who were well known in the community. He was facing the death penalty.

The other was Joseph James Blake, who in 1975 had abducted his girlfriend's two-year-old little girl and taken her to the top of the 136-foot Talmadge Bridge that spanned the Savannah River and thrown her off. The tragic death of this child had infuriated everyone in the Savannah area, both white and black. He was also facing the death penalty.

As a result of having to represent these two men for crimes that had everyone hating their lawyer, I thought that I had done enough for the furtherance of society in promoting justice and fair play. Under no circumstances did I think I should take on the cop killer and get all law enforcement officers within a hundred miles of Savannah against me. But the judge didn't see it that way.

Judge Dunbar Harrison was the senior judge in our circuit and was quite a character. As Louie the Tailor was the prototype for the Mafia, Judge Harrison was the prototype for what a Southern judge should look like. He was of average height, tanned, and had wavy silver hair that he kept neatly groomed. He never looked older than sixty-five, even when he was in his late seventies. He was truly a war horse and greatly respected among his peers.

During all the years I practiced before him, he always began a private conversation by telling me how anxious he was to retire. He enjoyed scaring young attorneys and testing the older ones every chance he got. Those attorneys who knew what they were doing and saying had no problem. The rest were targets for the good judge. The fact that he was cantankerous, impatient, snobbish, and hated all women judges and attorneys (there were very few women in those roles back then) didn't change my opinion of him. He knew the law and he expected those who came before him to know what they were doing. I guess that was the reason he liked me, because I was always prepared, and I always gave the district attorney a hard time. I suppose that his dislike for the DA's office increased my fondness for him.

When I arrived at his office early the next morning, the judge was thumbing through the lawyer's directory and yelling for his secretary to keep trying to get me on the phone. When he saw me, he wasted no time getting to the point.

"Don't give me any argument and no excuses. You've got to go down to the jail and represent the guy that shot up half of the police force Saturday. He's got to be arraigned by noon."

"But Judge—" was all I could say before he continued on ranting.

"I'm not going to risk bringing him to the courthouse. That sucker is so mean and crazy that Judge Elmore is going to arraign him at the jail instead."

"Judge, what have I done to deserve this? I've taken every case you've appointed me to and fought as hard as I could. Because of Sprouse and Blake, every classification of human being in Savannah hates me. If I take Washington, I'll have every police officer in this area gunning for me. It ain't fair. Why can't another attorney take this one?" I pleaded.

Judge Harrison heard me out and said he understood my sentiments. Then he said, "Mr. Haupt, you are the only attorney in Savannah that qualifies for appointment under the new rules of the United States Supreme Court. In order for me to appoint a lawyer for Washington, which I have to do, the lawyer must have at least represented five defendants in death penalty cases. As far as I know, you're the only one who meets these criteria. So, Mr. Haupt, I'm in a box."

Then he paused and smiled, and said, "Go along with me on this one, and I'll owe you one. How about it?"

We both knew what 'I will owe you one' meant to a trial lawyer. To my readers, it meant that he would rule with me on a close issue in a case that meant a lot to me. Having the chief judge of the circuit 'owe me one' meant a lot. I left his office and headed to the jail for the arraignment, and thus began the case that would rewrite the entire code section in Georgia on the treatment and judicial procedure on the handling of mentally ill offenders.

When I arrived at the county jail, I met scores of news media and protesting citizens angry that a rookie policeman was dead. Inside were all the high-ranking law enforcement officers in the county completely encircling Judge David Elmore. Judging from the noise and the shouting, the atmosphere was not that of a courtroom arraignment. It had the air of a lynching.

I was led to the cell door where Washington was bound in chains on his wrists and feet. Washington was yelling obscenities at the judge and the police officers. Seeing me, a white man with a briefcase, only inflamed him the more.

"Matthew, I've been appointed by Judge Harrison to represent you."

Before I could continue with the rest of the ritual of advising him to remain silent until we could talk privately, he interrupted me and said, "I don't want no honky lawyer. God is my lawyer!"

I responded quickly: "Matthew, that's fine with me. I'll just be His local counsel and relay messages for Him."

With that said, he calmed down and the judge arraigned him through the cell door. The wheels of justice would begin to roll. Unfortunately, it was not a smooth ride. Shortly after the arraignment, the young officer was buried with full honors with over five thousand mourners attending. The city was besieged with sorrow and vengeance. The newspapers printed full-page photos of the funeral, his pretty young widow, and their small child.

The evening after the funeral I entered the clubhouse where Lou was reading the media coverage of the shoot-out, the funeral, the arraignment, and me. He looked up and shook his head. "You got yourself a tough one! You gonna need a bodyguard."

"Lou, I didn't ask for it. It was forced on me. And yes, I probably will need a bodyguard before it's over. Can you help me out with a couple?" I responded half-joking.

"Ain't no way you gonna keep him out of the chair. If you do, I'm going to name you 'Houdini'," he continued, still displaying a slight grin.

"Lou, I don't make them. I only speak for them," I replied.

"What defense you lookin' for?" he asked.

"He's obviously crazy. Someone is going to have to explain why this guy was not in a mental hospital." I paused, and said, "To make matters worse, he hates white people and anyone wearing a police officer's uniform. He also hates the judge and his lawyer."

Lou grinned and said, "You gonna need my help, Cracker."

This remark surprised me and I really thought he was joking. A few weeks later, I discovered that he meant it.

In the weeks that followed, our charming Southern city responded in its sorrow by preserving the memory of the young rookie policeman. The new county police headquarters was dedicated to Hodgson's memory with an appropriate monument. A major city thoroughfare was renamed 'Hodgson Memorial Boulevard' and trust funds were established at several local banks for the welfare of the widow and the small child.

On the vengeful side, the citizenry responded by egging my office and automobiles. Death threats became the norm at my office, and I was forced to change my home telephone number to an unlisted one. A brave person named 'Anonymous' wrote me threatening letters almost daily. Unfortunately, I had grown accustomed to such antics over the previous ten years representing the worst of the worst, and Anonymous didn't frighten me.

Our country, and in particular, our charming Southern city, that boasts of the greatest judicial system in the world and brags daily about the protection of everyone's human and civil rights and fair play, could not accept the fact that someone among them had the responsibility to protect the human and civil rights of even the evilest citizens among us. Besides, I was never given the choice whether to defend Washington or not, and that seemed immaterial to those who chose to hate me. However, looking back on it, it fired me up the more to keep Washington out of the electric chair.

With appropriate notices to the DA, I obtained all the written statements of the many officers who had been present during the gunfight. On a dismal rainy morning, I went to the shotgun-riddled house that used to be the home of the Washington family and began diagramming the layout as if I were going to redesign it. Per their own statements, I placed each officer in the location at the scene. I created a huge chart and layout of the battle. I placed Washington where each of the officers said he had been when Hodgson had been hit by a shotgun blast in the chest. All agreed that Washington had been in the attic of the house and firing his weapon through an opening in the ceiling of the hallway leading into the kitchen.

They also placed an officer in the doorway leading from the hallway to the backyard where Hodgson had been standing ten feet from the bottom of the steps facing the door and the hallway. Another officer had been inside the hallway area firing his weapon upward towards the opening in the ceiling where Washington had been located. I assumed that the opening was used for the entrance into the attic. Other than these three officers, there had been about forty others in positions surrounding the house, including the backyard. All had been using twelve-gauge shotguns similar to the one Washington had been firing.

Markers were still present defining the exact spot where Hodgson had been hit and the position of his body at the time of his death. He'd been exactly thirteen feet from the doorway to the hall. I looked at the autopsy report and saw that he'd been hit in the chest with the shotgun pellets making a circle nine inches in diameter. I put a flag marker where Hodgson's feet had been as he was lying on the ground as per the statements and the diagram furnished by the police supervisor on the scene that day.

I went into the house through the hallway door and placed a ladder I had brought under the opening in the ceiling. I climbed up into the attic and assumed the position where they swore Washington had been firing from. I looked out of the opening and through the doorway to where Hodgson was supposed to have been shot. At that moment, lying in the battle-worn hole in the ceiling of the shattered home of Washington's mother, I realized that Washington had not killed Hodgson!

I hurriedly left and went to find Lou. I knew that he was not on the golf course because of the rain. I found him in the locker room playing gin with some members who routinely paid Lou several hundred dollars a week hoping to beat him one day.

"Lou, when you can take a break, I need to talk with you for a few minutes."

Lou looked up, took the cigarette out of his mouth and said he'd take a break after the hand he was playing. I watched as Lou won and he slowly got up and walked to the outside door with me.

"Cracker, this better be good. I gotta hot hand today and I'm paying my mortgage right now."

"Lou, I need to show you something. Can we go to your cottage so I can lay it out?"

This made his dark eyebrows rise and his forehead wrinkle. I could see I had aroused his curiosity, and we walked faster towards the cottage. We went in and I laid the diagram of the Washington house over his dining room table. I explained all of the markings and showed him the sworn statements of the officers. Then I told him I needed the best shooter in America. I needed his clout. Then I asked him to ride with me to the shattered home and see it in person. Louie the Tailor had a grin on his face when he said, "I get it. You think that crazy marine didn't shoot the rookie cop, don't you?"

"Yep," I replied.

Lou looked sternly at me and raised an issue that I had never thought of. "Cracker, in order for you to prove the marine didn't do it, you have to prove a police officer did, because all the guns that were not in the black guy's hand were in the hands of the cops."

I digested that true statement a moment, and replied, "Yep."

On the way to the crime scene, I stopped by a friend's house and borrowed a twelve-gauge Remington shotgun identical to the one Washington had used and then dropped by a store and bought some shotgun shells identical to the ones Washington had fired. My passenger's interest increased with each stop. He knew that we were going to shoot some rounds.

When we arrived at the crime scene, we proceeded to the side yard and went into the hallway door to the ladder I had left under the opening in the ceiling. I handed the gun to Lou and asked him if he would climb up and take any position he could in order to see the flag markers where Hodgson had been lying in the yard. Needless to say, it took some effort for a man of his size to go through the hole and then try to position himself for a shot out of the door. But he made it. I handed him the now loaded shotgun and told him to try and hit the flag on the ground outside.

After a few minutes (and after I had left the hallway and gotten a good distance from the outside door), Lou hollered, "Cracker, I can't hit the flag from here. In fact, I can't even see it!"

I hollered back, "Lou, you see why I need the best shot in America?"

There was silence and I saw Lou struggling to get down from the ceiling hole. I walked in and held the ladder while Lou and his 250 pounds strained every rung on the ladder. Finally, being safely on the floor, Lou handed me the shotgun and said, "You're right. The marine didn't shoot him. That's if the cops are telling the truth." He paused and continued, "Cracker, I'll get you a shooter you'll be proud of. We're gonna win this fucking case." Louie the Tailor was now my assistant and loving every minute of it.

A week went by before Lou got back to me on the shooter. We met in his cottage for a case meeting, and I don't mean on a case against *Playboy*. Lou had made a contact with a highly decorated army captain from Chicago who was then stationed at Fort Benning, Georgia. At that time, he was the Armed Forces Skeet Association shooting champion and considered the best marksman in America. Lou called him and I negotiated a price for him to come to Savannah for a firing test the following week.

I want to pause here and reflect on something. Here I am, a young Southern trial lawyer, running around Savannah with a man most crime commissions throughout the United States believed to be one of the top Mafia figures of a Chicago crime family, trying to solve a murder case on behalf of a crazy black man who everyone believed had shot four cops and killed one, and there was no money involved. The odds of this happening would have been greater than lightning striking the same man ten times in one day. But it was happening, and I assure you it gets stranger.

The captain arrived in Savannah the following Saturday and we (Lou and I) drove him to the bullet-riddled house. The captain brought with him an exact replica of Washington's shotgun and the ammunition he'd used. I brought with me two wooden human figures made out of four by eight-foot plywood panels cut to the victim's exact height.

I placed one of the figures in the exact location the police reports indicated the victim had been lying after he'd been shot. Lou helped me lift the figure to a standing position. We then helped the captain into the attic hole in the ceiling where Washington was supposed to have been. Lou handed him the shotgun and ammo and both of us stepped outside, out of the line of fire. On cue, I asked the shooter if he could see the wooden figure standing outside. He said he could, but only the bottom where Hodgson's feet would have been. I told him to fire. He did and hit the feet of the wooden figure.

Lou and I helped him down and I placed the shooter in a location where another officer had been standing in the doorway of the kitchen entering the hallway under Washington. I told him to aim at the chest area of the figure from that position and fire. He did, and he hit the area where Hodgson's chest would have been. I walked over to the figure lying on the ground. Giving the captain a highlighter, I asked him to circle the area where the pellets had hit. He did, and then I handed him a twelve-inch ruler and asked him to determine the spread or diameter of the pellets. The spread was nine inches, the exact spread found on the victim in the autopsy report.

I went to the truck and brought out the other wooden figure that was exactly like the one we had just used. Lou looked puzzled.

"Lou, let's stand this one next to the other one and get the captain to fire another shot into the chest area from the exact distance the report said Washington shot him from."

Since the captain couldn't do this from where Washington was supposed to have been in the attic, he asked me if he could just make the shot from the ground at the same distance. I replied, "Yes, and I want you to read the distance in the police report and then I want you to measure the exact distance from the figure to where you are going to fire from."

He made the shot as planned and then I asked him to mark and measure the spread on the second template. The spread was thirteen inches. Hence, the victim was not shot from the attic hole, nor could he have been shot by Washington if Washington had dropped down out of the attic.

Lou looked at me and with a sheepish grin said, "Cracker, the cop wasn't killed by the marine; he was shot by the cop in the doorway to the kitchen!"

I nodded in agreement and turned to the captain and asked, "Do you agree?"

He quickly replied, "Yes, the victim was shot from the doorway and not the hole in the ceiling."

I had him initial his marks on the two figures and I photographed him in the doorway and in the attic. After agreeing to come to court, we took him back to his car at the inn and he returned to Fort Benning. As we watched him drive away, Lou turned to me and held out his hand indicating a good handshake was in order, and said, "Cracker, I am proud of my lawyer today. Ain't no way they can convict the crazy marine. But man, are you going to catch some shit if you get him released. We gonna have to get our own shooters down here to protect you. I ain't kidding. I got your back."

I soon forgot about Lou's offer of protection; that is, until the morning of trial. Lou was one of the first in the courtroom accompanied by four men who looked as if they had just left the set of *The Sopranos*. As Lou and his delegation advanced to the front of the spectators' section just behind where I was setting out my files, Lou nodded and with a slight squint assured me that no one would harm his cracker lawyer during this trial. Of course, Lou's presence did not go unnoticed. Several of the deputies moved away from the area where he had set up camp. None would eyeball him. A few walked by me and just grinned, glancing back at my 'crew.' Some even shook his hand and welcomed him to the courtroom.

Meanwhile, back to the case. Savannah was more than saturated with the belief that Washington had killed a young police officer in cold blood and had tried to kill three others. I couldn't fault them for believing that he had tried to kill them all. But finding a jury in this town that would listen to evidence that not only would prove Washington innocent but would find a police officer guilty of killing a rookie friend would probably be impossible. Plus, Washington was a crazy, violent black man who hated white people and anyone in a uniform and made no secret of it.

When they brought Washington into the courtroom, he was handcuffed to his waist and had shackles on his feet. He was escorted by four deputies, one on each side. Needless to say, this was a picture of a guilty, violent killer whom the officers feared, and a picture of a man the jury would rush to strap into the electric chair. Simply said, he was a danger to society, and I couldn't argue with that. Washington was severely mentally ill, but he had not committed the crime of murder. He had, however, assaulted the other officers whom he had wounded at some point during the shootout. But he had not shot Hodgson!

On the other side of the courtroom was District Attorney Andrew Ryan Jr., a friend of mine. His nickname was 'Bubsy' and he always tried his cases fairly and with a lot of passion. Unfortunately, he was plagued in most of his cases by poor investigations by the various police agencies in the county. As the DA, he tried all the major cases for political reasons and, therefore, he and I faced each other many times.

As far as Ryan knew, I was defending Washington on a plea of not guilty by reason of insanity. He got this opinion through the many news articles planted by me and some of the motions I had filed. To put it in layman's terms, I had set Ryan and the investigators up. They had come to trial to prove only that Washington was legally sane. As in fishing, I had cast a lure and Ryan had taken the bait. Only Louie the Tailor and I knew what my defense was going to be, and the more Ryan introduced the mental evidence and expert opinions of state doctors testifying that Washington met the sanity test in Georgia, the more Lou smiled. He knew that Ryan was on the wrong battlefield and had no weapons. Lou knew the truth. Ryan wouldn't know until after he'd closed his case. I actually felt sorry for my friend and the deception played on him, but in death-penalty cases, the rules of engagement change. I knew that I was going to make a fool of my friend and he probably would not survive his next election if Washington was found not guilty of murder.

As Lou and his crew watched, Ryan proved all of his mental evidence in good fashion with very little cross-examinations by me. It took Ryan five days to prove that Washington had been in the attic hole when he'd fired his shotgun and hit Hodgson. He brought several officers who said they'd been in the gunfight and that they had seen Washington shoot the victim. He placed Hodgson exactly where the statements placed him at the time of his death and then he introduced the autopsy that showed the cause of death was from a nine-inch diameter spread of buckshot to the chest and heart. He proved all of the statements and positioned an officer in the doorway from the hallway to the kitchen. After five days, he closed his case in a very confident manner late in the afternoon.

The most damaging evidence was the statement made by Washington after his arrest. Ryan proudly submitted to the jury that the defendant admitted he had killed a white pig and had tried to kill more. The fact that Washington attempted several times to attack Ryan and me during the trial didn't help his cause. As Ryan announced his closure, I asked and received permission to begin my evidence the next morning.

That night I had dinner with Lou and the army captain, whom I had purposely kept from being seen in the courthouse. He was hidden at the inn at the expense of the Teamsters. Obviously, I had only one witness. And that witness was going to present himself as a highly decorated war hero and the best shooter in the country. He was going to testify in his full-dress uniform with 'Old Glory' draped next to him. He was going to talk about the firing tests he had conducted based on the police reports and diagrams. Ultimately, he would testify that Washington could not have shot Hodgson and the shooter was the officer in the hallway. The fact that the army captain was a white man would give credence to his believability in this fair city.

I met Lou and the crew as they came in the courtroom. I took Lou aside and asked him not to be in the courtroom while the captain testified. Seemingly hurt, he asked why.

"Because I don't want him to see you and refer to you as being with us when he made the tests. Lou, I don't want a distraction or a hint that something is odd here. Someone may think it odd that Louie the Tailor and I are working a murder case together. And you are a celebrity and I don't want to put you in the limelight and the press."

He looked at me as if he understood, but I knew he was disappointed. I would need to talk further with my assistant from Chicago. Lou had done such a valuable job for me and Washington; it would be a let-down for him not to watch his work come to fruition.

When the judge opened trial, I put the captain on the stand to the utter shock of Ryan and his investigators. Ryan quickly rose to his feet and asked to approach the bench. He wanted to know why a full-dressed army captain was going to be a witness. "Judge, this case has nothing to do with the army!" he stuttered.

I said nothing as the judge looked at me for an explanation.

"Well, Mr. Haupt, what is the purpose of this witness's testimony?"

"To prove the innocence of my client."

"How?" Ryan countered.

"Right now that is none of your business. You'll have to wait until I ask him some questions, and then you can make up your own mind," I replied. "Judge, I have the right to put on the stand anyone I choose in defense of my client without either of y'all's approval. After that, he can object all he wants to."

The judge looked at Ryan and said, "I believe Mr. Haupt is right. So, let's get on with the testimony."

I slowly walked the captain through all the verified measurements of the house and yard. After I established his expertise in firearms and noted his decorations given by the army based upon his skills, he testified about his firing tests.

The captain placed the position of Washington and Hodgson on a large diagram or plat of the scene at the time of the murder. He demonstrated how he had fired six shells through the opening and none could go higher than the feet of Hodgson. He then testified that the sill of the door leading to the backyard where Hodgson was standing had prevented the shells from going higher than the victim's feet. I introduced a photograph of the sill that showed no damage by gunfire from the inside where Washington had been shooting from. Then to the astonishment of everyone assembled in the courtroom, the captain gave his expert opinion that Matthew Washington could not have fired the weapon that had caused the pellet spread of nine inches in Hodgson's chest, if the officers involved in the gunfight were telling the truth.

Ryan sat motionless knowing that he could not object to the captain's opinion as an expert. He would only draw more attention and significance to the damage that the testimony had done to his case. I waited a few moments to allow an objection, but it never came. I continued.

I handed the captain a shotgun that I had subpoenaed from the county police department the night before. It was the weapon the officer who was standing in the kitchen doorway had used during the gun battle. He happened to have been the first officer on the scene when he'd driven the dogcatcher truck to pick up Washington. I then handed the captain several red shotgun casings that had previously been identified as being found by one of the detectives on the floor of the kitchen doorway.

"Captain, could any or all of these casings been fired by the officer who'd been pointing his weapon in the direction of Hodgson?"

"They could have," the captain replied.

The autopsy report was next. I went over the details of the report with the captain showing that the pattern of pellets that killed Hodgson was nine inches in diameter. He testified on questioning that the pattern would show from what distance the fatal shot was made. He explained his firing tests on the wooden images of the victim. He said that he had to fire from exactly thirteen feet to obtain a nine-inch spread. Then he'd fired from a distance of twenty-three feet and had obtained a thirteen-inch spread. He testified that from where they said Washington was shooting was twenty-three feet from Hodgson. Hence, had Washington fired the shot, the spread would have been thirteen inches.

Then the shocker came. "Captain, would you please look at the supervisor's report of the location of the officer who used the shotgun you're holding in your hand and tell the jury how far from Hodgson the officer was standing."

"Exactly thirteen feet from where the victim was hit."

"Captain, you testified a moment ago that you stood exactly thirteen feet from the wooden image and fired a shot at the position where Hodgson was standing. Did you measure the spread pattern of the blast from the thirteen-foot position?"

"Yes."

"What was the spread pattern diameter?"

"Nine inches."

"Then if the autopsy report said that Hodgson had a spread pattern diameter of nine inches, then the shooter had to be standing thirteen feet from him. According to the police reports, who was shooting thirteen feet from Hodgson?"

"A police officer."

"Based upon the police statements and sworn testimony of all the officers that have testified the last several days, who fired the fatal shot?"

"The officer in the doorway to the kitchen. The sill prevented Washington from shooting the victim in the chest, and at twenty-three feet, the spread pattern would have been thirteen inches. The spread pattern of nine inches meant that he was shot from thirteen feet, and that was the distance from where the officer was standing and firing."

I turned and faced the jury while I asked him my final question. "Captain, do you have any interest in this case?"

"No, only as an expert shooter stationed at Ft. Benning, Georgia."

"Based upon all the evidence that has been given to you, the statements of all the police officers present, could Matthew Washington have possibly fired the weapon that killed Officer Hodgson?"

The captain turned his head and looking directly at the jury said, "No, sir. Matthew Washington did not kill Officer Hodgson."

Several members of the jury looked at each other while observers in the courtroom shifted in their seats. "Thank you, Captain. I have no more questions."

Obviously shaken by a surprise defense that never mentioned the issue of sanity, Ryan fumbled around and tried his best to find an error somewhere in the captain's expert testimony, but he couldn't. The case ended with the obvious fact that if the officers were telling the truth as to where Washington had been firing from, Washington couldn't possibly have shot Hodgson. One of their own did, and they were covering for him.

When the judge recessed for the day, a room that had been full of police officers slowly emptied. The glares I received from their shocked faces did not matter. What mattered was that I had proved they had been dishonest and tried to send an innocent man to the death chair. Ryan was the last one to leave and he came over to me and told me that I had done a good job and the investigators had botched the case. He said that if he had known the truth, he would not have indicted Washington. Then he made a comment that has haunted me for years: "Bubba, the jury is still going to convict him. He's too dangerous to release on the streets. He's too mentally ill to be let go!"

I made no reply. I just left, leaving Ryan with a sad look on his face. I knew he was right, and I was ashamed to admit it.

That afternoon I walked to my office with Lou. I told him as much as I remembered about the testimony and the looks of the shocked officers. To Louie the Tailor, their dishonesty was no surprise. It was only an affirmation of what he'd believed since his days on the streets of Chicago.

"Cracker, the only difference between the Mob and the police is the police wear uniforms. The truth don't matter to either side." He looked away and said he would see me in the morning and went to his car where B. Days was waiting.

I turned and went into my office building. As I entered the building, I noticed that a couple of Lou's guys were standing at the end of the hall. They nodded. Where the other two were, I didn't know. However, I did know that Lou still had my back.

Three days later the jury found Washington guilty of murder with a recommendation of 'mercy.' That conclusion affirmed what Ryan had said. Had they thought that Washington had shot a rookie police officer in cold blood and wounded three others, they would have surely sent him to the electric chair. But they didn't. They believed that he was not the shooter of Hodgson, but that he was an extreme danger to society and needed to be locked up for life. They believed Washington when he said that he wanted to kill all the 'pigs.' The fact that he didn't kill the officer for which he was on trial did not matter. They also knew that he'd tried to kill President Ford, so they knew that he was not bluffing.

Matthew Washington has been in prison now for close to forty-one years, and I have visited him many times over the years. I even petitioned the Parole Board for his release several years afterward knowing that he would never be released. His mental condition improved so much that he eventually became my friend. To me, and to Louie the Tailor, Matthew Washington is a living example of how a segment of dishonest law enforcement officers and our criminal justice system operates. The line between the cops and the robbers had blurred.

That wasn't the only line that had been blurred. Prior to this case, Washington had walked into a carwash and killed a man. He'd been tried and found not guilty due to insanity. Apparently, killing a man at random is a crime of insanity. On the other hand, trying to kill forty police officers is not considered an act of insanity. Yet, Ryan correctly stated that Washington was too mentally ill to be let go, regardless of whether he was innocent or not. This was another case that would have an impact on the way Georgia perceived mental illness and crime.

I remained under the protection of Lou's crew for several months after the trial. The attitude of the police agencies towards me did not improve until a couple of years later when I was asked to represent a rookie police officer whose father was a popular police captain. His son had killed a man at night in a dark alley while on patrol. He had given chase and the victim had stopped, appearing to pull out a gun, and the officer had shot and killed him. The evidence showed that the victim had no weapon. The captain asked me to defend his son. He told me that he had attended each day of the Washington trial and during that time he'd hated me, but he sat in my office and told me he would sell his house to pay my fee if I would defend his son. I said I would, at no fee, as long as Louie the Tailor could be my assistant. I tried the case and won. The father and son remain good friends of mine.

21. The Great Escape

My paternal grandmother died in the fall of 1973 with me and my father present in her hospital room in Savannah. Effie Tyson Haupt was eighty-six years old and, to my knowledge, had never been sick a day in her life. In fact, two days before her death she'd push-mowed the grass on the grounds of her motel in Port Wentworth, Georgia, known as 'Haupt's Cabins.' This was after she'd cleaned the rooms and baths of the seven cabins she rented by the week to construction men working in nearby Savannah. This had been her regimen for the previous thirty years since Grandpa Haupt had died.

She was every bit of four-foot, five-inches tall. She raised six boys, one of which was my father, Reginald C. Haupt Sr. All her boys fought in, and survived, World War II, with the exception of my Uncle Alvin, who all of my relatives said looked like me. In fact, all the brothers looked alike, and were successful when they joined together after the war to form a liquefied petroleum gas company known as Coastal Butane Gas Company.

After the funeral, held in her Baptist church in Port Wentworth, I rode with the rest of the pallbearers (all grandsons who were able to hold her casket) to Laurel Grove Cemetery in Savannah where her earthly remains were laid to rest. After a brief service, my father and I lingered at the Haupt vault, waiting for all the beautiful flowers to be arranged around her grave and the vault.

As we were standing there admiring the arrangements, an unmarked police car parked near our lot with a couple of men sitting in the front seat. It's strange how 'unmarked' police cars are so obvious and noticeable. As I walked towards the car the passenger got out, and I immediately recognized my friend, Andrew Ryan Jr., the DA.

"Bubba, I hate to interrupt your grandmama's funeral. I know that this is a terrible time to ask you if we could talk a few minutes," Ryan said as an unexpected drizzle began.

"What's wrong?" I asked while wondering why anything could be this important.

"Get in the car with me and let me explain," he said, as he waved at my father who was watching the event with a concerned look on his face.

I got in the back seat with Ryan. A police detective named Edwards was the driver, and he turned around and faced me with a sheet of paper in his hand. Both of them had somber looks and seemed nervous.

"Bubba, you know about the jailbreak three days ago. Sixteen prisoners escaped. All of them are murderers and very dangerous. We've got nine of 'em, but we didn't know the area where the other seven were until two hours ago."

"Bubsy, what does this have to do with me?"

"Bubba, your clients Robert Hartwell and Theodore Brown are in that group. Hartwell's grandmother called and told us that Robert had called her and wanted to talk to you. She told me that Robert would give himself up if you'd come get him."

"Come get him? You mean go to where he and the other men are?"

"That's right. And...I know this is asking a lot because it's extremely dangerous. Here's a list of the ones we suspect are hiding out with Hartwell."

He handed me the list that Edwards had been holding and it read like a 'who's who' list of the most dangerous killers in the history of Savannah crime. The list read: Robert Hartwell, murder; Theodore Brown, two murder convictions; Michael Quarterman, one murder conviction and waiting for trial on another; Boisy Thomas, one murder conviction and two armed-robbery convictions. Then the list had three more, each waiting out appeals on murder convictions.

Ryan handed me the mobile car phone and asked if I would speak with the woman on the line. "Mr. Haupt, I'm with Robert's grandma. She insists on talking to you. Will you?"

I took the phone and the voice on the other end was the voice of the woman I had talked with many times about her grandson, whom she'd raised from birth. "Hello, Mrs. Hartwell. They just told me about Robert."

"Mr. Haupt, he called me and he wants to talk to you. He's scared that they gonna kill him if they find him. Mr. Haupt, he trusts you and he'll do what you say."

After assuring her that I would help, the line disconnected and I handed the phone back to Ryan. At that moment, another 'unmarked' unit drove up alongside of us. A detective got out and informed Ryan that they knew the house where the seven were holding up. He said it was in a very densely populated black neighborhood.

Ryan turned and said to me, "We have to move fast."

I agreed to go, but I first wanted to explain to my dad why I was leaving. I went over to him and quickly told him of the situation. He hugged me and said that my grandmother would be proud of me if I could help save Mrs. Hartwell's grandson. I left him in the drizzling rain as he stared at the car I left in.

We drove to the courthouse and hurried to the office of Sheriff Walter Mitchell where he and his crew wired me for sound. Mitchell briefed me on the situation.

"Bubba, we have the house under surveillance, but we don't know how long they'll stay there. Some of the men we captured told us that the men in that house are armed to the teeth. They said they're not going back to prison. They'd rather die first. But if they make a move, we're gonna take'm down."

I looked over at Ryan and wondered why my friend was getting me involved in such a dangerous situation. Ryan wouldn't look me in the eyes.

Mitchell continued, "We're gonna let you out of an unmarked unit at West 38th and West Broad. You'll have to walk alone about eight houses down 38th. Here's the house number you're looking for. We don't have a lot of time because if one of the neighbors gets wind that the house is being staked out, they'll warn them and then there will be a bloodbath."

A bloodbath concerned me. "Walter, why don't y'all announce that you have the house surrounded and give them an opportunity to come out?"

"We would do exactly that if we didn't have Hartwell's call to his grandmother. We can't ignore his plea that he'll come out voluntarily. If the others find out he made the call, they'll kill him. We gotta give this a chance to work."

After Walter ended the briefing, they finished wiring me with a tiny microphone taped to my chest so that they could hear every word and react accordingly. As I was putting my shirt back on, Detective Edwards came over to me and showed me a very small pistol; I believe it was called a derringer.

"Mr. Haupt, let me tape this under your left armpit; you may need it. I don't believe they'll kill you, but we need to give you some protection when you get inside."

Now those words made me nervous, and I stepped back and reassessed my decision to help, particularly since the gun only held one bullet. After a few moments, I realized that with all the guns aimed at the house by cops located on the adjoining neighborhood roofs, and behind me as I would approach the house, my fear was increasing.

I looked over at Ryan and said, "Okay, let's do it and get this over with."

Within ten minutes after taping the pistol under my arm, they'd let me out at the corner of West 38th and West Broad. Someone handed me the written address on a note and a small flashlight in case I needed it to read the numbers on the houses since it was now getting dark. This did not help to lower my anxiety.

As I walked down the street counting houses, I kept thinking of why this was not a good idea. The houses were chock-a-block on top of each other. You couldn't look out your side window without looking directly into your neighbor's. When I looked up at the roofs of the houses on the other side of the street, I could see sharpshooters hiding behind chimneys with their rifles aimed at the door of the house I was approaching. Then it occurred to me: if I could see them so easily, then why wouldn't the neighbors? Turning around seemed like a great idea. I thought about all the times I had faced some of the sharpshooters in court. They were not fond of me and I could easily be taken out along with the seven felons. I considered turning around, but for some reason, I didn't.

Then I began thinking about the men I was getting ready to meet. I thought of how Boisy Thomas had taken a fifteen-year-old kid into the back room of the Bottle Shop Liquor store and coldly shot him in the head. I remembered how he and Quarterman had lined up two elderly employees of the store and fired high-powered bullets into them. I remembered it too well because Robert Hartwell was with them during the robbery and I represented him.

I couldn't get out of my mind the images in the photographs of the dead young boy and the blood on the wall where they had him lean before brutally executing him. Neither could I remove the images of the two elderly men lying on the floor with most of their brain matter spattered on the walls. But I tried to brush aside such thoughts as I continued walking towards the house.

As I approached the steps to the house there was an uncanny silence, as if everyone in the neighborhood had suddenly left. My steps sounded loud on the concrete sidewalk. I looked across the street to make sure my would-be protectors were still there, but this time I could see no one. Was this a good thing or bad thing? I didn't know.

I walked up the front porch steps and noticed there were no lights coming from the closed curtained windows. After knocking on the door, it seemed like an eternity before someone peeked between the shades of the window adjacent to the front door. After what seemed like another eternity, I knocked again. This time the door opened about an inch and an eye viewed me.

"I'm attorney Haupt. I want to talk to Robert Hartwell. I know he's here. Tell him his grandmama sent me."

There was no response for about three minutes and then the eye closed the door. I waited another three or so minutes, and the door opened slowly again. This time I was face-to-face with Robert Hartwell.

"Robert, I need to come in and talk to you. I am here to save your life. Your grandmama wants me to help you come home."

About two minutes passed and the door opened wider. I stepped into a dark and dismal living room where seven accused killers were standing glaring at me. The light from a small candle allowed me to see that all of them had handguns with reserve weapons lying on a ragged dirty couch. The room smelled of dense smoke and burnt grease.

All of them were black and appeared not to be happy with my presence. They were afraid because they knew that my being there meant that the police knew where they were. Thomas and Quarterman held their pistols up to my face and quickly rationalized that all the cops in the world would not fire on them as long as I was there.

Robert Hartwell addressed me first, "You shouldn't have come here."

"Robert, you better be glad I did. Every police officer in this city is hiding out there waiting to shoot every one of y'all."

Boisy Thomas stepped in front of Robert and gave me every reason to believe that I had done the wrong thing by coming to this house.

"They ain't gonna shoot us while you here."

I knew that I was going to have to make the best closing argument I'd ever made or I would lose my life.

"Boisy, every one of those cracker cops out there are itching for a chance to take some shots at each one of y'all. Do you think they care if I get hit in the process? They don't like me either!" Then I paused for a few moments to let what I was saying sink in.

"If Robert's grandmother had not called and asked them to let me come and get him out safe, they would have stormed this place two hours ago. She messed up their plans. Man, they been wantin' to shoot their shotguns for years. This is an opportunity of a lifetime for them. Don't be stupid and don't give them a chance to be heroes. They don't deserve it."

I could tell that Boisy was rethinking the situation. He lowered his weapon and turned to Quarterman. "Robert can go. Take him. I don't wanna go back to prison. I'd rather die here."

I struggled for words and suggestions from a God that I knew as a young Baptist teenager. Thankfully, I would return to this God later, if not this night.

I knew that the next words from my mouth would seal my fate. Eight death penalties were at stake, including mine.

"Boisy, your case is on appeal, isn't it?"

"Yeah, but it ain't no good."

"Yes, it is! John Calhoun told me just yesterday that he was gonna win your appeal. He said the police failed to give you your rights when they arrested you." Calhoun was Boisy's attorney and I hoped my lie would be believed and forgiven in the circumstances.

"That's right. They never read me my rights!" he responded with excitement in his voice.

"Then, give him a chance to win for you. Don't you see, you got a chance to walk free in a few months. Staying here and shooting it out with the cops means that you will lose and die tonight. You've got more sense than that, Boisy. Your momma wants you to come home someday, and she wants you to try and win your appeal. She wants you to win, not die!"

I turned to Robert and said, "Robert, you're coming out with me. I got orders from your grandmama to get you out of here safe." Then I looked over at Boisy and said, "Robert's going to win his appeal because I'm gonna fight for him."

"How you know they ain't gonna shoot us when we get out on the porch?" Robert said nervously.

"Because I'm going to be in front of you."

"How you know that they ain't changed their minds about lettin' us come out with you?"

"Because I can talk to them from in here."

"What?" a couple of them shouted in unison.

"Here, let me show you the microphone." I didn't know whether I was supposed to do that or not, but it sounded like the right thing to say at the moment. I opened my shirt and pulled the medical tape loose and exposed the mic. They seemed impressed by my honesty.

"Now they are taking orders from me. They wouldn't dare give an order to shoot at us because District Attorney Ryan and Sheriff Mitchell are listening and taping every word of this. I would have never come in here if there was a slight chance I would be double-crossed. Some of those guys hate me more than you. So you see, I can guarantee that I can get all of you out safely."

I turned to Robert and gave the order to follow me. When I reached for the inside doorknob, I didn't know what to expect. Would I be able to open the door, or would I be stabbed, shot, grabbed, or stopped in some fashion? But I wasn't. They let me open the door and step out onto the porch.

I turned to see if anyone was following. Robert was just standing there, not knowing what to do. "Robert, your grandmama is listening to every word I'm saying. If you don't come with me, it will kill her. You know her heart ain't doing so good. She doesn't want to hear her child tell her that he doesn't want to ever see her again. Robert, you gonna kill her if you stay here. I know you better than that. You love her and she wants to see you. And Robert, if I didn't think you were worth saving, I wouldn't have come down here tonight and risked my life. I buried my own grandmama today. Don't you go and bury yours by staying here with these guys."

I turned towards the steps and began walking. I could hear footsteps behind me. I glanced backwards and saw Robert following me. I stopped him on the porch and told him to take off his shirt so that the itchy sharpshooters could see that he was unarmed. He followed the instructions as I tilted my head downward and told my listeners that Robert Hartwell was on the porch with me and that he was unarmed.

As we started down the steps, Boisy Thomas yelled out, "Wait up! We coming too!" I turned to see Boisy Thomas and five other men coming out of the front door with no weapons in their hands. I stopped and gave them the same instructions I had given Robert. They complied and followed me to the sidewalk where I lined them up and told my invisible listeners that all seven were ready to be picked up.

At that moment, about thirty heavily armed plain-clothes police officers came out from behind bushes, cars, houses, and posts. Although I should have been glad to see them, strangely enough, I wasn't. I knew some of these guys and knew that it wouldn't take but a flinch by one of these escapees for them to open fire. I wouldn't feel safe until Ryan and Mitchell arrived, which was within minutes. Each escapee was handcuffed and placed in single unit police cars and transported back to the jailhouse.

Before they drove off, I went over to one of the units and asked the officer to let me have a word with Hartwell. He agreed, and I told Robert that he had done the right thing. I told him that I would call his grandmama and let her know that he was safe. I assured him that I would see him the next day and that we would get working hard on his appeal. He smiled and thanked me.

"Bubsy, you need to take me home now. I need a stiff drink. I'm exhausted and I need to change my clothes. But first, let's get a drink," I said.

We got into Ryan's car and headed to our favorite watering hole. On the way home, I made Ryan promise that no one would ever know of my participation in the capture, especially my family.

"Bubba, the city will give you a special honor for what you did tonight."

"First, I don't want my family to think that I was this foolish, particularly on the day my grandmother was buried. My dad knows I went there with you, but that's all. Second, I don't want the world to know that I cooperated with the police in bringing in fugitives that I didn't defend. I'm a defense lawyer, not a partner of the prosecution. I'm believed to be a hard-nosed, double-fisted trial lawyer. I want to keep it that way."

Ryan considered my response as he drove and chuckled somewhat. "I understand, and God forbid that anyone would ever get the impression that you helped some cops apprehend the worst and most violent felons in Savannah's history."

Until this day, no one ever revealed my participation in that event. Ryan died with the secret and Walter Mitchell still lives with it. However, by revealing it now, Walter is released. Obviously, I never told my friend Louie the Tailor.

22. The Disappearance of Jimmy Hoffa

Prior to my representation of Louie the Tailor, I'd paid little attention to the exploits of Jimmy Hoffa. Like everyone else who watched television news and read newspapers regularly, I knew he was the powerful boss of the country's largest union. Like everyone else, I couldn't have cared less about his conviction and prison sentence in 1967. It came as no surprise because all of us in the Deep South believed him to be a crooked northern union boss, and 'good riddance' was the attitude.

This all changed for me in 1972 during the first few months of my representation of the Teamsters. Hoffa had been pardoned by President Nixon the year before. Now he was causing some problems that troubled the hierarchy of the union and eventually the Chicago Outfit.

As I understood the conditions of the pardon that was allegedly brokered by the Teamsters and some Chicago friends, Hoffa had agreed that he would never seek a high office within the International Brotherhood of Teamsters, especially the presidency. I don't believe that it was a special condition of the parole, but I know for a fact that it was a condition, or promise, given by Hoffa, the Chicago Outfit, and friends of influence close to Nixon and Hoffa.

Regardless of this agreement, it didn't take long for Hoffa to begin seeking support for another run at the presidency of the union. This infuriated many people, especially those who'd gone out on a shaky limb to get the pardon for him. What really fueled the fire was that he was trying to unseat Frank Fitzsimmons, the man who'd led the drive to get Hoffa out of prison. The Hoffa issue came up many times at the meetings I would attend with the union trustees at the inn. It also became a big issue to my primary client, Louie the Tailor. Lou was a man who strongly believed in such overused clichés as 'keeping your word' and 'my handshake is my bond.' To him, breaking an agreement or going back on one's word was not only disrespectful but was an act that demanded recompense.

Because of Lou's anger and constant criticism of Hoffa, I eventually knew that Lou had been part of the committee that had given its word that Hoffa would live up to his promise. To Lou and a few trustees, by Hoffa breaking his word, they were breaking their word to Nixon and his negotiators.

By 1974, Hoffa had a full-blown campaign going to unseat Fitzsimmons. The rank-and-file union members were shifting their allegiance to Hoffa, along with some of the union officials. In our meetings, there were many discussions of friends that the trustees believed were switching over to Hoffa. Then, when the articles came out in the July 1975 issues of *Playboy* and *Penthouse*, both detailing a meeting in San Diego, California, at the La Costa Health Spa between Fitzsimmons and a group of mobsters, the anger of the Teamsters and Chicago family increased exponentially. The *Playboy* article read:

Watching Fitzsimmons and Nixon that morning, a California investigator shook his head in dismay. "I can stand crooks," he said, "but it bothers the hell out of me when a guy meets with mobsters and then with the president." For in the days prior to the flight, in addition to playing golf, Fitzsimmons had attended a number of interesting meetings. At the Mission Hills Country Club and the Ambassador Hotel in Palm Springs, and then at La Costa, he had been joined in long secret conversations by a host of California mobsters, including Sam Sciortino, Peter Milano, Joe Lamandri, Lloyd Pitzer, and a crew from Chicago, that included Accardo, Marshall Caifano, Charles Greller, and Lou Rosanova.[20]

For the general public, this 1975 article brought into full view what had only been a rumor: the Mafia's involvement with the Hoffa pardon. It became a political issue that embarrassed Nixon and the Republican Party. But their embarrassment did not come close to the effect the articles had on the Teamsters and their friends in Chicago. All this national anger was a direct result of Hoffa not keeping his word.

As you already know, I filed lawsuits against both *Playboy* and *Penthouse* at the insistence of both Louie the Tailor and the Teamsters within weeks of the publications. I've already told you of Sam Giancana's interest in the success of the suits, but I have not told you of the Godfather's meeting with Lou, Charlie Greller, and me.

The Godfather in 1975 was Tony 'Big Tuna' Accardo. I received a call from Lou to clear my calendar for the following Monday morning at 7:00. He said the 'Don' wanted to meet with me. Of course, by then I knew that the Don was

Accardo and that such a meeting was not an option. At that time, he was bigger than Uncle Sam.

As I approached the entrance to the inn, I saw that the resort was empty except for the workers on the golf course and at the clubhouse. The usual Lincolns were parked in front of the hotel, and as I pulled my Jaguar into a parking place, the Godfather's crew approached to make sure that I did not carry weapons into the meeting. I'm sure I looked nervous as I got out of my car. My smile faltered as they patted me down. I thought they might search my car and I was trying to remember if there was anything in the trunk that could get me in trouble. Finding no weapon on me, one of them nodded towards the inn and I walked away relieved.

As I entered the conference room, I remembered certain things Louie the Tailor had told me about Accardo. First, he hated publicity and became enraged when his name was in print. Second, he was presently under investigation by the Department of Justice and needed a low profile and certainly no allegations of any connections to the many businesses of the Chicago Outfit or the Teamsters. Third, he hated Hoffa and wanted the Hoffa issue to go away. He believed that Hoffa's arrogant betrayal would keep him and his friends in the headlines for months to come. According to Lou and Greller, Accardo wanted closure to the entire Hoffa problem. What that actually meant I did not know or want to know at the time.

Tony Accardo was the classic Don as I had envisioned one to be. You could tell by his appearance alone that he had come from a culture in which 'survival of the fittest' dictated a way of life. In a way, he reminded me of Louie the Tailor. His appearance also convinced me that he was not a man someone betrayed or messed with. He was a big man, very stout with penetrating eyes. Knowing how he got the nickname of Joe Batters gave him instant respect. Being a protégé of Al Capone made him the center of attention when he was around.

As the door closed behind me there remained only five people in the room. Accardo, Greller, Lou, me, and an intimidating family soldier who stood silently by the door. Accardo began the meeting by asking me to explain the suits pending in federal court and our chances of winning. I went into great detail of how truth is a defense to a libel suit under Georgia law. I explained to him that even though we were trying the case in federal court, the law of Georgia applied because the libel had occurred here. I told him that if we proved that the article was false, we could still be dismissed if the defense proved that Lou was a public figure. If they did, then we would have to show personal malice towards Lou by *Playboy* and *Penthouse*. That was the most difficult issue in the case.

Eventually Accardo got to the real reason why the meeting was called. "Can you get the writer and fed to reveal who gave them the information about La Costa and Fitz? How would they know about the sit-down?" This is the same question Giancana had asked me at my first meeting with him.

Knowing beforehand that any statement I made at this meeting could have long-term repercussions for my life and wellbeing, I took my time and gave a very deliberate answer, just as I had done with Giancana. I wanted to give Accardo the same answer.

"Mr. Accardo, the only method at my disposal is what is known as 'discovery.' That allows me to take the sworn deposition of both of them. At the depositions, I can and will bear down on their sources. Unfortunately, they will probably assert their constitutional right to not reveal them. So, I doubt we are going to get the names."

"Don't tell anyone what you just said. I want the fuckers to believe that the suits gonna give 'em up. I want to sweat the shit out of them. Hoffa is in this up to his ass. He did it to me to take me down. He knows about the investigation and once I'm down, the Teamsters are his again. That ain't gonna happen."

He stopped for a moment, trying to judge my reaction. He turned to Lou and said, "You understand what I'm getting at? You with me?"

Lou nodded and replied, "The cracker understands."

Accardo turned towards me to see if I agreed, and I quickly nodded. "I can get some good press releases out that will express our intent to secure the information. I believe that we have a right to know the sources, and I will take it up on appeal if we can't get it in the district court."

The next issue was Hoffa, and I really felt uncomfortable listening to the rhetoric about a man that these guys hated and wanted to dispose of. At the outset, Greller left the room. I wanted to go with him, but Lou looked at me and silently indicated that he wanted his lawyer to sit still.

Accardo asked Lou about Dorfman and others who were rumored to be defecting from the union and Fitzsimmons. Lou threw out a few more names and men were assigned to verify each of their positions.

Accardo glared at Lou and said, "Let the fuckers know that they deal with me if they go against Fitz."

The two-hour meeting ended with a statement from Accardo that I will never forget: "Louie, maybe we won't have to deal with the rat much longer. I'll be back in touch."

With that, the meeting ended and I quickly left the room. I honestly thought that he had some information that Hoffa was going to drop his bid to unseat Fitzsimmons. I never thought for one minute that he may have meant that Hoffa would be dealt with in a more sinister fashion a few months later, on July 30, 1975—until the national headlines read, 'HOFFA DISAPPEARS OUTSIDE OF DETROIT.'[21]

This may sound strange and unbelievable, but I never mentioned or discussed Hoffa's disappearance with Louie the Tailor until the FBI made an appointment with me to interrogate Lou about Hoffa's assumed demise.

Tony Accardo (Photograph from Wikimedia)

23. The Hoffa Investigation in Savannah

The Jimmy Hoffa mystery is not new to the city of Savannah. For example, the *Savannah Morning News* wrote two very informative articles. In 1999, the newspaper quoted a Chatham County Commissioner who speculated that Hoffa was beneath a helicopter pad located at the Savannah Inn and Country Club.[22] Again in 2003, a newspaper article noted the association of the helicopter pad with Hoffa's final resting place.[23] In both articles, the *Savannah Morning News* pointed out that this particular helicopter pad was built overnight under cover of darkness. While this may be true, this is not the final resting place of Jimmy Hoffa. But the newspaper was close. They were on the right playing field, but on the wrong yard line.

Now let's go back forty-seven years to when the FBI was seeking an interview with Louie the Tailor Rosanova concerning the death and burial of Jimmy Hoffa.

I received a call in late 1976 from Lou asking if I could meet with him and the FBI in my office sometime that week. I looked at my trial schedule and gave him a date for 10:00 that morning. In keeping with Omerta, Lou did not mention Hoffa in the phone call, but in the back part of my mind I believed Hoffa would be the topic.

Louie the Tailor arrived at 9:30 that morning dressed as if he were approaching a tee time. We had coffee and talked a few minutes about the lawsuits. Finally, at about 9:55, I asked Lou if the FBI had told him what the subject would be. He answered, "The Hoffa shit."

"Lou, is there anything that you could give them about Hoffa that would help them either solve the case or locate his body?" I asked.

"Nah, I ain't seen Hoffa since '72 when he was down here for a meeting. He had a few drinks with me and a few friends at Dino's, but we didn't talk. Get this straight. I could've, but I didn't."

"Lou, then why don't you just refuse to make any statement whatsoever? You don't have to answer any of their questions," I advised. "It would be better if you remained silent. That's your right."

As we talked, Lou began looking at his diamond-clad watch and seemed to be irritated that it was now 10:20 and the feds hadn't shown up. Seeing that it would not be to Lou's advantage to be too mad when they finally appeared, I got us some more coffee and offered to play a hand of gin with him. He agreed and after drinking another cup and playing one hand of gin, my secretary buzzed me and told me two FBI agents had arrived.

I only recall one name because it was so off-the-wall. His name was Joe Friday. (For those of you who do not recognize the name, Joe Friday was the main detective character in the long-running television series *Dragnet*.) Friday was the agent in charge of the Savannah office. At 10:45, he and his partner were led into my office where Lou was still sitting with a smirk on his broad face. Both offered to shake hands with Lou after I shook their hands during the introductions. Lou did not offer his hand in response. Instead, he told them that he would not permit the interview until they apologized for being late. Lou, drawing out the pronunciation of his favorite stereotypical Southern term, "Ya'll set this up at ten. Me and my lawyer were here. He hits me for a hundred bucks an hour. Whose gonna pay my lawyer seventy-five for sittin' here waiting on ya'll? I'm not. So, ante-up the seventy-five and then we talk. If not, I walk."

The agents were taken by surprise. Agent Friday replied, "Are you refusing to be interviewed?"

"No. Pay my lawyer for wasting his time. You feds think you can treat people anyway you want. But you ain't gonna treat me or my attorney this way. Ante-up or I'm leaving."

Again, the agents looked at each other. After a couple of moments, one of the agents pulled out his checkbook. Lou held up his hand in 'halt' fashion and said, "No checks. Only cash. I don't trust the feds."

I was getting antsy. I thought Lou was pushing them too much. But my client was seemingly having fun with federal agents that he'd detested all his life.

Agent Friday reached in his pocket and counted out seventy-five dollars in cash and handed it to me. I buzzed my secretary in and told her to give the agent a receipt for his payment, which she promptly did. Then the interview began.

One of the agents pulled out a tape recorder and advised us that the interview was going to be recorded. This brought no reaction from either of us, so the other agent began reading Louie the Tailor his Miranda Rights. Simply stated, he could remain silent and he could have an attorney present if he chose to make a statement.

Lou interrupted and said, "Save it. I got my attorney here."

They opened the interview by advising Lou that they were there as a part of the investigation to determine the whereabouts of Jimmy Hoffa, who'd disappeared in July 1975.

They told Lou that they had information that Lou knew Hoffa and was not a fan of his. Then the interrogating agent tried to ask Lou about his relationship with the Teamsters and Tony Accardo.

Lou promptly stopped him and said, "I'm an employee of the pension fund as the director of the inn. I know Accardo through relatives we have in Chicago. I'm just a friend, a distant friend."

"Mr. Rosanova, we are aware that you were in San Diego with Accardo and Frank Fitzsimmons discussing Mr. Hoffa's future prior to his pardon," the agent responded.

"Who told you that? Whoever did, don't know what he's talking about. I ain't met with anyone discussing Hoffa for any reason, pardon, or whatever," Lou countered.

I interrupted and said, "Gentlemen, Mr. Rosanova has two lawsuits pending in federal court that involve the subject matter that you just brought up. I'm not going to allow him to respond to any questions that involve the cases." They acquiesced to my objection and switched the topic.

"When was the last time you saw Hoffa? Dead or alive?" This question brought a smile to Lou's face.

"What do you mean, dead or alive? I last saw him in Savannah in '72. He was alive and drinking a lot of booze."

The agent then asked the $64,000 question: "Do you know where he is now?"

"Sure," Lou responded, shocking me and the two agents. I sat up in my chair and quickly asked Lou if we could leave the room a moment before he answered further.

Lou said no, and continued, "I wanna help them find the guy. I know where he is."

The agent in charge, after having interviewed four thousand people about Hoffa's disappearance, couldn't believe what he was hearing. I'm sure that his mind was racing forward to the awards and accolades he would receive for solving the greatest mystery of his time. Finally, after making sure the tape was running and taking all of this in, he asked: "Where is he, Mr. Rosanova?"

As I stared in disbelief and utter shock, Louie the Tailor said, "It depends on what kinda life he led before he bought the farm. Knowing that, he's in hell. What's your next question?"

His answer shocked me even more. I was afraid to look at the agents, so I just stared down at my desk. Lou chuckled as the agents put the tape recorder away, got up, and left.

"Lou, don't do that to me again. I almost had a heart attack. Why did you do it?"

Lou continued smiling and said, "Because I wanna jerk 'em around. I loved it. It cost the rats seventy-five bucks to find out Hoffa is in hell. They should've known that Cracker." He left my office laughing out loud. His last comment to me and my staff that day was: "What a great day this is!"

I learned something from that encounter. I learned that the FBI had information that my client knew something about Hoffa's disappearance or his burial place. I was absolutely convinced that Lou had had nothing to do with Hoffa's demise, but I was uncertain as to whether or not Louie the Tailor had had something to do with the burial place.

From that moment on, I began following the news more closely, and I listened more carefully to my clients who never would—when sober—discuss Hoffa after July 1975. That, alone, was strange to me.

As to the articles in the *Savannah Morning News*, they were close. They believed that the helicopter pad could be the resting place. To the newspaper's credit, this was a pad built in a hurry in the heat of the night. If I didn't know better, I would have agreed with them because during all the meetings I attended with both Teamster officials, the Chicago Outfit, and Louie the Tailor, I never heard a single discussion or comment that a helicopter pad was needed or wanted at the Savannah Inn. Further, I never heard of a helicopter landing there, and I specifically recall that when I noticed the pad the morning after it was built, I asked Lou about it, and his reply was, "Beats the hell out of me."

But in answer to all the inquiring minds, it was only a ploy! I would later get the answer while playing golf with Lou, Irving Greenberg, Charlie Greller, and while drinking at Dino's with several inebriated Teamsters.

24. The Thundering Herd

If you wanted an uncertain future on this earth, then you made it a point to damage the beautiful golf course at the Savannah Inn and Country Club—specifically, if you trampled the finely manicured greens. That, to Louie the Tailor, was sacred ground.

I recall the beautiful spring morning as I arrived at the golf club one Saturday to enjoy a round of golf with Lou and a couple of the members. It was a perfect morning, and the smell of the fresh-cut grass made it even better. I was in a good mood.

Assuming that I would find Lou in a similar mood, I entered the clubhouse eating area eager to see my friends and enjoy a good Bloody Mary that only my favorite server could fix. But I was wrong. Lou was there and everyone was silent. It didn't take a brain surgeon to know that something was drastically wrong.

While giving Lou my customary 'good morning' greeting, I took my usual seat at the table. The only response I received was, "Cracker, let's take a ride." On cue, I got up and walked with Lou out to where his golf cart was waiting.

As Lou mumbled some obscenities under his breath, we drove out to the eighteenth green, which was the closest green to the clubhouse. As we approached the green, I could see that there was significant damage to the once immaculate grass surface. We stopped and Lou got out and led me over to what looked like deep hoof marks in the grass. He pointed out to the fairway, and I could see similar hoof marks approaching the green that led back around the lake to the tee area.

I understood why Lou was so upset and why it rendered him almost speechless. It appeared to my untrained eyes that a herd of horses had stampeded through Lou's precious golf course; he felt extremely violated. He looked as if a member of his immediate family had departed. He stated, "Cracker, someone's gotta hate me a lot to do this. This hurts." He turned and as he walked back to the cart he mumbled in a low voice, "When I find out who did this, I'll make cufflinks out of their eyeballs. They'll wish they'd never been born."

I involuntarily rubbed my eyes.

He drove me out to the seventeenth fairway where there was more damage, more obscenities, and more promises of retribution. I said very little beyond expressing my sympathy and disdain for the offenders. However, I assure you that I never concurred with the 'eyeball/cufflinks' threat.

When we arrived back at the clubhouse, there was a telephone call waiting for me. It was my wife reminding me to remind Lou that he was to have dinner with us at our home on Wilmington Island that evening. She had invited Lou several days prior, and up until this morning, he'd been excited about spending the evening with my family.

Louie the Tailor loved being around my family. My daughter was around thirteen at the time, and he referred to her as his 'pretty ballerina.' Two years before, he'd anointed himself as her godfather and he took his title seriously. I can't count the times that he asked about my family while we played golf and the numerous times he went to the pool to see them when he heard of their presence. He always predicted that the pretty ballerina would be a beauty queen and a real ballerina.

When I got off the phone, I went over to the table where Lou was sitting and reminded him of the dinner engagement he had with my family. This perked him up a little, and he smiled and said, "Cracker, this could take my mind off it, for a little while. Just make sure you got good vodka and not that rot-gut you served last time. That sent me to the john for a solid week."

"No problem," I replied and left without playing that day since I had concluded that this was not the day to be with Lou on his trampled golf course. I anticipated that he would shut down the back nine for immediate repair. I also knew that it would cost the Teamsters a few hundred thousand in damages. No, the best move for me was to leave and go home.

I guess this is as good time as any to tell you more about my daughter, the pretty ballerina. She was a talented equestrian and had won several ribbons in horse shows. When she was eleven, we moved to Wilmington Island into a home that had a pool, a wooden fenced corral, and a horse stable. On arrival, she immediately wanted a horse. So, in conformance with our usual pattern of giving her whatever she wanted, we began to search for a horse.

Newspaper ads led us about thirty miles from Savannah where we found a strawberry roan thoroughbred with a magnificent pedigree. I immediately pictured my daughter riding this animal to victory in dominant fashion in the years to come. The price of $10,000 (two Chevy automobiles, loaded back then) didn't faze me. But to my surprise (and her mother's) the ballerina wanted to look further. So, we went to the next ad in Pooler, Georgia, a little town a couple of miles outside of Savannah.

This horse was a solid black male quarter/thoroughbred mixed breed horse that reminded her of Black Beauty. His name was Diablo. The owner was a retired police officer who'd ridden Diablo as a mounted policeman. He told us that the horse was formerly a barrel racer and was kid friendly. However, he showed us where the horse's ears had been clipped and a healed gash on his right rear flank. He related how the horse had been abused and beaten with a board. Reacting to the abuse, Diablo had responded by kicking the man. Thus, he'd been labeled as 'having a mean trait' requiring his ears to be clipped. I watched my daughter's reaction to Diablo's history and knew what she was thinking. She had a soft heart, particularly for animals, abused or not, so I knew that she wanted Black Beauty.

I nodded to her and informed the owner that she wanted the horse for hunter-class competition. He said that the horse was Western saddle but that it wouldn't be hard to change him over to English saddle for show purposes. Not knowing a lot, in fact, nothing about horses, I took him at his word and bought the horse, especially when he gave me a price of $800.

That led to buying a horse trailer and an enormous amount of tackle and related horse things. 'Horse things' included an English saddle, blankets, bridles, etc., including several riding outfits for the ballerina. After spending several thousands of dollars that week, we set her up with riding lessons on the island and her equestrian career began.

She took to the lessons remarkably fast and it was not long—perhaps ten to twelve months—before she entered a horse show. I recall as if it were yesterday the way she looked and the excitement on her face. She was outfitted in formal khaki riding pants (called a Jodhpur), brown boots made in England, a plaid jacket over a white lacy shirt, and a velvet black hard hat. She was absolutely beautiful.

On the morning of the first competition, we loaded Diablo into the trailer. She had groomed him the day before and platted his mane and tail earlier. He too was beautiful and looked very impressive. How good a show horse and jumper he was, remained unknown.

When we arrived at the show in Savannah, we unloaded Diablo and his tack. I noticed for the first time that Diablo appeared to be sway-backed and not 'show horse' quality as the other thoroughbreds appeared to be. Not thinking anything of it, we got him ready for competition. I pulled my daughter over to the side just before she was to advance to where she was to begin her competition. I told her not to expect to win a ribbon in her first show. I said this only to assure that she would not be too disappointed when she lost. As if she didn't hear a word I was saying, she looked at me and said, "Daddy, I'm going to win." She hugged me and her mother and walked her horse to the starting gate.

Standing next to me was another father whose daughter was riding a beautiful chestnut thoroughbred. He had seen Diablo and his sway-back and clipped ears, and the man appeared to be snickering. He looked at the event program and said, "Your daughter's horse's name is listed on the program as Diablo. You know what the name means?"

"No."

He quickly responded, "'The devil' in Spanish."

I had to get away from this guy who'd just told me that I had put my child on a horse that was so mean that he was called the devil. As I was contemplating what to do, I noticed that she was already riding and getting applause. I also noticed that Diablo looked totally different in his movements and appearance. He looked like he was a different horse without any signs of being sway-back. He was responding to the competition as if he knew that he had to carry my daughter to victory. To my surprise, he did! Both of them looked and performed as accomplished jumpers and not as first-timers. Together, they were hard to beat, and my worries about him hurting her subsided.

As she rode back to us on her black beauty, I looked over at the man who had snickered. He was consoling his daughter after the loss she took from my rookie rider and her devil horse. He wouldn't look in my direction and moved away from us for the rest of the competition.

Now, back to our evening with Lou. When Lou arrived, we all gathered in the family room. He teased my daughter, joking with her about school. I could tell Lou was still tense and after a few drinks, he began telling Jean of the thundering herd on his golf course. As he was relating the story, Jean noticed the reaction of our ballerina. When Lou had finished, Jean expressed her horror and sympathy to Lou. Then she told our daughter to come help her while I poured us another drink.

Both Jean and I knew that our daughter was a terrible liar. She absolutely could not conceal a lie. Neither could she hide the truth. So, with this background, my wife confronted her: "What do you know about the horses trampling Mr. Rosanova's golf course?"

It only took a few seconds for the child to come clean. This was her story: The day before (Friday) she'd gone to her riding lessons. While there, she and three other girls had wanted to run their horses outside of the training corral, but their instructor had not allowed it. So, the girls had made plans to ride back to the training center to meet up around midnight and run their horses on the trails on the island. She'd sneaked out that night under a full moon, ridden Diablo to the center, met up with her friends, and off they'd gone. Unfortunately, they'd ended up on the open range of the fairways at the inn at about 1:00 Saturday morning. She'd gotten back home around 4:00 in the morning.

Jean's first reaction was to quickly pack some overnight clothes for our daughter and send her to a friend's home for the night. "Your father and I will talk to you tomorrow, little lady, but for right now we have to hide you from Mr. Rosanova. Do not, and I repeat, don't you ever mention this to anyone the rest of your life. Do you understand me? Do you?"

Our remorseful and frightened young daughter left with one other caution given by her mother: "And, please, don't ever think that you have to confess this to anyone, especially Mr. Rosanova. Do we agree on that?" She agreed with her mother. And, to her credit, she never spoke of this again while Lou was living.

When Jean finally joined Lou and me, she seemed somewhat troubled. However, after a few more drinks, we all settled down. Lou forgot the shock of the morning's revelation of the thundering herd, Jean forgot her knowledge of the culprits, and I just enjoyed not knowing anything until the next morning when Jean told me of our daughter's confession.

I stayed away from Lou for a few days to let things simmer down. We grounded our daughter for a month and prohibited her from going to the inn for any reason. Louie the Tailor never knew that the lead rider of the thundering herd was his lawyer's daughter riding bareback on the former barrel racer Diablo.

25. The Lack of a Bond

I often marveled at how beautiful a city Savannah was with her extraordinary history and how she had charmed tourists from around the world. However, Savannah had its dark side as well—a dark side that exposed its judicial system to injustices that were too obvious to see and far too bothersome to correct by the righteous leaders of this Southern city. Unfortunately, as a trial lawyer, I was exposed to this dark side much too often. Two cases, in particular, affected me to such an extent that I wanted to walk out of the courtroom for good.

The first involved the brutal rape and extensive beating of an elderly woman who owned and operated a well-known antique shop, the Old Arch Antique Shop. This shop was located at the foot of the Talmadge Bridge that spanned the Savannah River and connected the state of Georgia to the low country of South Carolina. As mentioned earlier, it is also the bridge where a man threw a two-year-old child from its highest point above the river.

I learned of the crime through Louie the Tailor as we played golf on a brisk Saturday morning at the inn. The article in the newspaper had angered Lou and brought out many Sicilian phrases that I had never heard. I am sure that most were curse words and ancient curses directed towards men who rape elderly mothers and grandmothers.

"Cracker, in the country of my ancestors, the devil who raped and beat this little lady would never make it to court. They'd blow his head off and feed him to the dogs."

After this opening observation, I decided not to respond quickly. So, I walked over to my golf ball, lined up my shot, and stroked it down the fairway. I was hoping that we could concentrate more on golf that morning than the brutal rape and Sicilian justice. My wish would not come to pass.

Staring at me through his squinting Sicilian eyes, he said, "Cracker, when they get that motherfucker, what lawyer with a heart is gonna defend that piece of shit?"

As I watched my ball come to rest in the rough not far down the fairway, and much too far from the green on this par four hole, Lou continued, "Cracker, he don't deserve a lawyer. He don't deserve a trial." I knew where Lou was going with this conversation and I also knew how to respond, because as a criminal trial attorney, this statement was made to me many times over the years as I defended the indefensible in our quiet little Southern city.

"Lou, you know my answer to that. You're assuming that whoever they arrest will be the one that committed the rape. How many times have you been with me when the man they tried was innocent? Applying your 'justice' before trial would have meant that you would have killed the wrong man and taken a father from his family or a son from his mother."

Upon hearing my response, Lou stared at me for a few moments looking for words that could challenge my statement. Finding none, and still squinting, he pulled his club from his golf bag, walked over to his ball, lined up his shot, and stroked the ball down the middle of the fairway to the edge of the green. He turned to me, smiled, and said, "Cracker, you know your stuff." He turned and pointed his club towards a ball that I could hardly see because of its distance from me, and continued, "And, I know my stuff."

I smiled and nodded affirmatively. We got into the golf cart, and for the rest of the day, neither of us mentioned the devil that had raped the old lady at the Old Arch Antique Shop located at the foot of the bridge.

News of an arrest dominated the media for several days following the crime. The man had been identified by an eyewitness as being a black male, in his mid-twenties, slender, and medium height. Unfortunately, this was a description that fit half of the black population in Savannah. His name was Frank Williams, a twenty-five-year-old black man who worked on Hilton Head Island, South Carolina, as a bricklayer. Williams was married to a teacher at Savannah State College and they had three children. He had no criminal record. But unfortunately, he was already being tried in the newspapers and being convicted on the streets and bars of this lovely town.

I became involved in the case through a telephone call from the Washington, DC office of the black activist Jessie Jackson. I was asked by the caller if I would talk with the wife of Frank Williams later that afternoon. I was told that she was the cousin of Jackson and that he would appreciate me representing Williams in what Jackson thought would be a lynching. Without committing to represent Frank Williams, I agreed to meet with his wife.

Mrs. Williams was a very pretty lady who was nicely dressed in fine clothing and jewelry. She had little makeup on and presented herself as very obviously stunned by the arrest of her husband.

"Mr. Haupt, Frank didn't do this. He's a good father, a good husband, and he has a good job in Hilton Head. Mr. Haupt, he is a good man," she said as she wiped tears from her eyes.

She showed me several photos of Williams with her and their children. The photos demonstrated to me that the Williams family was well thought of in the black community in Savannah.

"Please represent him. He needs a bond right away or he'll lose his job. His supervisor said they'll hold his position for a week. So please get him out," she pleaded.

Without much ado, I told her that I believed her, and that I would represent her husband, but I could not guarantee her that I could get him out on a bond. I tried to explain it to her as best I could.

"Mrs. Williams, Frank has been accused of a terrible crime against an elderly white woman. To the police and the vast majority of this city, he is already guilty because he's a black man. You know what we are dealing with, and I believe you know that a bond is not an option. I believe that you know that I am going to have a tough job overcoming what the newspapers have already printed about Frank."

I paused, allowing her time to digest what I had just said. From what I could determine from watching her reaction, she was understanding but not accepting it.

"Mr. Haupt, if he was white, he would get a bond. It's not fair. It's just not fair," she replied while drying eyes swollen and red from crying.

"I know it's not fair. I also know what is reality, and I don't want you to get any false hopes that I can't deliver on. Do you understand?" I hesitated and then continued, "Mrs. Williams, I promise you that I will fight for him and that I will do everything in my power and knowledge to get Frank back home to you and the kids."

With that said, she looked up at me and with a soft smile said, "I believe you." Mrs. Williams stood up, shook my hand, and left my office knowing that she and her children might never be with Frank Williams as a family unit again. She also knew that her life, that had been so organized and successful, was probably over. She would have to contend with social shunning at the college and her community.

Within minutes of her departure, I called Jackson's office and informed them that I was representing Frank Williams. The voice at the other end thanked me and assured me that Jessie Jackson would help me in any way he could, even by coming to Savannah and marching in the streets. I thanked the voice and modified my acceptance to represent Williams by conditioning my representation on Jessie Jackson not coming to Savannah or getting involved in any way with the case. My last statement to the voice was, "I have enough to overcome in this case without Mr. Jackson's involvement. Please, tell him not to interfere."

I called my friend the DA, Bubsy Ryan. "Bubsy, can we agree on a bond for Frank Williams?"

Bubsy chuckled and replied, "Are you serious? Ain't no way! That man beat that little old lady in the face while and after he raped her. She's lucky to have survived it."

"Bubsy, what happened to the principle 'innocent until proven guilty'?" I replied to deaf ears.

"Bubba, an eyewitness was in the store and looked directly in his face immediately before he attacked the woman. It's open and shut if there ever was an open-and-shut case," he exclaimed. "You need to read the police report and witness statements. This man is extremely dangerous," he continued.

"Bubsy, that's ridiculous. This man has no record, has a good job, a nice home and family, and his wife is a teacher at Savannah State. We're not talking about the average black hood running the streets. He'll lose everything if he has to stay in jail for the next six months, and he has no reason to not show up for trial," I pleaded.

"Bubba, I'm sorry, but you know that no judge is going to give him a bond. This is a brutal case of a black man raping and beating a white grandmother. I can't help you. I'm opposing bond."

Within minutes of hanging up with Ryan, I had my secretary prepare a bond petition and I headed for the judge that I had the best chance with. As I entered Judge Cheatham's office, I passed Ryan coming out. With a smile and a nod, Ryan quickly disappeared.

"Good afternoon, Judge. I need to talk to you about a bond."

The judge nodded as he displayed a slight smirk. "Is it about Frank Williams?" he asked.

I gave him an affirmative nod and waited for his expected response. "From what I know of the facts, I cannot risk a bond in this case," he replied.

I pleaded with the judge for several minutes about what I knew of Williams, but the judge wasn't buying it. Ryan had done a good job of convincing him that the police had sufficient evidence that Frank Williams was the man who had brutally beaten and raped a helpless elderly white lady in broad daylight, just after a tourist left the store. I quickly realized that my pleas were falling on deaf ears and further discussion was useless.

"Mr. Haupt, file your formal petition and set a day to hear your motion. Send Mr. Ryan a copy, and I'll hear what both of you have to say. But I don't mind telling you that I am not inclined to grant a bond in this case."

I stood and before turning towards the door leading to his reception area, I gave it one more shot. "Judge, by all of this court's criteria in bond cases, this man would be getting a bond without any effort. He owns his home, has family roots in this county, he has a good job, and has no record. But because he is accused of a crime involving a white woman, he is disqualified and the presumption of innocence goes out the window. That's justice?"

Judge Cheatham stared at me and then looked away. The absence of a reply told me I had said too much, and I had worn out my welcome if I'd had one that day. I left and didn't bother to say goodbye or close his door behind me. Hopefully, he got the message that I wasn't pleased either.

That evening, before I began my investigation, I called Lou because he had warned me, in his own way, not to take this case. I told him of the events surrounding the case and of my conversation with Jesse Jackson's office. He wasn't pleased, to say the least, but he accepted it because he knew my call was out of respect for him. I knew then that the case would not affect my relationship with Louie the Tailor.

My first stop was at the county jail to interview my client and to inform him that I was going to fight for him and that he was not going to get a bond anytime soon. On the way in, I ran into the lead investigator for sex crimes in our fair community.

Alonyia Haisten was a mid-fortyish, five-foot-two feisty detective who knew her job better than any of the many other detectives I had faced. She was dedicated to her job and was an untiring workhorse. Her only fault or weakness, according to her co-workers, was that she had a tendency to express her opinion too much in the accused's favor when she thought the man innocent. To me, this was not a fault. I thought it was her strongest attribute.

There is nothing wrong with a good police officer having a strong conscience or sense of fair play. When Alonyia believed that a woman was lying about a rape or an assault, she would lay back and help the defense get the man a bond and an acquittal. Of course, this didn't bode well for the DA's office or her fellow detectives.

However, when she thought the defendant was guilty as sin, you could forget any cooperation from her. She would double-down on her investigation and build a case for the DA's office that was hard to overcome. Unfortunately, she believed that Frank Williams was the rapist.

"Bubba, I got an eyewitness!" were her first words to me after I informed her that I was Williams's lawyer.

With a grin that reached from one ear to the other, she continued, "You're going to lose this one, sport. As Williams was coming in the door of the antique shop, a woman employee was leaving and she got a good look at him. She picked him out of a photo lineup with no hesitation."

Her grin disappeared as she reached into the file she was holding and removed some photos of a severely beaten elderly lady. "Look at these photos of the victim. Look what he did to her face. Pretty, ain't it? He also broke two of her ribs. And you want him out on bond? No way, Jose! If he ever sees the light of day again, that would be a shame."

"Alonyia, I know nothing about the case yet, so I can't answer you. I'm here to interview him for the first time, so take a deep breath and let me read your witness statements," I replied, without deliberately showing any emotion in order not to fuel her anger and lose all hope of getting any statements before filing a bunch of motions.

"Sure, but they won't do you any good. Your best bet is to plea bargain on this one. You ain't gonna pull any rabbits out of your hat on this one." With that said, she went back to her file and handed me copies of the initial police report and statements from the victim and the eyewitness. I thanked her and told her I would get back to her after I had talked with Williams and did some investigating. She nodded and walked away.

Two deputies brought Frank Williams into the interview room where I was sitting with the statements spread out in front of me on a desk. While waiting for him, I read the statements.

"Frank, I'm Bubba Haupt, and I have been retained to represent you by your family," I said while shaking his shackled right hand.

Frank was a slightly built light-skinned black man who looked to me to be about five feet eight and weighing no more than 145 pounds. He had an afro-type haircut that was very popular in those days. There was nothing unusual about him that would have distinguished him from a considerable percentage of the black male population in Savannah, except for his very sad eyes and slumped-over defeated posture.

"Frank, I've just read these statements that were given to me by the lead detective in your case. Would you sit down and read them carefully?"

I watched him as he read. When he finished, he looked up at me and said, "Mr. Haupt, it wasn't me that did this. I've never been in this lady's shop. I pass by it every day coming home from work on Hilton Head, but I never stop there. They got the wrong person."

"Frank, did you stop somewhere up the road on the Carolina-side of the bridge?" I asked.

"No, I drove straight from the job site to home."

"That doesn't help us because that would place you in the area of the crime at the time the crime was committed," I countered.

"Mr. Haupt, I drove straight home and that is the truth," he replied.

Having talked to him for over two hours and getting as much information from him as I could, I left him in the custody of the deputies after assuring him that I would fight for him.

We had no alibi and they had an eyewitness. That made the outcome of this case very doubtful as far as my client was concerned. At the outset, I could see no weakness. The only chance that Williams had to go free depended solely on the credibility of the eyewitness. I had to discredit the witness any way I could. That hope was diminished when she refused to talk with me.

Because of the refusal to grant a bond, the judge directed the DA's office to expedite the pretrial proceedings so that the case could come to trial more rapidly than normal. Within about four months, the case was called for trial under heavy media coverage. Because of the Williams family's standing in the black community and Jessie Jackson's connections, race relations were at its lowest point in our fair city and the courtroom spectators reflected this chasm. Blacks sat on one side while the whites sat on the other side. Deputies were situated in between.

Ryan came out of the gate swinging. He had an air of confidence that I hadn't seen in a while. He had a good solid case, and everyone in Savannah knew it, including me. His lead-off witness, Detective Alonyia Haisten, attired in her best conservative dark suit with a nice scarf framing her freshly done hairdo, laid out the crime from the time the police had received the initial call to the final identification and arrest of Frank Williams. As she exited the witness stand, she gave a hard glance towards my client as if to show the jury her disdain for him and what he had done to the little old lady.

The next witness was the victim. She was a frail white lady who looked to be about five feet six and about ninety-five pounds. She spoke very softly as she described what had happened that afternoon within a few minutes of closing her shop. As she related how a black man came into her shop, approached her from the rear, and hit her in the head, the women on the jury gasped as if on cue from a conductor. She then described how he pulled up her dress, pulled it over her head, and was careful to do the evil deed from a position where he couldn't be seen or identified, except for the color of his hands. She then told the jury how he held her head by her silver hair and repeatedly smashed her face into the hardwood floor.

When she finished describing and recounting one of the most vicious crimes I had ever had the displeasure of defending, the judge intervened and recessed the trial as Ryan and one of his assistants helped the very emotional grandmother from the stand. I didn't look at the jury during this process because I didn't want to see their reaction and prejudice my own thinking. I had to stay optimistic for my client's sake.

The flaw in the State's case came with the introduction of their eyewitness. Because she had refused to see me so that I could interview her, I was unaware of the weakness that could possibly make a difference in the case. All I had access to was the recorded statement she had given to Alonyia Haisten, and it didn't help my case.

Ryan put her on the stand as his last witness of the day. The woman was a middle-aged, attractive married white woman who had been working at the shop for over a year. She followed her prior statement to a tee and testified that on this particular afternoon she had left a little early since business had been slow and there were no customers in the shop. As she was leaving through the front door a young black man passed her walking into the shop. She testified that she saw his face as he passed by. She was not alarmed in any way, nor did she suspect that he was there to harm the owner. In fact, she claimed that she thought nothing of it, or she would have turned around and gone back into the shop.

She testified that when she left the shop, she had gone next door to the Holiday Inn restaurant for her usual cup of coffee after work. She also stated that she had gone for a cup of coffee before work each morning as well. An hour later she had driven home and that's where she'd heard the news broadcast of the rape of the elderly woman-owner of the Old Arch Antique Shoppe. She'd stopped what she was doing and hurried to the police station to report what she had seen. On arrival, she'd been interviewed by Detective Haisten and had been shown a photo lineup that consisted of seven photos that included one of Frank Williams. She'd immediately picked out the photo of Frank Williams as the man she'd passed leaving the shop that afternoon.

Ryan had the clerk mark a photo he had in his hand as evidence for the State. He walked over to me and permitted me to examine the photo before he showed it to the witness. The initials of the witness and the name of Frank Williams were on the back of the photo. I nodded that I was through examining the photo, and Ryan walked to the witness stand and presented it to her. She looked at the photo and told the jury that this was the photo she'd picked out of the lineup.

"Are you sure that the man you passed leaving the shop is the man in this photo?" Ryan asked. "Is he in this courtroom today?"

She looked towards my client and pointed at him and said in a very bitter tone, "That's him! That's the man I saw entering the shop as I left. I will never forget his face. He did it! He's the one!"

The jury stirred and stared at Frank Williams as Ryan announced to the court that he had no further questions from the witness. The judge looked at the clock hanging on the wall and announced that he was recessing the trial until the next morning at 9:30. He dismissed the jury for the day and advised me to be ready for my cross-examination of the witness. I acknowledged his advisement, and as I was packing my briefcase preparing to leave, I realized for the first time since I was hired to represent Williams, that my client had a chance to go home again. I knew that the witness was lying, and I knew how to prove it.

The following morning, I entered the courtroom with a smile on my face that caught my friend Ryan by surprise. He came over to me and asked me why I was

154

so happy? I looked at him and said, "Bubsy, my client is innocent and I will prove it this morning." Ryan smirked and walked away wondering what hat-trick I had in store for him and the jury.

The jury was brought in, followed by the judge and the witness. She was reminded by the judge that she was still under oath. He then asked me if I was ready to proceed with the cross-examination of the witness. I acknowledged that I was and told the jury good morning.

"Mrs. Smith [not her real name], yesterday you swore under oath that Frank Williams was the man that passed you going into the shop that afternoon. Is that correct?"

She replied, "Yes," while staring at Williams.

"How long did it take for you to walk past him? A second or two?" I asked.

"Maybe four or five, because I wasn't in a hurry to leave."

"So, your identification of this man was made within that four or five seconds."

"Yes."

"Did either of you stop and talk to one another?"

"No, certainly not!"

"Was there anything about him or the occasion that would have made you notice him more than normal?"

"No."

"So, you are asking this jury to convict Frank Williams on an identification that lasted no more than four or five seconds as you passed him at the doorway to the shop?"

"Mr. Haupt, I know what you're getting at and I can assure you that I have always had the ability to remember faces, even when I just glance at them. He's the man I passed that afternoon."

"Yesterday in your testimony you told this jury that when you left the shop you went over to the Holiday Inn for coffee, as you did every afternoon after work. Isn't that right?"

"Yes, I sure did."

"Now, other than walking past a black man, you had no reason to pay extra attention to him or suspect him of anything?"

Showing signs of tiring from my few questions, she replied, "No, there was no reason to pay extra attention to him. I've already said that."

I turned and walked away from her to my counsel's table and picked up a file and returned to face her once again. "Mrs. Smith, you had your usual cup of coffee this morning at the Holiday Inn, didn't you?"

"Yes, but I don't think that that has anything to do with this," she replied as Ryan stood to object to this line of questioning.

"Judge, what does this have to do with this trial? He's harassing the witness."

Before the judge could respond, I interrupted, "Judge, I assure you that this has everything to do with this trial and the innocence of my client. I am going to prove that this witness did not have the ability to identify my client as the man she passed in the doorway."

"Okay, Mr. Haupt, but get to the connection as quickly as you can."

"Thank you. Mrs. Smith, how long were you at the Holiday Inn this morning drinking coffee?"

"About thirty to forty minutes."

"Did the same waitress who took your order bring you the coffee?"

"Yes, I think so."

"What color hair did she have?"

"What?" she responded with a raised voice.

"What color hair did she have? You should know, you saw her twice in a thirty to forty-minute span and talked with her when you gave her the order. Tell this jury what color hair she had."

There was no immediate response, so I continued to press her. "Mrs. Smith, I have the lady outside in the hall. Tell this jury what she looked like."

Obviously agitated, she turned to the judge and asked, "Do I have to answer him?"

"Yes, you do," the judge politely answered.

After hesitating once again, she reluctantly replied, "I don't remember."

I walked over to the court reporter's table and picked up the photograph that Ryan had used in identifying my client as the rapist. I went over to the witness stand and handed it to Mrs. Smith.

"Read to this jury the date that's printed on the back of the photograph you selected as the man you passed that afternoon in a total span of four to five seconds."

"It says December 5, 1966," she replied.

"Did you know that this was the date that the photo was taken, eleven years before this crime?"

"No," she responded with a puzzled look on her face.

"Is the hairstyle on the young man in the photo the same as the hairstyle on Frank Williams as he is sitting here today?"

"No."

"The kid in the photo has short hair while my client has a full afro, right?"

"The hairstyle is different," she reluctantly admitted.

"Did the man that walked past you have short hair or an afro?"

"About average. Not short, but not an afro," she replied.

"Mrs. Smith, if Frank Williams had an afro hairstyle on the afternoon of this rape, then he could not have been the man you passed and you have identified the wrong man. Am I correct?"

She said nothing. She stared at Frank Williams and continued to think of a reasonable response. I stopped the drama and announced to the court, "Judge, I have no further questions for this witness and I want the record to reflect that the witness never answered my last question. Thank you."

After Ryan announced that he had no further witnesses, I placed Frank Williams on the stand for the sole purpose of having him identify his driver's license that showed a photograph taken a week before the crime. I then introduced several photographs of Frank with his wife and children taken two weeks before the rape. The final photograph I introduced was the arrest photograph taken at the jail that showed Frank's hairstyle. All of the photos showed Frank Williams with a full afro.

When I concluded my evidence, the case was given to the jury to determine Frank Williams's fate. As the jury left the courtroom to deliberate, I walked back to where two of my friends were sitting. Louie the Tailor was sitting next to a friend, David Powell, commonly known as 'Eat'em-up.' He had that name because the guy was always hungry and ate anything that didn't eat him.

The three of us left and walked back to my office for a few drinks and chatter. When we finally sat down with a 'cool one' Lou spoke first, "Cracker, you busted them. The man is innocent. They got to let him go."

Then Lou put his drink down and asked, "Was the lady from the Holiday Inn really outside in the hall?"

I looked at Eat'em-up and smiled. My hungry pal had gone to the Holiday Inn that morning at my request, to observe the witness as she had ordered her usual coffee. Since he had been in court the day before when the lady had testified, he'd known who she was. That morning he'd watched as the witness had ordered her coffee, chatted with the waitress, and received the coffee a few minutes later.

David wrote down the time, the table location, and the description of the waitress with a fresh blonde hairdo. He then called me and told me her name. I quickly filled out a subpoena for her to be at the courtroom two hours later. A deputy served it for me and when she'd arrived, Eat'em-up had given me the high sign.

"Yes, Lou, she was there and ready to walk in and testify as to having talked with the witness two hours before. She was also ready to testify that she had waited on Mrs. Smith many times before."

Lou smiled and said, "That's my lawyer!"

An hour later the jury returned a 'not guilty' verdict, and Frank Williams had to have been the happiest man on earth that night. He was free, still had his job, and his family was still intact. He hugged me and I watched as he and his wife left arm-in-arm walking out of a stunned courtroom.

As I was leaving, Alonyia Haisten came over to me and congratulated me on the victory. She admitted that she'd been wrong on this one, and we departed still friends. The next day, Jesse Jackson called to thank me for standing up for his family and invited me to attend an Atlanta event where he would be speaking. I thanked him for the invitation and the call.

But it was not over.

Two months later, I received a call from Frank's wife and she told me that Frank had been arrested again for the rape of a young white sales lady at a local dress shop in the historic area of Savannah near the Old Arch Antique Shoppe. She said that he was being held in the county jail without bond. Again, she pleaded with me to get him out on bond because he would definitely lose his job and they would lose their house. I assured her I would do whatever I could to get him home. She was crying as we ended the call.

On the way to the jailhouse, my mind was running a hundred miles an hour. Was I wrong in the first case? Was Frank really a black rapist that hated white women? Was he insane? Unlike my normal attitude of not wanting to know whether my client was guilty or not, I needed to know this time. If he was guilty, I would still represent him, but I didn't address the consequences of breaking my long-standing rule; would I defend Frank any differently if I knew he was guilty? I didn't know.

I decided to meet up with Alonyia Haisten before I interviewed Frank. I found Alonyia in her office with a series of photographs in her hand. They were the same photographs used in the first Williams case. She waved at me to come over to her desk as I entered the room.

"Bubba, I hate to tell you this, but this same pack of photos used in the Old Arch case was used in the photo lineup in this new case. I wasn't on duty, and no one called me. How stupid can someone be?" she said in an apologetic tone.

"We had a recent photo of him sitting on my desk, but they used the same eleven-year-old one," she continued.

She knew what that meant. She knew that the case would now have problems in the identification area. She also knew that she would have serious doubts about his guilt in this new case. She knew that Frank Williams did not look like the old photograph the young girl had selected, and the identification was now tainted with a fatal flaw. Fortunately, unlike the first arrest, Alonyia Haisten was not convinced that Frank Williams was guilty of this one.

Ryan and the trial judge were convinced that in view of the second rape charge, Frank Williams was guilty of the first one at the Old Arch. This logic once again denied Frank the right to a bond and the presumption of innocence. But in Frank's situation, it meant a lot more. He would lose his job and home.

However, in this case, we had a lot more firepower than we'd had in the first. On the day and time of this charge, Frank had been picking up his little girl's birthday cake to take to her Saturday afternoon party at their home. At the same time the rape occurred, he'd been in a bakery owned by the chairman of the Chatham County Commissioners waiting for the cake decoration to be completed. After waiting for almost an hour, he'd given them a check and left for the party with the cake. The rape had occurred fifteen minutes after he'd arrived at the bakery, making it impossible for him to have been at the scene of the rape since it was on the other side of town approximately forty-five minutes away.

The owner of the bakery was a popular political figure in the Savannah area. He was white, very conservative and had no problem with the KKK's ideology. No one in Savannah would have ever accused him of helping a black man get out of a charge of raping a young white woman. His name was Robert McCorkle and he had been in office (the highest political office in Savannah) for the previous twenty years. He was known for his honesty and uncompromising attitude when he thought he was right on any point.

I called McCorkle and arranged an interview at the bakery. He greeted me warmly since I had been his favorite high school quarterback as well as a Baptist in a Catholic school. "Hey, Bubba, what can I do for you?"

"Judge McCorkle, good to see you again. I'm representing a guy who came to your bakery last Saturday and bought a birthday cake for his daughter." I showed him a copy of a recent photograph of Frank.

Staring at the photo, McCorkle looked up and said, "Bubba, I remember him."

"Judge, do you remember the time he arrived?"

"No, but I can get the order ticket because it'll have the time he picked up the cake." Disappearing into a back office, he soon returned with the ticket. "Here it is."

I looked at it and it placed Frank at the bakery during the time of the rape. McCorkle went a step further and introduced me to the lady who had waited on Frank. She looked at the photograph and confirmed the time.

Showing them a copy of the incident report that included the time of the rape and where it took place, I said, "Judge, Frank is in jail this moment for raping a girl on the other side of town at the same time he was here at your bakery."

Looking at the time on the incident report, McCorkle emphatically replied, "There's no way he could've done it."

"Judge, I need you and this little lady to testify so that he won't go to prison for the rest of his life. Judge, he's black and she's white. Does that present a problem?"

His eyes opened wide and then he said, "If he's innocent, he's innocent."

"Then will y'all testify on his behalf?"

Without hesitation, they both agreed.

On the morning of trial, eight months after Frank's second arrest and no bond, I could sense a change in my client. He was no longer the hopeful, smiling Frank Williams who had a future before him. He appeared to be defeated and my words of encouragement did not help. He stared down and never offered a smile as he sat slumped over at the defendant's table. Unlike the first trial, Frank no longer had the Afro he was accustomed to wearing; he had a 'jail cut.'

The trial went as expected with the victim positively identifying Frank from an eleven-year-old photograph out of a series of eight. I was startled since the original series used in the first trial only had seven. When Ryan handed them to me for review before he offered them into evidence, I thumbed through them to see the added photograph. There, staring at me in such a sad manner, was the photograph taken of Frank on his arrest in the first case. That photo had Frank with an afro. The old photo still had him in short hair.

When it came my time to cross-examine the victim, I confronted her with the eight photos. She admitted that she had identified Frank by his eleven-year-old photo when he'd been seventeen years old. The second one, the one taken during his arrest, she had not selected.

With this evidence and the testimony of Robert McCorkle and the little lady who worked at the bakery, the jury took only twenty minutes to find Frank Williams not guilty of the second crime. Once again, I watched Frank leave the courtroom a relatively happy man, but this time, he was not arm-in-arm with his wife.

A year later Frank Williams came to my office for me to represent him on a driving-under-the-influence-of-alcohol charge. The man I saw that day was not the man I had known the year before. The man who appeared that day was jobless, homeless, and an alcoholic. He looked like he had shrunken into himself since the last time I had seen him. He was thin, frail, and unshaven. I told him that I would help him, and he left.

I called his wife and asked her what had happened. She told me that when Frank had come home from the second trial that he'd begun looking for a job. She said that he'd started drinking heavily when he couldn't find one. She told me that the black community had abandoned him because they thought he was guilty of raping the women. She said that no white employer would talk to him. There were not many black employers in Savannah at that time.

When he couldn't work to help with the bills, they'd lost their home and his car. When that had happened, his whole personality had changed and they'd ended up in a divorce. He'd left and was living in inner city shelters somewhere downtown.

What a sad commentary these cases presented. A gainfully employed family man had been charged with rapes based on photographs that did not resemble him, had spent eighteen months in jail because he couldn't get a bond since he was a black man accused of raping white women. His life had been ruined because he'd been denied that presumption of innocence that the Constitution guarantees.

But more upsetting was that his fate and the gross injustice served upon him went unnoticed. No one in the system, except Alonyia Haisten, expressed remorse or an intention to correct the illegal custom of not granting bonds to black men in Frank's situation. It was as if Frank Williams didn't matter and never existed.

When I shared my discontent and thoughts with Louie the Tailor, he agreed. However, like the perpetrators of this injustice, he offered no solution. But unlike them, he did tell me I was right and that it was a shame the way they had dealt the cards to Frank.

I never saw Frank again. When he didn't show up for court on the DUI charge, I called the voice in Jessie Jackson's office and told her of Frank's plight. She told me she would see what they could do for him. I never received a call back.

26. The Kennedy Assassination

During my tenure as the attorney for the Teamsters, their friends, and Louie the Tailor, I couldn't help but hear various conversations about the Bay of Pigs and the assassination of President John F. Kennedy. Never did I think that many years later I would come to a conclusion about who had killed the president. Nor did I entertain the notion that the Warren Commission was wrong in naming Lee Harvey Oswald as the lone shooter that fateful day. But after all these years, I believe I know, and I will give you the information I received from men who were involved—to some extent—in the events and one who took part in the assassination. Then, you make your own decision.

Louie the Tailor was a great host. In fact, this talent was a factor in choosing him to run the Teamsters' resort. He took great pride in hosting such men as Accardo, Giancana, and the celebrities I've named before. However, there are some others that, heretofore, I have not mentioned that inspired my interest in the assassination.

Although Lou was a heavy vodka drinker, I never saw him drunk. However, after having several drinks he enjoyed telling me of his experiences as an enforcer for the Chicago Outfit, the Teamsters, and a few of his highly connected friends. He also would boast of his part in the preparation for the invasion of Cuba in 1961. I would listen intently because it was not only entertaining, but extremely interesting, and the information was nothing like what I had heard or read before.

For a while, I thought it to be an exaggeration of memories of a guy who liked to be the center of attention while enjoying his favorite booze. But when men such as John Roselli and Santo Trafficante joined in the conversations, I listened closer.

John Roselli was a highly connected mobster in California, Florida, and New Orleans.[24] During the discovery procedure in the *Playboy* case, Lou and I would often meet up with Roselli in Florida. Roselli was always our host. Roselli was known in some circles as 'Handsome Johnny,' and he claimed that Louie the Tailor was one of his best friends. The more they would drink, the more they talked about the Kennedys. However, one of the more interesting conversations that I heard at these meetings concerned the late Marilyn Monroe.

Roselli alleged that Tony Accardo had ordered him to get a girl named Norma Jean into the movies. Roselli, at one time, was a Hollywood producer of some sort. Consequently, Norma Jean was signed by a studio and changed her name to Marilyn Monroe. Whether Roselli can take credit for launching Monroe's career, I do not know. It was rumored that Giancana was the last person to see Marilyn Monroe alive.

One of the many subjects discussed between Lou and his friends during that time was the Bay of Pigs invasion. Over the many years since then, news and magazine articles have seemed to confirm most of what Lou and his buddies discussed in my presence.

The Bay of Pigs was a beach area on the island of Cuba where, initially, Cuban exiles were to come ashore in 1961, hoping to drive Fidel Castro from Cuba. The invasion plans had been proposed by the Eisenhower administration before he left office. On leaving office, his successor, John F. Kennedy, assumed the task. The task was to liberate Cuba from communism. Unfortunately, for the exiled Cubans in the Miami area, Kennedy was not as enthused as Eisenhower.[25]

Kennedy was very particular in keeping the United States in the background. He did not want the world to believe that the United States would deliberately attack the small country of Cuba. So, he insisted that the CIA take total charge of the effort and leave the US military out of it until a certain condition was met. That condition: Once the exiled Cubans were able to establish a beachhead on the shores of Cuba, they could call on the United States for assistance in defending their country. He agreed to have the carrier *Essex* standing offshore in the Gulf of Mexico. The *Essex* was to be accompanied by two destroyers, the *Eaton* and the *Houston*. American landing crafts (LCI's) were offshore with a brigade of marines known as Brigade 2506.[26]

Without getting into the details given to me by Rosanova, Roselli, and Trafficante at this time, let me jump to what actually happened on April 17, 1961, as related by the mainstream media. Thirteen-hundred Cuban exiles using small private boats as landing crafts invaded the island of Cuba at the Bay of Pigs. As they moved ashore, they established a beachhead and radioed for American assistance. While waiting for the air cover and the marines and with no means of retreat, they fought an army of two hundred thousand Cubans for two days. The call for assistance was in vain because Kennedy rescinded his previous orders. As a result, the Cuban army killed sixty-eight Cuban exiles and captured 1,209. The survivors were given life sentences.[27]

Now, let me tell you what I was told by the men who took part in the invasion and the planning, and why there was so much anger towards the Kennedys.

With President Kennedy's permission, the CIA originally engaged in negotiations with Sam Giancana and Santo Trafficante to assassinate Castro. The negotiator for Giancana and Trafficante was Johnny Roselli. A deal was struck for $150,000 (a bonus of one million dollars was added by Meyer Lansky). The method was to poison Castro. The CIA was to supply the poison pills to be given to Castro by several women who attended Castro's meals at some time or another. The handler of the women was to be Trafficante.

Why was the Mafia involved? Because the Havana Casinos were owned and operated by multiple crime families, including that of Trafficante (affiliated with the Outfit) and Lucky Luciano (out of New York).[28] Roselli estimated that when Castro took over the casinos, they lost at least a million dollars a day. Hence, the one-million-dollar reward offered by Lansky. Unfortunately, the poison efforts failed for various reasons that are not important here. Suffice it to say, the failure to eliminate Castro brought on the necessity of the invasion.

In organizing the invading Cuban exile flotilla, the CIA contracted with the Five Families to supply personnel for the invasion. Confident that Cuba and the casinos would be liberated with the full support of President Kennedy and the expected marines, warships, air support, and US carrier sitting offshore, the Dons of the Families authorized many of the sons of Italy and Sicily to lead the attack.

According to Roselli, the story told by the mainstream media was very incomplete. He related: The invasion began one night by several hundred exiles storming the beach led by the young soldiers of Italian and Sicilian heritage. Once on the beach, a flag of the new Cuban government was planted and the call was made for assistance, as promised, in defending their country. But on the advice of his brother Bobby, President Kennedy refused to take the call and no order was given to the armada to join the invasion. Had the president answered the call, it would have meant certain victory and capitulation by Castro's army. Instead, the Cubans were picking the brave young men off like flies. The betrayal resulted in the deaths of many young Italians, Sicilians, and brave Cuban exiles.

If you know anything about the Mafia, you know that they exact revenge on those who personally kill or order the killing of their members, especially their young sons. (*The Godfather* movies graphically show this Mafia trait.) Sicilian culture required revenge and the Godfathers had to implement it or lose face and power. This betrayal and the resulting death of the Sicilian sons doomed President Kennedy. That revenge was exacted eighteen months later in Dallas, Texas, on November 22, 1962.

Why did I believe them? For many reasons. First, each time the assassination was mentioned or discussed under various circumstances, each of the men got angry, and nothing about their countenance suggested that they were lying. Second, they had no reason to lie to each other! Third, Roselli and Trafficante said things that I had already heard from Louie the Tailor. Fourth, Lou had participated in the invasion as confirmed by Roselli and Trafficante.

Whenever Lou would talk about the invasion—and that was when he had had too many vodkas—he'd tear up. He would describe the events and the deaths of some of his buddies with a face that betrayed the toughness he'd acquired as an enforcer on the streets of Chicago. Lou had been a participant in the invasion and never forgot the experience. He certainly never forgave the Kennedys. When the tears came, Lou would get up and leave me sitting for some time. On occasions, he would not return and then would call me the next morning to apologize. So, I am totally convinced that the three men, who are now dead, told me the truth under Omerta.

During the conversations, I gathered from their innuendos that Roselli had participated in the assassination of President Kennedy. None ever mentioned the identity of the other shooter, except to say that there had been one in the grassy knoll. Lou said that Roselli, in his weak moments, claimed that he'd been a shooter from a storm drain near or in the grassy knoll. Lou told me he didn't take Roselli's claim seriously, but Lou also told me on numerous occasions that Oswald had been only a 'patsy' who'd believed that he was working for the CIA. Each time Lou mentioned this he would snicker and say, "His CIA contact man was Roselli." Then he would laugh.

Lou said that Jack Ruby, who fatally shot Lee Harvey Oswald, was an informant for the CIA on the activities of the Families. According to him, Ruby was a marked man by the Families and believed that Ruby was ordered to kill Oswald either by the CIA or Giancana. Both sides were convinced that Oswald was going to talk his head off about his contacts with the CIA and probably

Roselli. Neither could afford for Oswald to live. Louie the Tailor felt no remorse as to the deaths of the patsies, Oswald and Ruby.

Lou was very clear on the fact that Ruby had killed Oswald on the promise that the Families would forgive him for informing on them to the CIA on various activities centered on Ruby's nightclub. Lou said that it was redemption.

I was totally convinced when I read in the newspapers at the time that a Senate investigative committee had concluded shortly after Roselli's death that he had been involved in the assassination. Roselli disappeared on July 28, 1976, a few days after one of our visits. He'd told Lou that he was scheduled to be interviewed by a Senate committee within the coming months about the Kennedy assassination. His decomposing body was found in a fifty-five-gallon steel drum floating in a bay near Miami on August 9, 1976.[29] Outwardly, Lou took the news hard.

Because of my position as an attorney, friend, member of Omerta, and a frequent participant in meetings and conversations that no one else had with these guys, I felt they were telling me the truth. Giancana orchestrated Kennedy's assassination with the approval of the Five Families in retribution for the deaths of their sons at the Bay of Pigs and for the loss of the casinos and the enormous funds the Families had been receiving. Oswald and Ruby were only two of their tools.

The mafia's revenge extended to Bobby Kennedy as well. His death in 1968 was close to the time of my insider position with men that knew far more facts than the pundits in the media. And, as in JFK's assassination, my information has been confirmed many times since then.

John Roselli (right) (Photograph from Wikimedia)

27. Another Assassination

At the time, Robert F. Kennedy was assassinated on June 5, 1968, I was not connected in any way with the Teamsters or Louie the Tailor. I was busy trying horrific murder cases and serving in various capacities in efforts to improve our local community. I was very civic-minded and politically ambitious.

Unlike his brother's assassination six years before, Robert Kennedy's death did not shake the world, at least not where I lived in sedate Savannah. However, it was a sad commentary on what was happening in this country; we were fast becoming a banana republic by killing our leaders. Coming on the heels of the assassination of Martin Luther King Jr. on April 4, 1968, the general public was not shocked that another leader had gone down. Being in national politics had become a dangerous occupation in the world's most powerful country.

Unlike President Kennedy's assassin, Bobby Kennedy's killer was never in doubt. He shot Kennedy three times in full view of many witnesses in the ballroom of the Ambassador Hotel in Los Angeles, California. Unlike Lee Harvey Oswald, Sirhan survived to be tried for murder and convicted. It was open and shut.

However, in the United States nothing seems to remain open and shut. Upon assuming my duties as the attorney for Rosanova, the Teamsters, and the Chicago Outfit, I began hearing of the hatred between the Kennedys, Teamsters, and the Mafia. As I pointed out in a previous chapter, the Teamsters and the Mob made no secret of their feelings at any event or meeting. Hating the Kennedys was in vogue at the inn.

At first, I had a problem with their long-standing grudge against the two dead men. After a while, I realized that the anger they held for the Kennedys would never subside during their lifetimes. The important notions of honor and revenge meant that the Kennedy betrayal was a 'forever' act and the grudge would probably be passed down for generations to come.

According to Louie the Tailor and his friends, the death of President Kennedy had been orchestrated by Giancana, Roselli, and Trafficante. I wondered if Bobby's death was related to his brother's. But knowing the much-publicized facts of the Sirhan trial and conviction, it was hard for me to believe that my clients had had anything to do with it.

But what about Ted Kennedy, the third Kennedy? Did their hatred include him? Yes, but not in the same way. To put it in Lou's words, "Chappaquiddick saved his life." After Kennedy left Mary Jo Kopechne to drown in the wrecked car that night, Lou and his buddies were convinced that becoming president was not possible for the younger and sole surviving brother. Plus, Ted Kennedy was not an avowed enemy of the Teamsters or organized crime, as his brothers were. Simply put, he was not a danger to them; furthermore, he had not been involved in the great betrayal—the slaughter of their sons or the loss of the vast funds of the Havana casinos.

However, Bobby Kennedy had been *the* persuasive voice in his older brother's ear to withhold American armed forces at the Bay of Pigs. He was an avowed enemy of the Teamsters and their relationship with organized crime.[30] When he'd become attorney general under his brother, he'd sought to take control of the Teamsters' finances and especially the Central States' Pension Fund. He'd come after the goose that was laying golden eggs. Knowing all this, I wondered if there were a link between Bobby's assassination and JFK's.

At first, as I said above, I was convinced that Sirhan had been the assassin and it was an open-and-shut case. But as I heard conversations on trips and at the inn, I gradually became a skeptic. One conversation I had with Lou stands out above all the rest. That conversation was on an airplane and resulted from a meeting that Lou and I had with Tony Accardo that stoked my curiosity.

We were in Chicago for the deposition of Lou and the editor of *Playboy* magazine in 1976. While at dinner with Accardo the night before, and after a few drinks that loosened some tongues, Accardo asked Lou if the lawyers for *Playboy* could ask Lou about his connections in Los Angeles. Lou looked at me for the answer.

"They can ask Lou about anyone that is suspected of being involved in organized crime. The article mentioned a meeting in California. So, any friendships that Lou has are in play, especially in California," I responded.

Accardo looked at Lou and said, "Louie, you need to forget some people. You need to forget any connections and trips to LA when the second Kennedy hit the dirt."

Lou nodded in agreement and said with a grin, "I can only remember playing golf with Dean, Hackett, Greller, and Fitzsimmons at La Costa back then. On my mother's grave, that's the truth," he replied, grinning.

Accardo kept it going. "Louie, if they mention either of the Kennedys, don't answer, no matter what the question is."

I joined the conversation by responding, "Mr. Accardo, they can fish for information, but they are limited to information that pertains to the article or that might reasonably lead to information relevant to Lou's suit. Questions concerning JFK and Bobby Kennedy are not relevant. At least in my opinion."

"What if they try to go into the assassinations with Louie?" he asked.

"I will object and make them explain the purpose of each question as it relates to the suit. I will also tell Lou not to answer."

Big Tuna's eyes scanned the room and then he leaned in and said, "Louie, one of my lawyers up here warned me about this. They think *Playboy* wants to show all of your connections. They say *Playboy* can go back to your days on the streets of Chicago. I asked the lawyers if that meant they could ask you about meetings with Roselli and Marcello in LA before Bobby hit the dirt. He thinks they are digging for a bigger story and that they can use this case for that."

While I met numerous times with Roselli and Lou, I only met Carlos Marcello on one occasion in New Orleans. Lou did not tell me that Marcello was the boss of the New Orleans crime family. Lou never disclosed the positions of mobsters to me, and I never asked for details.

"Mr. Accardo, I will object to any question about meetings before the Bobby Kennedy assassination. I will also instruct Lou not to answer. Then they will have to connect the question to the case and I don't think they can. What would meetings back in 1968 have to do with a meeting with Frank Fitzsimmons at La Costa in 1971? Am I missing something?" I asked, looking at Lou and then at Accardo.

"No, but just be aware of what we've discussed tonight. Make a note of it, a big note!"

I agreed, and we had no more discussion about Bobby Kennedy.

The next day at the deposition, the lawyer did attempt to question Lou about various meetings he'd had in California in the sixties and immediately prior to the meeting at La Costa. As planned, I objected and asked him to connect it to the case. He tried to, by saying that he had the right to go into any meetings or events that Lou had with so-called mobsters prior to La Costa because we had alleged that Lou was not a mobster as the article depicted. Therefore, they had the right to prove he was a mobster because truth was a defense to the suit.

I turned to Lou and asked, "Have you ever met with a mobster in California before the round of golf you had with Fitzsimmons at La Costa in '71?"

"No."

"Do you remember the names of anyone at a meeting you attended in California before '71?"

"The only ones I can remember is Dean Martin, Buddy Hackett, John Raitt, Vic Damone and some of their buddies. I don't think they are mobsters," he responded with a broad grin.

I turned to the lawyer and said, "That's his answer to your question. Other than that, he has nothing more to say about any so-called meetings in California."

The other attorney was persistent. "Do you know Johnny Roselli?"

I quickly objected and instructed Lou not to answer.

"We contend that Roselli is a mobster and we want to know if Roselli is a friend of Rosanova."

Lou interrupted, "I am a friend of a lot of Catholic priests; are you saying that makes me a priest?"

I was surprised at Lou's logic. It was a perfect response and true. I should have used it myself. I looked at the lawyer and said, "He's right. Let's get on with some questions about matters that are pertinent to the case. Besides, the article did not say that Roselli was at the so-called meeting."

Eventually, the lawyer relented when he was satisfied that he was going nowhere with this line of questioning.

On the flight back to Savannah we played a hand or two of gin and drank a few vodkas. My curiosity had been aroused.

"Lou, what was all the discussion about some meetings in California before the Bobby Kennedy assassination?"

"Okay, Cracker, that's a touchy subject. There are some people out there that want to tie the two hits together."

"How can they? Sirhan did it. Everyone in America saw it. It was on television."

"Cracker, some things appear to be what they are not. That's all I can say," said Lou as he took another sip of his vodka.

"Lou, is there a link?"—a question I would not have asked if I had not been drinking at thirty thousand feet above the earth.

Then he answered, "Yes. No more discussion about that jerk."

"No more discussion," I agreed.

Another conversation occurred in 1976 during a week-long Teamsters' trustee meeting at the inn. Lou, Jackie Presser, and I were having drinks at Dino's one evening. Jackie Presser became an international vice president of the Teamsters during my tenure as a Teamster attorney. He and his father, Bill Presser, were trustees of the pension fund.[31] I'd met Presser before at the inn and at the Teamsters headquarters in Washington, DC.

Unlike his father, Jackie Presser was deeply involved in Mafia affairs, to the chagrin of Louie the Tailor. Lou thought that Jackie Presser was a big-mouthed, overweight slob who boasted too much about his authority and influence in the Teamsters and the Chicago family. Although Lou had to tolerate him since he was a trustee, he didn't have to spend any time with him except when Presser was at the inn for trustee meetings.

This night Lou got sole custody of a very drunk Presser when everyone, except me, had vacated our table. Presser began talking about Ted and Bobby Kennedy. He said that there were some rumblings that Ted was seeking revenge on those who his family believed had killed his brothers. He told Lou, in a voice that was much too loud to suit Lou, that Ted Kennedy was pushing to reopen the Warren Commission in view of some new evidence that linked to the Mob. Then he said, "Louie, my source tells me that they're gonna look at Bobby's death. They think there's another patsy who took a shot. They want to connect it to the Family." Then he laughed and held up his glass as if he were toasting.

Lou did not immediately respond. He looked at me in disgust. Finally, he responded to Presser in a very deliberate and low voice, "Jackie, you need to zip it. We ain't talking about this tonight. Too many ears are here."

Before Presser could respond, Lou continued, "You need to shut up. It's none of your business in the first place. You know nothing."

Lou was obviously referring to the fact that Presser was only a Teamster and not involved in Family business, even though Presser liked to brag about his influence and Mafia ties.

Presser didn't challenge Lou because Louie the Tailor outranked him. While Presser was a trustee and, theoretically would be one of Lou's bosses, Lou had more clout because of his role in the Chicago Outfit as well as connections to other Mafia families. Butting heads with Louie the Tailor was not in Jackie Presser's playbook.

Lou got up from the table and pulled Presser up by one arm. Then he looked at me and said, "I gotta get this shithead to his room before he gets us all arrested. I'll call you tomorrow. Forget what you heard tonight." With that, Lou ushered a very drunk Jackie Presser out of Dino's Den.

Looking back on all that I heard and saw, I concluded that organized crime had played a part in Bobby Kennedy's death. How? I could never figure that out. Sirhan was the shooter; it was open and shut. Yet, over the past forty years, I believe that evidence has come out that may suggest a more complicated scenario.

Over the years, I've reviewed or become aware of several books and reports beginning in 1977 that give some evidence that there was a second shooter.[32] (Familiar?) Collectively they claim the following as uncontroverted facts: Robert F. Kennedy, whom I will refer to as RFK, went to the Ambassador Hotel in Los Angeles, California, to speak to his supporters shortly after being proclaimed the winner of the Democratic Primary on June 5, 1968. As he was proceeding to the Colonial Room where he was to speak, someone suggested that he should take a shortcut through the kitchen. A security guard by the name of Thane Eugene Cesar, a Cuban American, took hold of RFK's right elbow to escort him through the room when Sirhan opened fire.

According to the autopsy report performed by Los Angeles County Coroner Thomas Noguchi, RFK was struck by three bullets from the rear in a flight path from down to up, right to left. Noguchi maintained the shot that killed RFK was fired less than an inch from the head and less than three inches behind the right ear. Yet, all witnesses to the shooting said that Sirhan had been in front of RFK when he'd fired, and not behind him. In 1973, criminologist professor Herbert MacDowell signed an affidavit stating that the bullet that was removed from RFK's neck could not have been fired from Sirhan's gun.[33]

Recently, Robert F. Kennedy Jr. has requested that his father's assassination case be reopened based on autopsy and police reports that indicate the real possibility of a second shooter. Ballistic tests and the number of bullets fired show that two guns were fired during that fateful night.[34]

Grant Cooper, Sirhan's lead trial attorney, never followed the trail of evidence that indicated another shooter. Cooper persuaded Sirhan to plead guilty, so there was never a full trial that would require all the evidence to be presented and examined publicly. Cooper was criticized for not investigating whether his client was actually guilty.[35] Then there came the revelation that Cooper also had been the attorney for Johnny Roselli in another case in California. Simply said, a quick conviction of Sirhan closed the case and ended any idea of pursuing another shooter or perpetrator.

Like JFK, Senator Robert F. Kennedy had been shot by another fanatic who'd been an easy patsy for someone. Organized crime families had many motives to be involved in both assassinations, and none greater than revenge for the shedding of Sicilian blood on the beaches of Cuba. I believe my suspicions in the seventies have been confirmed with the passage of time. I now understand why Lou shut Presser up.

28. Blacks Don't Bruise

Lou was sitting at his usual table in a chair that faced the door, laughing at whatever he was reading in the *Savannah Morning News* one bright Saturday morning that was perfect for golf. I sat down and gave my usual salutations to my friend and client. Then I waived at the server to bring me a cup of coffee and asked Lou what was so amusing in the "Morning Mistake," a nickname given to our local news by most attorneys.

"You gotta read this. This gal beat her husband to death with a telephone 'cause he made her leave a party too early. They're charging her with murder. You don't find murders like this in Chicago. You Southern folk are very ingenious when it comes to selecting murder weapons," he chuckled. When he finished, I read the article.

Briefly stated, Bernice Moultrie was a thirty-five-year-old black woman who'd allegedly beaten her husband to death with a telephone. According to the lead detective, Horace Case, she admitted killing him because she hadn't wanted to leave a party where both of them had been drinking because she'd been having a good time. When they had arrived home, they'd started arguing and he'd hit her. She'd hit him back with the new bicentennial telephone they had recently bought. She was quoted as saying, "I guess I hit him too hard."

As I put the paper down, smiling at what I had just read, Lou asked, "What is a bicentennial telephone?"

"It's a commemorative, old-time, long-necked telephone, made of brass and painted red, white, and blue. It weighs about nine pounds. It would be considered a formidable weapon when swung at your head."

"Had the fool stayed long enough for her to pass out, he'd be alive this morning," Lou replied.

Shortly thereafter, we went to the cart and headed to the first tee. Neither of us spoke of the unusual case until the following Monday.

When I arrived at my office on Monday, I was met with an urgent message to come see a Bernice Moultrie who was lodged at the local jail. Obviously, I needed no further information on the crime she was charged with, so I headed to the jail to interview her.

Bernice was a husky black woman who appeared to be very shy and introverted. She was despondent and looked down as she sat across from me in the interview room. I found it difficult to get any reaction out of her as I questioned her on the incident. She admitted that she had hit her husband a few times.

"I bopped him a few times, 'cause he kept hittin' me."

She admitted that they both had consumed too much booze and they had argued over having to leave the party. She expressed her sorrow for killing her husband.

After about an hour, I ended the interview and told her that her family was coming to my office that afternoon to make arrangements for my fee. As I left, she thanked me for coming.

I went up to the detectives' office to locate Horace Case. I was sent to the desk of Detective Tom Izzo who was a friend of mine and a very competent and honest cop. He was a balding Italian in his thirties with a sense of humor that was lacking in most of the detectives working out of the city office. I was glad I had drawn Izzo.

As I approached his desk, Izzo was holding up the bicentennial telephone apparently used as the murder weapon with a broad smile spread across his face.

"Bubba, she beat him to death with this phone."

"Yeah, that's what she told me. She said she hit him in self-defense after he started beating her with his fist."

Izzo, while still smiling, said, "Maybe you oughta see these photos."

He handed me a few eight-by-ten photos of Bernice and her dead husband. The first one showed the victim slumped over in a recliner. His head had been flattened and was nothing but a glob of blood. A couple more showed the same scene from different angles. The next photo was of Bernice and it stunned me. It appeared like she had posed for the photographer with one foot on the recliner while holding her arms high with the fingers on each hand giving the 'victory' sign, reminiscent of Nixon's and Churchill's famous poses. She was wearing a straw hat cocked to one side and was smiling. She also looked very intoxicated and happy she had won the fight. I had never seen a more incriminating photograph than the one I was looking at. The two others depicted the same scene at different angles, as if they needed the additional ones.

"Tom, where were these photos of Bernice taken?"

"In the living room of their house where she killed him. We'd already removed the body. We arrested her right after the photos were taken." Then, he said with the same broad smile on his face, "She sure looks happy, don't she?"

"Tom, I need a copy of her statement and I want copies of the photos."

"Sure, you can take these. We have plenty more."

As I was leaving his office, he walked with me to the door still smiling. "If there is anything else I can do for you, let me know. Bubba, you'll have to perform magic to win this one. I don't envy you, but you probably can plead her out for manslaughter and twenty years."

"Tom, I like the ones I can't win. That way I can't lose."

As I exited, he was scratching his head.

On return to the office, I read the statement Bernice had given the police. She had spelled out the details of the battle with her husband. She had confessed that she had bopped him a few times with the bicentennial phone. She left nothing out. All the evidence that the prosecutor needed for a conviction was there. Further investigation on their part was unnecessary.

Several days later I went to meet with Bernice at her home. She had gotten out on bond, unlike Williams. Williams had been accused of raping a white woman and Bernice had killed a black man. Do you see the difference? A black defendant could not get a bond if the victim were white but could if the victim were black.

"Bernice, let me show you some photographs of you shortly after the police arrived at your house that night. Do you remember posing for these as if you were celebrating a victory after your husband was killed?"

"No. I don't remember any of that."

"Were you drunk?"

"We both were high 'cause we both been drinking at the party."

"Tell me again about the argument?"

"I didn't wanna leave. I was havin' a good time. He got mad and made me go home with him. I wanted to go back, but he wouldn't let me. Then he started hittin' me. That's when I started hittin' him. I guess I hit 'im too hard."

"How many times did you hit him?"

"A few times. I don't know how many. I don't remember, but I remember him hittin' me three or four good ones."

"All right, I understand what happened. Y'all just had a husband-and-wife fight."

"That's it!"

A few days later after my second meeting with Bernice, I met with Lou concerning a meeting we were going to have the next weekend at the inn with a couple of Teamster trustees. I needed to be well prepared and to the point when meeting with these guys. However, before we got down to business, Lou said that he had read in the paper that I was representing the woman who had killed her husband with the phone.

"Yeah. It's a total loss. She confessed to everything and took a victory photo for the cops giving the Nixon victory sign with both hands in the air."

"What kind of defense you got?" he asked.

"None right now. I'm looking for one. You got a suggestion?"

"How about spouse abuse?" he said with a grin.

"No. She's actually bigger than him. I'd lose that argument."

"I want to be there for the trial," he chuckled.

"No problem. You bring me good luck in the courtroom. I haven't lost one since you've been tracking me."

We finished the telephone case discussion and opened the Teamsters file and got down to the task at hand.

A few months later, the Moultrie trial began with me having no defense except self-defense, and I knew that dog wouldn't hunt. My only chance of helping her was to get a plea of involuntary manslaughter because of the heavy intoxication of both of them and the mutual combat. But the judge killed that possibility an hour before the trial began. In the judge's own words, "She hit him too many times and she flattened his head. She went further than she had to. The photos are gruesome. No, it's murder or not guilty."

As I left the judge's chamber and entered the packed courtroom, I scanned the spectators for Louie the Tailor. He wasn't there. That was unusual in view of his interest in a case he thought to be amusing.

The trial opened and Ryan had a field day. He opened with Horace Case, the detective who'd been at the scene and had conducted the basic investigation. He identified the phone as the murder weapon, the photos of Bernice and her husband, and the voluntary confession of my client. Ryan questioned him as to the mutual combat theory they knew I was going to foster.

"Did Bernice Moultrie tell you at the scene that she fought with her husband?" asked Ryan.

"Yes," answered Case.

"Did you find any evidence of mutual combat? In other words, did you see any bruises or marks on Bernice Moultrie that would be a resemblance of having been struck by her husband?"

"No, sir. Had I seen any bruises on her I would probably not have arrested or charged her with murder."

Ryan turned to where I was sitting and said that he had no more questions and walked to his table and sat down with a lot of confidence. An open-and-shut case!

I approached the detective and asked, "Did I understand you correctly when you answered the last question Mr. Ryan asked you? You said that if you had seen any bruises or marks on Bernice Moultrie, you would not have charged her? Why is that?"

"It would have confirmed her story that he was beating her and I think a wife should be able to defend herself."

"Are you sure that you didn't see some bruises or marks?"

"Mr. Haupt, I'm not blind. After she told me he had been beating her, I looked very carefully at her arms, neck, and face and I could find nothing that confirmed her story."

"Your Honor, I have no further questions for Detective Case at this time. But I reserve the right to call Detective Case back to the stand when I present my case." I paused, then said, "I call Bernice Moultrie to the stand."

Bernice walked slowly to the witness stand in a black short-sleeved mourning dress. She looked humble and nothing like the photo of her at the scene. She looked much older than thirty-five. She was depressed and scared.

I questioned her about the events that led up to the fight she'd had with her husband that night. She admitted that both had been drinking heavily and had been drunk. She told the jury that her husband had started hitting her in the face, arms, and stomach. She demonstrated how she had held up her arms to block some of the blows.

"Bernice, would you come down here next to me and stand here in front of the jury?" She complied, and I positioned her about three feet from the first row of jurors.

"Bernice, would you hold out your arm?" I asked.

Then I did something that I had never done before. I hit my client. I hit her very hard on the arm and it knocked her against the jury rail and three jurors fell backwards in their seats. Bernice, the jury panel, Ryan, and the judge were shocked at my actions. As Bernice bounced off the jury rail she moved quickly away from her lawyer, probably thinking that he was going to hit her again.

The judge began hammering his gavel on the great desk before him and began calling order to the courtroom.

"Mr. Haupt, did you just hit your client?" he shouted.

"Yes, sir!"

He quickly motioned his chief deputy (bailiff) to remove the jury and instructed Ryan and me to meet him in his chamber. I complied and knew that I had a huge problem in explaining my action that probably was a first in Georgia jurisprudence.

"Mr. Haupt, you have a lot of explaining to do before I hold you for assaulting Mrs. Moultrie."

"Judge, I'm defending my client on a charge that could put her in prison for the rest of her life. I'm doing the best job I can under the circumstances. All I ask you to do is to permit me to complete this case, and if you think I should still be charged, then so be it."

The angry judge stared at me and then looked at Ryan. "I'm going to adjourn for the day and start again at 9:00 in the morning. Mr. Haupt, you will complete your case and then I'll make a decision on what to do about what you just did. I caution you to not touch her again and to somehow make amends with her in the meantime."

"Thank you, Judge, I appreciate the opportunity to finish."

The judge continued to stare at me because he had yet to hear an apology. I turned and left.

That evening I called Bernice's mother and told her to make sure Bernice wore a long-sleeved blouse for trial the next morning. She agreed but wanted an explanation. I gave her no explanation. I then called Lou to see if he was okay. He was not at the inn. I was told he was out of town.

The next morning, I went to the jail to talk with Bernice before they brought her over to the courthouse. She was wearing a white long-sleeved blouse, as requested. I told her to trust me and that I would not hit her again. She appeared to believe me.

That morning there were long lines waiting to get into the courtroom. Word had apparently spread among the law enforcement world that I had hit my female client in the courtroom. Knowing their love for me and lawyers in general, I suspected that they believed that the judge was going to put me so deep in jail that they would have to pump sunlight to me. They wanted to be there for such an occasion.

The bailiff brought the jurors in after Ryan and I got seated. All of them, and I repeat, all of them were staring at me in a way that I couldn't explain. They had truly become interested in what I was going to do next. What Ryan might do was no longer of any interest. The focus was entirely on me.

My first witness was Detective Case. He still looked confident that Bernice was going to be convicted.

"Officer Case let me remind you that the last thing you told this jury was that if you had seen bruises and marks on Bernice's arms, you wouldn't have charged her. You said that a wife had the right to defend herself. Do you recall that?"

"Yes. I looked very carefully and I didn't see any bruises. There weren't any, so I thought that she was lying about gettin' beat," he responded as he turned his head towards the jury to make sure they heard him.

"Detective Case, would you please step down here in front of the jury?" He hesitated and turned to the judge. I quickly took the opportunity to tell him I was not going to hit him. By this time, the judge was not so sure of my motive.

"Mr. Haupt, I am going to permit him to do as you ask, but I caution you that under no circumstance will I permit a reoccurrence of yesterday's events. Are you clear on that?"

"Yes, sir! I just want him to see something for me."

As Case approached the jury panel, I motioned for Bernice to come over to where Case and I were standing about two feet from the jury rail. I could see that the jury was totally involved.

"Bernice, would you please roll up the sleeve of your left arm all the way to your shoulder?" Slowly she complied, still not completely convinced that I would not hit her again.

"Detective Case, would you please show this jury any bruise or mark on the arm I hit so hard yesterday."

Case looked hard but couldn't find any. I then walked Bernice up and down in front of the jury panel so that all the jurors could see that she had no bruise. After a few minutes, I asked Bernice to return to her seat and told Case that I had no further questions from him.

"Your Honor, I rest my case," I announced as the packed courtroom began murmuring.

Ryan just sat there knowing that he could do nothing to counter or demean the dramatics he had just witnessed. There was no way he could respond by offering any further evidence. In his closing argument, he said a lot about how hard she had hit her husband, but he couldn't refute that Bernice's husband could have beaten her as she said that night. He knew that his own lead detective had given away the case by narrowing the truth of the case to whether or not a black person bruises. Ryan's balloon had burst and he finished his argument awkwardly, knowing the probable outcome.

In my argument, I pointed out that Bernice was a dark black person and that for that reason no bruises would show up on her. I acknowledged that Case was an honest detective and that he'd learned a valuable lesson that would serve him well in his career. I highlighted the fact that had Bernice been white she would not have been charged because the bruises would have been evident. But she wasn't.

The jury stayed out about twenty minutes before coming back with a verdict of 'not guilty.' As the courtroom emptied of spectators disappointed in not seeing any more fireworks, Bernice hugged me along with her family.

As was customary in that day, the DA came over and shook my hand congratulating me on the victory. As Ryan offered me a cigarette, he said with a half-smile on his face, "Bubba, I didn't know that blacks don't bruise."

I slowly closed my file, took his cigarette, and responded, "I didn't either! She never pulled up the sleeve of the arm I hit."

I smiled, took a long puff from the cigarette, and walked away, leaving Ryan mumbling something about the chastity of my mother.

Thank God there were no blacks on that jury.

29. The Car that Couldn't

As I've said many times, Louie the Tailor delighted in following local crime highlights in the newspaper, and he was proud of the fact that his lawyer, or 'mouth-piece' as he put it, was the defender-in-chief in most of the horrific cases. It connected him to each and gave him a seat at the table when it came to winning the bad cases. He loved beating the cops!

One particular case occurred in 1979 when the local papers began reporting a series of rape incidents involving the use of a small red Volkswagen in the Southside area of Savannah. Several articles appeared alerting women to be aware of a white man driving the red car. The suspect was reported to offer young females a ride late at night, and then once in the car, he would sexually attack them.

According to the reports, the victims were not able to identify him through mug-shot books and lineups. None of the victims were able to positively describe his features or get a good look at his face. The police had little to go on and needed a break.

My first involvement with the case came with a midnight call from my former college basketball coach. He lived in a nice subdivision in the Southside area and had a small red car. He also had a son who was brain-damaged at birth and was now in his late twenties. His son was mild-mannered and a responsible worker at a local grocery store. His family and all of the former players loved him and liked being around him at team functions.

"Bubba, they arrested Greg and impounded my car. They've got him at the jail, and they think that he's the rapist they're looking for. Can you help us get him back home?" he asked in a trembling voice.

"Coach, there is no way he could be the one. I didn't know that he could drive."

"He can't. Greg's just backs the car up and down the driveway. He's never gone past the driveway."

"Coach, I'll go down there tonight and see what I can do. They've made a huge error. Tell your wife I'll bring him home."

When I arrived at the jail I was met by the lead detective, Alonyia Haisten. I spoke first. "Alonyia, he's not the one. He's brain-damaged and cannot drive. He only moves the car a few feet up and down his family's driveway. He's a good young fellow, but he has only a twelve-year-old mentality."

"Bubba, you verify his mental capacity and show me proof that he can't drive, I'll cut him loose pending further investigation."

I went to a phone and called my coach. He came down to the station with his son's medical file and the name of the caseworker who helps his son. Alonyia was touched and let him go home.

The next morning, I called Lou and told him of the arrest of my coach's son and his release. While I was talking to him, my secretary came in and motioned for me to put Lou on hold.

"They have made a definite ID on the red car and a tag number. It's on the radio now," she said.

I returned to Lou and said, "Lou, they've made an ID on the red car. They'll probably make another arrest today." Lou said to keep him informed. Upon hanging up, I started work on a pending murder case. An hour later, the wife of an oil company executive in the area entered my office and informed my secretary that she needed to talk to me because her husband had just been arrested for rape.

Inman Averitt was a fifty-year-old owner of a fuel oil company in Savannah. He was short, medium build, with wavy salt-and-pepper hair. His wife, Linda, almost matched his description. She was understandably nervous and stunned by what was going on.

"Inman can't possibly be the one. It's impossible!" she said as the tears began to flow.

"Mrs. Averitt, do you or your husband own a red Volkswagen?"

"No. But Inman's son does."

"Does your husband have access to the car?"

She hesitated and appeared as if she didn't want to answer the question. Finally, she responded. "His son works for Inman and the car is kept at the plant most of the time." That was not the answer I wanted or was expecting.

She asked what the fee would be and I quoted a sum that would have bought two fully loaded Chevys at that time. She wrote the check and I headed out to get a bond for her husband.

When I arrived at the jail, it was déjà vu all over again. Alonyia Haisten was standing there with a file in her hand. This time she was smiling. She thought she had her man, and for all I knew at that time, I couldn't disagree with her.

"We've got him nailed. He's the one. The fourteen-year-old victim gave us a tag number that matched a red Volkswagen owned by Averitt's son and she picked Inman Averitt out of a photo lineup. Ain't no way you gonna spring this one. No way, hotshot!"

"Alonyia, I don't make them, I only make y'all try them," I replied.

"Well, I'm so sure of this one that I'm gonna give you a copy of the victim's statement and the photos of the car and tag and you don't even have to go to the judge. Anytime you want to look at the photos we used in the lineup, let me know."

I accepted her offer, thanked her and left her wallowing in confidence. I then went to the courthouse to get a bond for the release of my client.

Inman Averitt was a prominent local businessman who had a reputation for overindulging in the spirits. He was a functioning alcoholic. Interviews with some of his employees revealed that every day, around three in the afternoon, Inman disappeared to an early cocktail hour somewhere.

But Inman had another and bigger problem in his personal life. After marrying thirteen times to five different women, the last one he'd picked would turn out to be his chief tormentor. Linda was domineering and had a temper that bordered on insanity. She let everyone know that she'd married Inman for security and whatever else came her way, including the oil company.

A week later, we had the preliminary hearing to determine if there was enough evidence to hold Inman over for trial. At the hearing, the girl stated that the defendant had pulled up beside her as she'd stood outside a small strip mall on the Southside of Savannah around 7:30 at night. He'd asked her if she'd wanted a ride. She said the car was a little red Volkswagen and the man was white, around fifty years old, with grayish wavy hair.

When asked how a sexual act could be performed within such a small car, she replied, "He folded down my seat."

After testifying that the whole episode took about thirty minutes, she gave the most damaging part of her testimony; she told her mother that the license plate had a 9, 6, and 3 in it.

Detective Haisten took the stand and stated that when she was given the tag numbers the night of the incident, she'd run the three digits on her computer and had found a red Volkswagen registered to a Carl Averitt of a downtown address. She'd dispatched an undercover agent to stake out the residence and verify young Averitt's description. The agent reported to her that he was a young man in his late twenties and had blonde hair.

On a hunch, she testified, she'd gone to closed files and dug up a seven-year-old DUI arrest photo of Carl's father and had placed it in a packet of other photos for the purpose of a photo lineup for the young girl. When she'd showed the girl the photos, the girl had promptly picked out Inman Averitt. This alone got the case bound over and set for trial.

In the coming weeks, I would meet with Averitt many times and I became sympathetic to his personal as well as legal problems. I could see that he did not fit the profile of what I considered to be a man capable of forcible rape of a fourteen-year-old girl. I had no doubt of his innocence, but I had plenty of doubt as to how he could escape a positive identification of his son's little red car and the young girl picking him out of a photo lineup.

At our first meeting, I asked Averitt to tell me where he'd been on the date and time of the assault. He said that he'd been with a group of friends at a local bar. He gave the names and locations of his friends. Thankfully, I knew a couple of his buddies and it allowed me to get these people together for a meeting.

The organizer was an old friend of mine, Billy Lee, who owned a small bar on the outskirts of town. Billy was adamant that Averitt had been with him and the others at the Ramada Inn lounge in downtown Savannah, many miles from the spot where the girl was picked up on the Southside. At the meeting with the witnesses, I established that Averitt and his wife had met Billy and two other witnesses at around 5:00 p.m. in the lounge. Around 7:30 p.m., they'd left and gone to Billy's bar on the Eastside of Savannah. All of them had stayed together until Averitt had left in his white Ford auto to go home at around 9:45. His wife stayed at the bar.

You would think that this was an ironclad alibi that would win the case. Unfortunately, you'd be wrong. First, they were all his friends and not disinterested parties. Second, and more important, Averitt had left around 7:30

p.m. alone to go to Billy's bar. The girl alleges that she'd been picked up around 7:30. The DA would argue that he could easily have left at seven, picked up the girl and raped her on the Southside, which was on the way to Billy's bar. The time frame was tight, but workable for the prosecution.

Averitt then related how he'd been arrested by a county policeman for drunk driving as he'd approached the road leading to his island home, still far away from where the girl had claimed he'd been. He'd been taken to jail and stayed overnight to sleep it off before being bonded out the next morning.

Within an hour of the completion of the meeting with the alibi group and Averitt, I reached the officer who had arrested Averitt the night of the assault and confirmed Averitt's story. I acquired the arrest photo and it was in color. The shirt he was wearing at the time of the arrest was a different color than the girl claimed. This was a good point in our favor. Things were looking up!

About two weeks before the trial, I played golf with my quasi-legal assistant, Louie the Tailor. While we walked the course, I filled Lou in on the positives and negatives of the evidence I had found.

"Cracker, is he innocent?"

"Yep. He didn't do it."

"Well, you better pull a rabbit outta your hat. There's too much of a coincidence with the three numbers in the tag, her picking him out of the lineup. They gonna believe her. I'm sorry. Wish I could help."

Then Lou said something that changed the whole case. "Cracker, have you re-enacted the crime like we did in the Washington case?"

"Why? How would it affect the case?"

"Why'd you do it in the Washington case? What's different about this one? Do it. Even if it's useless. Just keep doing the things that you do so well."

The next day was a Friday. I went to the oil company where Carl Averitt was working and asked if I could borrow the little red car. He said, yes, "anything that would help my dad."

From there, I drove the little red car to the spot where the girl said Averitt had picked her up. Then I drove to the spot where he'd allegedly raped her after laying her back on the front passenger seat. I re-enacted it as if she were there. At that point, I realized that I was going to win the case. Had Louie the Tailor been there, I would have hugged him. He'd changed the case! But I couldn't tell him yet.

The night before the trial, Inman Averitt showed up at my house around nine o'clock drunk as a skunk. His clothing and hair were in disarray. He obviously had been drinking hard and probably fighting hard with his wife.

"Inman, what are you doing here? We go to trial in the morning and you got to be at your best. I'll need your help or you're going to prison for at least twenty years." Then I realized that he was confused and needed help.

"What happened?" I asked.

"Linda's raising cane. She's threatening me."

"What do mean, threatening you? With what?"

"You gotta drink?"

"No. You got to get sober. I need you tomorrow." I paused and then asked again, "What did she threaten you with?"

"She wants you to do some papers that would give her my house, my car, and half my company or she's gonna testify for the police tomorrow."

"What? What would she testify to that would hurt you?"

"She said that she would tell them I admitted raping the girl when she picked me up after bonding me out from jail."

"Did you tell her that?"

"No. She's lying 'cause she thinks she can get everything she wants before trial. She knows I need her to go free. She knows she can send me away by lying. I ain't gotta choice. You need to do the papers 'cause she wants 'em tonight," he said as tears rolled down his face.

I'd never been angrier. I couldn't fathom a wife doing this to her husband. This was a first. All of this work for an innocent man could go down the drain because of a treacherous woman.

"Is she at home?"

"Yes."

"I'll take care of this right now," I said as I went to the phone to call his greedy bride.

"Linda, this is Bubba Haupt. Inman is over here wanting me to draw up some papers deeding everything over to you or you will testify that he admitted raping the girl. Is this correct?"

"Bubba, I'm sorry, but I've got to look out for myself. If they convict him, he'd lose everything and I'd have nothing. He owes me, 'cause this is embarrassing," she replied in a low sweet voice.

"And, it doesn't bother you that he's innocent and you'd be lying?"

"I'm sorry, but I got to look out for yours truly. I'll do what I have to. He knows I'll lie to get this done. I want the house and half of the company. I'll let him keep the car," her voice took on a sugary softness.

"Linda, there'll be no papers drawn up tonight, you'll tell the truth at trial, and you will act the good wife. You know why?"

"Why?"

"Because this conversation is being taped. If you try to lie on the stand, I'll produce the tape and get you charged with perjury. And, it'll be my life's mission to make sure you do at least ten years in the worst women's prison in Georgia."

"You bastard." She slammed the receiver down without telling me goodbye.

I called Billy Lee and asked him if he would come over and get Inman and let him spend the night with him. Thirty minutes later a happier Inman Averitt left with Billy and one of my best cocktail glasses in hand. As he left I promised him that I would represent him free of charge in a divorce case as soon as this case was over.

The next morning, walking into the courtroom, I spotted Lou and a couple of his friends from Miami. We shook hands and Lou asked me if I was ready. "Lou, you know I'm ready. And, thanks to you we're going to win," I said without any intention of explaining at the moment.

Looking puzzled Lou responded, "Cracker, that's all you gonna say? You're not gonna let me in on one of your surprises?"

"Nope. The surprise is that big! And you did it," I replied as I walked away to meet my client.

I was ready, but there were still too many unexplained incriminating facts to feel too confident. We were going to get hammered on the fact that the girl was able to identify three digits of the tag on a red Volkswagen and she'd picked him so quickly out of the photo lineup. A jury could believe her just on those two items and convict my client.

Then I looked over at Ryan and saw that he was more nervous than usual. Ryan glanced at the assistant DA, my best friend, Tom Edenfield. Ryan knew that I had been able to get a case dismissed by embarrassing Tom. Here's what happened: Tom had been prosecuting a client of mine for armed robbery. Judge Harrison had been irritated with members of the DA's office for coming late to court. During the case, I'd asked the judge for a bathroom break. He'd granted a fifteen-minute recess with a stern warning that if the DA's office came back late from the break, he would dismiss the case.

I'd smiled to myself as I'd followed Tom to the men's restroom. Finishing, I'd gone to the sink to wash my hands when Tom had come up beside me. Cupping my hands, I'd gathered up enough water to toss onto the crotch area of Tom's light tan pants in order to make it appear that he had peed on himself. I quickly left Tom, stunned and angry, and hurried back to the courtroom. When Tom had failed to appear on time, Judge Harrison had banged his gavel and announced, "Case dismissed."

Perhaps Ryan thought I had another 'dirty trick' up my sleeve. Whether it was with cigars, water, or hitting my client as in the Bernice Moultrie case, he knew something was coming, as did Lou and his buddies in the back of the courtroom. Hopefully, he would be distracted when I pulled the trigger on him this time.

Ryan and the judge were elated that I was not objecting to a lot of the evidence, but both thought that I was acting out of character. This added to Ryan's distrust.

Ryan led off by presenting Alonyia Haisten, who was her usual self and a good witness. She basically laid out the case and finished with the arrest of the 'man that raped this child.'

His next witness was the girl. For the first time during this whole process, I realized that her stepfather was an old friend of mine with whom I had played golf at the inn many times. He stared at me as his stepdaughter testified how my client raped her.

She backed up everything she said in her statement and reiterated her positive identification of Inman Averitt. Ryan walked away leaving her for me to cross-examine.

"Are you certain that you were assaulted in the little red car?"

"Yes, sir."

"You stated that he let the front seat fold back and then got on top of you. Is that correct?"

"Yes, sir."

"Are you positive that it was in this car and that Mr. Averitt is the one?"

"Yes, sir."

"Could you be mistaken?"

"No. I am not mistaken. At first, I wasn't sure, but when I saw him in person at his company, I was sure."

"What? What do you mean by 'saw him at his company'?"

"When I first saw the pictures, I couldn't tell for sure. My stepfather took me to the Averitt Oil Company and we sat across the street and watched Mr. Averitt go in and out several times. Then I was sure. That's when I called Detective Haisten and told her I was sure. Dennis took me back to the station and I picked him out of the lineup. I was sure then!"

"Who told you the name of Mr. Averitt and where he worked?"

"My stepfather got that from a policeman friend."

"Did you smell alcohol on the man that raped you?"

"No, sir."

"Thank you."

With that, I ended her cross-examination. The judge announced that the trial was in recess for the day and we would reconvene the next morning. When the jury left the room, Ryan came over to me and assured me that he did not know that the girl and her stepfather had staked out Averitt before identifying him. I believed him.

When Ryan told Detective Haisten of the stakeout, she was visibly upset. She came over to me and promised that she'd known nothing of the stakeout and that she would find out the identity of the officer who'd given the unfair information to the girl's stepfather. She said that the officer would be disciplined. A day after the trial, she did, and he was.

The following morning I presented my evidence. I started with the officer who had arrested Averitt for a DUI the night of the rape. When arrested, Averitt had been wearing a shirt that did not match the description given by the girl. Then came the four alibi witnesses, exclusive of Averitt's wife. I did not trust her and there was no way I would put such a runaway train on the stand. The witnesses did a good job on the stand, but even so, I was not going to rely on their testimony to win the case. I would use the evidence that Louie the Tailor had led me to.

As I called to the stand a representative of the US headquarters of Volkswagen, I turned to where Lou was sitting with his two buddies and winked. The clerk swore him in and I began qualifying him as an expert on Volkswagen automobiles. I showed him an enlarged photo of the red Volkswagen owned by Carl Averitt that Ryan had introduced without my objection.

"Sir, have you had the opportunity to personally examine, at my request, the vehicle that the police have identified as Carl Averitt's automobile?"

"Yes, sir."

"Did you match the serial number with the dealer's invoice to confirm that the red car you examined was purchased by Carl Averitt?"

"Yes, sir."

"Did I ask you to fold down the back of the right front passenger seat?"

"Yes, sir."

"Did you?"

"No."

"Why?"

"Because that particular car did not have that option on it."

"I show you a copy of the invoice. Does it reflect that the option was not included when Carl Averitt purchased it?"

"The invoice confirms that the car did not have that option."

I turned to the judge and announced that the little red Volkswagen was downstairs in front of the courthouse, and I requested that the jury be allowed to inspect it to confirm that the seat did not fold back as the girl claimed. And then I theatrically announced, "Judge, I want the jury to try to lay the seat backwards. If it can lie back as the victim says, then convict my client. If not, then free him, because she has identified the wrong red car."

Although the trial judge denied my request, the die was cast. The jury knew for sure that the victim had identified the wrong car which was the only evidence that had led the police to Averitt. As I walked back to my table, I glanced over at Lou, who was smiling and slowly shaking his head in disbelief. He knew that his cracker lawyer had struck again.

A shaken Ryan had been surprised again, almost as much as my client. I purposely had not told Inman Averitt out of fear he would have gotten drunk and told his wife of my surprise witness, and she could have sabotaged us.

Ryan completed his case unenthusiastically and gave a closing argument that rang with defeat. In my closing argument, I put the icing on the cake when I pointed out to the jury that the young girl said her assailant did not smell of alcohol, however, within an hour and a half of the time she was assaulted, Averitt was arrested for being stone drunk by a county policeman—another reason to eliminate Averitt as a viable suspect.

The jury took only thirty minutes to acquit my client. I shook hands with my friend Ryan and left with Averitt and his buddies for a celebration party at the Ramada Inn. When Averitt's wife joined the group, I left. I never told his wife that I had not taped her that night. The real assailant was never apprehended or struck again with the same motif.

I ended up that night at Dino's Den with Lou and his two buddies from Miami. I told Lou of how he'd led me to the fault in the case and how he'd re-taught me a lesson I'd already known. That lesson, "Re-enact the crime, no matter what the crime may be," was the same lesson I'd taught him in the Washington case.

30. Thirty Pieces of Silver

"Cracker, the only difference between the Mob and the police is the police wear uniforms. The truth don't matter to either side."

—Lou Rosanova

Louie the Tailor was often accused of not liking black people—mainly because he only had one black friend that I knew of, B. Days, his driver and caddie. But such an accusation was unfair. The society he lived in while he was growing up on the streets of Chicago did not include blacks. The same was true in Savannah, especially around the golf courses, including the Savannah Inn.

However, the cases that he took an interest in involved mainly black defendants. When he felt the black defendant was innocent, he doubled down trying to help me win the case. Those that he felt were guilty as sin he never helped nor expressed interest in. As you will recall, he actively participated in the Matthew Washington case. However, the case that emotionally affected him the most was the Floyd Brown case that was initially tried fifteen years before he came to Savannah to save the Teamsters.

Floyd Brown was a black handyman who'd been accused and convicted of raping and murdering a white woman in 1962 who'd been well known on the Westside of Savannah as the Sandwich Lady. She'd been in her forties, attractive, divorced, and raising a couple of children. Each day of the week she had delivered to local businesses sandwiches that were considered the best in town. One day after making her deliveries, she had disappeared.

A huge search had commenced, and after a couple of days, her body had been found in a field at the edge of a railroad track in west Savannah. She had been raped and shot several times. This had led to the arrest of Floyd Brown a week or so later, and the case had become the biggest murder case of its era.

I first learned of the case while I was attending law school. Like good law students, commonly known in those days in Athens, Georgia, as 'legal eagles,' we followed the proceedings in the Atlanta newspaper. I, like most of my colleagues, thought the verdict of 'guilty' was appropriate under the evidence that was published by the media.

I thought no more about the case and Floyd Brown until many years after I'd graduated from law school. I woke up one morning, fifteen years later, and read where the Brown case had been overturned by the Georgia Supreme Court and a new trial had been ordered. The reason he'd been denied a fair trial was because of the systematic exclusion of blacks from his jury panel and the grand jury that had indicted him. And it should be noted that Brown's attorneys had never filed a timely appeal on the conviction in 1962.[36]

As was the custom, I walked into the clubhouse at the inn where Lou was sipping on a cup of coffee and reading the 'Morning Mistake.' He looked up at me and smiled.

"Cracker, have you seen the morning news?"

"Briefly."

"Did you read where this black guy's case got overturned?"

"Yeah, I was in law school when it was tried. That guy was lucky that he didn't get lynched in those days. He killed the 'Sandwich Lady.' Who's going to defend him this time?"

"Lou, he had five appointed lawyers the first time he was tried. So, thank God whoever it is will have a lot of company."

We played golf that morning, and as we rode in the golf cart, I mentioned a few tidbits of the evidence I had read about fifteen years before. Lou's interest was increased.

Bright and early the next Monday morning I received a call from my mother. She invited me over for lunch and said that she wanted to talk to me about something. That was an invitation I couldn't or wouldn't refuse.

When I arrived at my parents' home, my mother was lying back in her reclining chair with her maid sitting nervously in the chair next to her. My mother was suffering from a rare terminal illness that would take her life six years later. During that span, and at least for five years before, Inez Perry, had waited faithfully on my mother—hand and foot as we say in the South—and my mother was devoted to her. They were also very good friends.

"Son, I want you to listen to what Inez is going to tell you. I promised her you would."

"Mr. Bubba, I know that you been readin' about Floyd Brown. He's gonna get a new trial. Mr. Bubba, he ain't killed that lady. He needs the best lawyer there is and me and your mama think that's you."

"Inez, I remember the case very well. I remember they found the murder weapon in Floyd's bedroom, and they identified his truck as being seen in the area where they found her body. I don't think that there was much question in anyone's mind that he killed her."

Struggling to control her sobs, she explained, "Mr. Bubba, Floyd was my man. He didn't have no green pick-up truck and he loaned that gun out to his friend Wilson, long before that day. Wilson ain't returned it. When that lady disappeared, Floyd was over at my house fixin' my fence all day. Folks were there and they knew Floyd was at my house. He picked me up that day from your mama's house in his blue truck. His truck was blue, not green. Wilson had a green truck. Mr. Bubba, Floyd ain't never been in no trouble before. He wouldn't harm a fly."

"Did you tell the police this?"

"Yes, and they told me they'd get back to me and talk to the people that saw Floyd at my house fixin' the fence, but they never did. Mr. Bubba, Floyd has a bad heart now and he's going to die in Reidsville if you don't help him."

I looked over at my mother and knew without asking what the next words were going to be out of her mouth.

"Inez says that Floyd Brown didn't kill that lady, and that's all I need to know. Inez has never lied to me before, and she has told me this many times over the last few years. She's been following your impossible cases in the papers for years and she's bragged to me how smart my son is and how fair you are to the blacks. She said this morning that when she heard Floyd's case had been overturned that it was God's will to talk to me. She believes that you can get him off and back home before he dies."

Then my dear mother closed the deal with this statement: "What good is a good lawyer if he's not going to free innocent poor people from crimes they did not commit? Son, Floyd Brown did not kill anyone!"

I looked over at Inez, and said, "Inez, I'll do my best."

She began crying out loud and praising God, invoking the name of Jesus every other word. When she finally composed herself, Inez fed my mother and me the best low-country shrimp Creole and rice I had ever tasted or will ever taste for the next forty years.

Instead of going to my office, I went to the newspaper office and straight to their morgue. I asked the clerk for all of the old files on Floyd Brown. Within minutes, she'd stacked two boxes of newspaper clippings and proofs of old photos. I spent the rest of the afternoon reading every one of them. The one that stuck out the most concerned the headline, 'Businessmen's Club Awards Detectives $3,000.'

I thought it strange that the two detectives in charge of the investigation had been honored by the largest civic club in Savannah and given $3,000 for just arresting a man who had not been tried or found guilty of any crime. The article stated that the chief of police had praised the detectives for 'busting' the case. What if the jury had found him not guilty once the trial had been conducted? Would the detectives have been required to give back the money since they had arrested the wrong man?

Another article gave me information I was unaware of. The article read: 'Brown Given Back His Clothes.' What? Given back his clothes? I read further. The article stated that upon Floyd Brown's arrest he'd been stripped naked and placed in an isolated cell for five days. On the fifth day, one of his five attorneys had petitioned the court for an order allowing Brown to wear clothes once again. The court had signed the order and Floyd had been allowed to put clothes on.

A third article concerned a telephone tip that had led the police to Floyd Brown's house. The tipster had said the gun would be found in a chest-of-draws in his bedroom. This was the tip that had led to the murder weapon and the arrest of Floyd Brown.

I made copies of all the articles and returned to my office and notified the trial judge that I was representing Floyd Brown in his new trial. Unfortunately, I was not given four other attorneys to assist me as had been in the case in the first trial. Actually, as I told Lou that night, I don't think I could have worked with a team of lawyers. Why? Because I didn't trust other lawyers when it came to keeping trial secrets and antics. One, maybe, but not four! Lou agreed with me.

After I had determined that two of the lead attorneys in the first trial were now dead, I contacted the daughter of one of them who was a lawyer in her own right. I obtained her father's files and brought them to my office.

One of the detectives who'd been paid for the arrest was Randolph Strickland, who was now dead. The other detective was George Bouchea and he was still alive and kicking. I headed to his office at the county police station. On my appearance, he voiced his surprise that after all these years someone was still looking into helping 'Old Floyd Brown.'

"Bubba, he had the best lawyers in Georgia defending him. Hell, the judge appointed him five. If he didn't get all of his rights protected by that crew, then he won't ever. The man was guilty and that's all there is to it. He would've gotten the death chair if the death chair wasn't illegal at the time."

"Did he ever confess?"

"No, but you know that ain't unusual. If he did, someone would've lynched him. No, we never got a confession out of him, but it wasn't because we didn't try hard."

"Can I look at your old file?"

"What?"

"Can I look at your file? Detective, I'll get a court order if I have to, but that's going to bring some media coverage and we don't need that this early in the process. I just have one or two questions in my mind that could possibly be answered by looking at your investigative file."

Removing the smirk from his face, he changed his tone, "You know they tried this before, but back then our investigative file wasn't available to a defendant. Since then they've changed the rules, and I know you can get it with a subpoena."

The detective slowly rose up from his swivel chair and said, "Wait here while I get it." He returned a few minutes later and handed me the file to review. I was about to see what the first team of lawyers had not been allowed to see. And I knew what I was looking for.

I wanted the name of the tipster and the last name of Wilson. The first statement I read gave the name of the tipster. It was a man named Wilson Jones. I read the information sheet on Wilson Jones and there was nothing in the file that connected him to the crime.

"Can I make copies of these statements?"

"Sure, you'll get them anyway."

"Did you ever have any information that Wilson Jones had borrowed Brown's gun a few months before the crime?"

"That's what Brown told us."

"Did you confirm this with Wilson Jones?"

"Not really. We didn't believe Brown."

"Did Jones own a truck?"

"I don't recall. What's that got to do with anything?"

"The news article said a witness spotted a green truck driven by a black man in the area where the lady was found. There's a statement in this file that Floyd Brown's truck was not green, it was blue. So, how did that witness link Floyd to the crime scene?"

Watching his reaction, I continued, "After reading your statement and the news article, Wilson Jones called the police after hearing on a radio that a black man driving a green pick-up truck is suspected of killing the lady. After hearing that, he calls the police and gives them the name of Brown and tells them that he has a gun stashed in his bedroom. Doesn't that seem awfully strange to you, since the man knew where Floyd kept his gun and also knew that Floyd's truck did not meet the description of the truck?"

The conversation suddenly changed. The detective became defensive. Gone was the friendly tone of earlier. Looking at me in a hostile fashion he said, "I have to end this because I have other and better things to do than mow cut grass again." He went into another office and slammed the door.

I left there knowing that the police had withheld major evidence in the first trial. In defense of the five attorneys, they had not been legally able to read the file I'd just copied. They'd never known of Wilson Jones. He'd only been known to them as 'the tipster.'

That night I had drinks with Lou and told him of the withheld evidence and the strong possibility that Floyd Brown had not killed the Sandwich Lady. Lou took the news in his usual manner. He mumbled a few well-chosen curse words that questioned the heritage and birth of the cops, and then he offered his support.

"Cracker, are you gonna need outside experts to help the guy? If you do, you can count on me to donate what you need."

"Lou, not at this point. If I do, I'll holler at you." We had a few more drinks and I left with a strong handshake from Louie the Tailor.

I knew that the key to the case was determining the color of Wilson Jones's truck, something that the detectives had never done, or if they had, had never revealed. I also needed to confirm from an independent source that Jones had borrowed the gun prior to the murder. I knew I had a lot to do if Floyd Brown had a chance on the retrial.

My first revelation was that Wilson Jones had died three years before. So I went to a witness, Vastie Blue, who claimed to have been the friend of both Brown and Jones. She verified that she'd been there when Jones had borrowed the murder weapon from Brown; she verified that Jones had had a green truck that he'd sold shortly after the lady had been killed; that Jones had had free access in and out of Floyd's house at all hours of the day and night; that they'd been friends and drank together; and that the day the lady had been murdered, Floyd had been fixing Inez Perry's fence. She strengthened that by saying that Floyd had worked on that fence for at least a week.

I went to the tag office and confirmed that Jones had purchased a 1962 tag for a green 1960 pickup truck that was eventually sold to a John Mann, a local State Farm Insurance agent. Luckily, I knew the man, and I went to him to get the exact date of the purchase. John told me it had been purchased on a certain date that happened to be within three days after the crime and before Jones had called in the tip. John also said that the man had been anxious to sell and at a very cheap price. The case was definitely looking up for Floyd.

I noticed in the original police report that when they had confiscated Floyd's truck, they'd dusted it for fingerprints. They had found a lot of fingerprints and old tools, but no fingerprints of the victim. Nothing in any of the reports supported any reason why the police had switched from a green truck to a blue truck. That was puzzling to me.

I contacted a friend of mine with the Georgia Bureau of Investigation and obtained the criminal records of both Floyd and Jones. Floyd had a couple of driving violations while Jones had a prior rape conviction for which he'd served three years at Reidsville.

And here are some more questions that remained unanswered for the next fifteen years: Why did the police ignore the statements of Inez, Vastie, and Floyd Brown? Why didn't they trace the truck of Jones to determine its color, and more importantly, why didn't they trace the sale of Jones's truck to John Mann? For some unknown reason, the police had rushed to judgment. Why had they settled on Floyd and not the better suspect, Wilson Jones? The answer would become obvious by the time the case was called to trial.

Three days before trial, the state brought Floyd from Reidsville to Savannah. I saw him for the first time the next day. As I entered the interview room, I saw a very tired old man who had aged greatly before his time. We shook hands and it became obvious that he was a sick man who had been mistreated for the past fifteen years in the worst prison facility in the state of Georgia.

"Floyd, I'm Bubba Haupt. I'm your new lawyer and it's a pleasure to finally meet you." He was clearly perplexed. Here was a young white lawyer trying to free an old black man for the murder of a white woman for no fee in a town that hated him.

He finally spoke after the tears began to flow. "Mr. Haupt, God bless you. Oh, God bless you. I ain't killed that lady. I didn't do it. I been praying all these years. I thought nobody cared no more. I thought I'd been throwed away—yes, sir, throwed away!"

"Floyd, you have a lot of people that have gone to bat for you. Inez, Vastie, and my mother. That may not sound like a lot, but I can assure you that the Lord moved for you through them, but we've got a lot to do. We're not home yet by a long shot."

I spent the rest of the afternoon with Floyd and prepared him for trial because I was going to break my own rule—I was going to put my client on the stand.

The first day of the call to trial of a major murder case was always a big event in small Southern towns and cities, particularly in Savannah. People would take a day off from work to be there to see the characters and the person accused of such vile crimes. In this instance, they were there to get a look at Floyd Brown, the man that all of them believed had killed the Sandwich Lady. The courtroom was packed, but only after the deputies relieved eight people of pistols as they entered the courtroom. Why a law-abiding citizen would bring a firearm to watch a trial always puzzled me. Eventually, I came to understand that it was normal in most of the cases I tried. Could it have been because of me? I never got an answer.

Ryan put up the surviving detective and went through all of the evidence Ryan's father (the former DA) had introduced fifteen years earlier. The detective carefully described the gruesome rape and murder of a very popular 'sandwich lady' who had harmed no one in her forty years of life. Then he went into detail, with photos of the body discovered near the railroad tracks in west Savannah. The photos showed a mangled corpse that animals had half eaten. The all-white jury mostly made up of women, became agitated, looking away from the gruesome photos. In that day and age, these photos alone could have convicted Floyd Brown.

The detective then recited how Brown became a suspect. His green truck had been spotted in the area of the corpse and a tipster had led him to Floyd's bedroom where the murder weapon was found. After identifying the gun as the murder weapon through ballistics tests, they arrested Floyd and charged him with murder. Their investigation was far too easy to suit me.

When Ryan turned him over to me for cross-examination, I took my time by having the court clerk mark exhibit numbers on copies of the statements I'd obtained from the detective and the news clippings I'd gotten from the newspaper morgue. When she completed her task, I took them in hand and slowly walked towards the man in the witness chair and began my examination.

"Detective, you understand that you are under oath, don't you?"

"Yes."

"Do you recall meeting with me and allowing me to copy the statements and reports that were in your investigation file?"

"Yes."

"Did you have in your file information that Floyd Brown's truck was blue, not green?"

"Yes."

"As a matter of fact, when the police impounded the truck, you led the search of the truck, isn't that right?"

"Yes."

"When you saw that the truck didn't match the description of the truck everyone was searching for, did that raise a question in your mind that this may not be the truck?"

"Yes, but when we found the gun in Brown's bedroom, we thought the witness was mistaken as to the color of the truck."

"So, because of the fact that a tipster led you to the murder weapon in Brown's bedroom, you excused the discrepancy in the color of the truck?"

"That's right."

"In view of what you just testified to, the gun was the only evidence you had against Floyd Brown?"

"I guess so."

"You guess so?"

"No, I'm not guessing. It was the only evidence."

"Detective, would you tell this jury the name of the tipster?"

"His name was Wilson Jones. He's dead now."

"Did you make a background check on him?"

"For what? He wasn't a suspect in the crime."

"Wouldn't that have been a help to you in determining his credibility?"

"I guess it would have, but we didn't."

I handed him a certified copy of Wilson Jones's criminal record and asked him to look over it.

"Am I correct in saying that the tipster had a previous rape conviction and had served time in Reidsville?"

"Yes."

"Was the victim in this case raped?"

"Yes."

"Don't you think, looking back on the situation, knowing that the tipster was a convicted rapist would have been important to your investigation?" I asked as I walked over to my counsel's table picking up a certified copy of Floyd Brown's criminal record.

"Hindsight is 20/20, Mr. Haupt, but it would not have changed my mind that Floyd Brown was the man."

"Would you look at Floyd Brown's criminal record prior to him being charged with this crime?"

He read it carefully and replied, "He had a couple of driving violations."

"You've never seen this before, have you?"

"No."

"So, having not seen the criminal records of the only two men involved in your investigation, you actually did not know who to believe, did you?"

Ryan jumped up and objected to the question, stopping the detective from giving an answer. I changed gears as the judge sustained Ryan's objection.

"What was the color of Wilson Jones's truck?"

"I didn't know he had one."

"Assuming he did and the truck was green, would that have made Jones a better suspect than Brown?"

"No."

"Why?"

"Because the murder weapon was found in Brown's bedroom."

"Did you ever ask Wilson Jones how he knew this?"

"Yes. He said that Brown and him worked together sometimes and that it was known by him and most of Brown's friends."

"Did Jones tell you he'd borrowed it from Brown before the date of this crime?"

"No. No one ever said that."

I walked over to the table and selected Brown's statement and the one Inez Perry had given to him shortly after Brown's arrest.

"Would you review these two statements and tell this jury if both of these statements, which were taken by you, informed you that Jones had, indeed, borrowed the gun before the murder and had not returned it until after the murder?"

He slowly read each statement and reluctantly answered, "Yes, both of them said that."

"Did you question Jones about it?"

"I don't remember."

"Let me refresh your memory. There is no statement in your file from Jones concerning the gun or the color of his truck. Wouldn't it have been important to ask him about the gun and the color of his truck?"

Again, Ryan stood to object before the detective could answer. And again, the judge sustained the objection.

"Now, let's go to money that you and detective Strickland were given, or awarded for arresting Floyd Brown."

With that, Ryan jumped up and shouted his objection, stopping me temporarily from going into the most important issue of the trial. (Incidentally, it was never mentioned in the first trial.)

"What is your objection, Mr. Ryan?" the trial judge asked.

"It has nothing to do with this case. There is no relationship between the award and the innocence or guilt of the defendant," he answered.

"Would you two gentlemen approach the bench?"

The judge asked, "Mr. Haupt, would you enlighten me as to the materiality of this line of questions? I am confused as to where you're going."

"Judge, I ask permission to connect this information to the case. I promise I will demonstrate to you and the jury why Floyd Brown was chosen over Wilson Jones as the defendant in this case. Further, the conduct of the investigating detectives is admissible if it affected the case," I replied, knowing that I was reaching.

The judge stared at me and said, "Okay, but connect it as fast as you can."

"After arresting Brown, you and Strickland received a lot of praise from your chief and the news media, isn't that right?"

"In a way."

"In a way? Let me show you the headline of a newspaper article appearing two days after Floyd's arrest. Do I need to read it to you?"

He looked at the headline and said, "It says that the chief praised us."

I took the article back and held it up for the jury to see, "It reads, 'Chief Praises Detectives.'"

"Now, let me show you another one a week or so later. 'Detectives Awarded $3,000.' So, am I correct in saying that you and your partner were receiving praise and money in the weeks following the arrest of Floyd Brown?"

He looked over at Ryan and said nothing.

"Never mind that, the articles speak for themselves. Detective, after you received the money, you couldn't investigate Jones could you?"

"I don't understand."

"Let me help you. You quickly determined that Brown was the culprit after confiscating the gun that Jones dropped a dime on, and had Brown arrested. The news media ran wild with it. But you knew that Brown's truck didn't meet the description. However, you had information that Jones had a truck that did. You also had information that Jones had borrowed the gun before the crime."

"You didn't trace Jones's truck or determine that he had hurriedly sold it to John Mann within three days of the crime. Hence, you never sought the criminal record that would have shown Jones to be a convicted rapist."

Ignoring Ryan as he jumped up, shouting some sort of an objection. I persisted, "Detective, had you continued your investigation concerning the information on Jones, you would have been placed in a position where you would have had to repay the Lions Club's $3,000. To be clear, Jones was by far the more likely suspect, but you couldn't take that road.

"You had spent the money! You had to get Brown convicted in order to justify keeping the money, regardless of whether or not you were convicting an innocent man."

The courtroom went silent. The judge told the deputy to remove the jury as he motioned for Ryan and me to meet him in his chambers. We followed him as instructed.

The judge spoke first, "Mr. Haupt, you just accused a well-known and respected law enforcement officer of accepting money in exchange for the conviction of an innocent man. I understand your logic, but I believe that you went too far. Now, tell me how you're going to fix it."

"I'm not," I said. "I believe every word I said, and I think that the real killer was never investigated because of the payoff to the detectives. The 'thirty pieces of silver' doomed Floyd Brown and now he is required to die in prison. If I can't tell the jury the truth in this case, then declare a mistrial and I'll go to federal court for help. I'm sorry, Judge, but I can't relent just because I've gravely insulted the detectives in this case," I replied. I expected to be held in contempt.

"Mr. Ryan, what say you?" the judge asked.

"I believe the question Bubba asked should be stricken from the record and that he should be allowed to argue his point in his closing argument if he desires to do so. Frankly, I think he angered some jurors by accusing the detective of a crime. But let's don't mistrial the case."

After accepting Ryan's suggestion, we adjourned for the day and I had drinks with Lou at Dino's later that night.

The following morning Ryan concluded his case, and I began mine. First, I put Inez Perry on the stand, then Vastie Blue, John Mann, and finally Floyd Brown. As much as we tried, we couldn't overcome the murder weapon being found in the chest-of-draws in Floyd's bedroom with the testimony of two black women who were personal friends of Floyd.

When the jury came back with a guilty verdict, I couldn't look my client in the eye. Never in my many years of criminal trial experience had I ever witnessed such an intentional miscarriage of justice, but Floyd broke the ice.

"Mr. Haupt, you did the best you could. I still know you gonna win it for me. God bless you and thank your momma for me."

As the courtroom emptied, I turned towards the judge. He surreptitiously motioned me over and lowering his voice he said, "Bubba, your man's innocent. File a motion for a new trial."

I thanked him and walked back to my client. Although I appreciated the judge's sentiment, I was planning to appeal in federal court. I didn't believe that Floyd Brown could ever receive a fair trial before a Savannah jury. I turned to Floyd as the deputies moved to shackle him and said, "Floyd, the fight has just begun. I am appealing tomorrow and I promise I'm going to get you home."

With that said, they walked him out of the courtroom in shackles to be returned to his hell on earth at Reidsville. I never spoke to him again; he died from heart failure a few days later.

Explaining the outcome of the trial and Floyd's death to my mother and her friend Inez was the toughest task I ever had as a trial attorney. Surprisingly enough, my mother understood and concluded the case with a simple statement that comforted Inez. "Floyd is free now; he's in heaven."

Unlike my mother, Louie the Tailor took a different approach to hearing the news of Floyd Brown's death. After mumbling some choice curse words under his breath about the detectives that took the 'thirty pieces of silver,' he said, "Brown never had a chance, did he? The photos of the lady did him in, didn't they?"

I nodded in agreement and said, "Lou, I'm ashamed of the system I'm in. It's going to burn me out soon. I can't keep taking these cases so personal."

He gave me a bear hug and said, "Not until we beat *Playboy*, okay."

"Okay."

31. The Simmons Family

During the seventies in Savannah, the city was rated in the top five cities in America consistently for murders per capita. For a couple of years during that time span, we were number one. Yes, that's right. We ranked above Chicago, New York, and Atlanta. This amused Louie the Tailor to no end.

Every time Lou caught flack in news articles linking him to Chicago's crime families, he would always bring to my attention Savannah's crime rate. "Cracker, you got more crime down here than Chicago ever had. Ours is just organized. Y'all's is random," he told me one bright Saturday morning sitting in the clubhouse minutes before we were scheduled to tee off.

"What brought this on?" I inquired.

"This article," he said as he handed me the 'Morning Mistake.'

I looked it over and realized that he was reading an article about a recent bout the police had had with the Simmons family. This led me to tell Lou about my long-time clients, the Simmons.

The Simmons family lived about three miles on the other side of the Savannah River in Jasper County, South Carolina. Papa Simmons was a huge man about six foot three and 280 pounds. His wife, whose name I never knew, was about two inches shorter and thirty pounds lighter. Together, they would have easily anchored the Atlanta Falcons' defensive line.

They had three sons: Paul, Tunch, and a younger son whose name I have forgotten. They also had a nephew, Mickey, who lived with them, and was raised as a son.

As far as I knew, the family income came from selling peaches from derelict old pick-up trucks and a small store that also sold fireworks on US Highway 17. Apparently, the income was good enough to support a modest cabin on about two hundred acres of land between Savannah and Hilton Head Island, South Carolina. However, they spent little on clothing attire since I never saw the parents or sons in anything but baggy overalls.

My first involvement came when Papa Simmons arrived at my office one morning and wanted me to represent his son, Tunch, and his nephew, Mickey. He explained the need for an attorney in this fashion:

Mickey and Tunch had gotten arrested for drunk driving at Tybee Island (Savannah Beach) the night before and been taken to the Tybee jail for the evening. Mama Simmons had driven to Tybee to bond them out at about two o'clock in the morning. Unfortunately, the jailer would not allow her to pay the bond, and he'd told her that they would have to go before the judge the next evening.

This had upset Mama Simmons, so she'd clubbed the jailer, taken his keys, and set the young men free. I believe that Tunch was about twenty-five and Mickey about twenty; both were big men, but smaller than Mama Simmons. The men had climbed into Tunch's car and sped off. The mama had followed at a distance in her car.

As they were driving the twenty miles back to Savannah, they had encountered about six roadblocks at various intersections and highways. As they'd crashed through each of them, several police units had been demolished.

By the time they'd reached the bridge that would allow them to cross over into South Carolina, police units from the City of Savannah, Tybee Island Police, Chatham County Police, and the Georgia State Patrol had joined the chase and the roadblocks. As the Simmons had crashed through the last roadblock at the foot of the bridge on the Georgia side, the chasing units and the various departments had decided to continue the chase into South Carolina under the legal doctrine of 'hot pursuit.'

When Tunch and Mickey had arrived at the Simmons homestead, they'd jumped out of the car and fled into the house where Papa and two other brothers had been waiting. When the police units drove into the Simmons' front yard, the Simmons had opened with a barrage of gunfire. The officers had then exited their units and begun returning fire.

One hour later, the police ran out of ammunition and surrendered, holding up white handkerchiefs. Seeing that, Papa Simmons had called the sheriff of Jasper County and asked him to come to the property. The sheriff arrived and determined that about forty law enforcement officers from the Savannah area needed a ride home because all the tires, headlights, and windshields had been blown out. The sheriff had called for a school bus and within thirty minutes the officers had been brought back to Savannah and released.

After hearing this story—which I had difficulty believing—I asked if Papa Simmons knew what the charges were against Tunch and Mickey. He said he didn't know, but he thought the various police departments were mad as hell and would try to 'railroad' his boys. He said he needed to get them a good lawyer, and that is why he was in my office standing in front of my desk in oversized overalls with a straw hat on.

I thought for a moment and considered the fact that the man sold peaches for a living and probably couldn't afford the fee that should be charged for such serious crimes.

"Mr. Simmons, I will represent them for a total of five thousand dollars," I said, thinking that he would need some time to raise the money.

He reached into his pants pocket and pulled out a huge roll of cash money. He counted out five thousand dollars in one-hundred-dollar bills and put the rest of the money—which still remained a large roll—back into his pocket. Then he said, "Man, that's a lot cheaper than I thought you would charge. I brought twenty-five thousand just in case you needed it. But thank you."

In that day, as I keep saying, five thousand dollars bought a new Chevy. Shock set in as I realized that I had left twenty thousand dollars on the table or four Chevys! It took a while for me to recover from this, particularly since the men were eventually charged with forty-eight counts of attempted murder of forty-eight police officers.

As I told Lou the story, he started laughing and said, "Cracker, what happened to 'em?"

I held up my hand and told Lou there was more and to let me finish my story before I told him of the outcome.

I began relating to Lou that several weeks later, I received a call from Papa Simmons that Paul and Tunch had been arrested for killing a marine recruiter near their property in South Carolina. This time I was ready to collect what I'd left on the table a few weeks before. I drove to South Carolina with a much larger fee in mind.

Later that day, I met Papa Simmons at the Simmons homestead and he related how he had taken a hog-hunting party to his property one foggy morning. After twelve hours of hunting and failing to sight one hog, the party had given up and driven away disappointed. Papa Simmons, being mad and tired, had gotten into his truck and yelled at Tunch and Paul to gather the damn dogs and bring them home to their pens as he drove away.

Upon hearing the instructions of Papa Simmons, Paul and Tunch had become angry, jumped into their truck after rounding up the dogs, and sped away. As they'd entered the highway about three miles from home, they'd had to swerve to miss a marine recruiting truck with two marines inside.

Tunch had shouted at them and shaken his fists out of the window. Paul, who'd been driving, caught up with the marine truck, and Tunch had fired his shotgun into the cab. The shell had hit one of the marines and killed him. The other marine then radioed ahead and identified Tunch and the truck to the Jasper County authorities. Paul and Tunch had been arrested a few hours later.

After hearing the facts, I'd quoted Papa Simmons a fee that had made him reach a lot deeper into his overalls than before; I felt redeemed. When I got to this point in the story with Louie the Tailor, I again held up my hand and told my listener there was more.

"Lou, a few months after that, and while all of these cases were proceeding through the courts in Georgia and South Carolina, I got a call one evening that Tunch and the brother [whose name I had forgotten] were pulled over by a county policeman on the Tybee Road for speeding. Not knowing the occupants were Simmons, the officer had approached the car and been quickly attacked, pistol-whipped with his own pistol, and left on the road with head injuries."

"Lou, the officer they'd attacked was Billy Fields, the guy that gave me the tapes. They sewed up his head, but he was never the same afterward. No one was arrested because Fields could not identify which Simmons had hit him."

I paused and looked at Lou, and said, "And, there is still a lot more to tell."

I told Lou that a few months after that, I had read in a Hilton Head Island newspaper where Paul Simmons had been involved in an automobile wreck that had killed a family of nine. He had run a stop sign in Hardeeville, South Carolina, and hit a station wagon full of black people going to a family reunion. Paul was never charged by the Jasper County authorities.

"Lou, there were two more incidents that involved four more killings. Mickey was charged with murdering a woman in Garden City—that's west of Savannah. And to cap it all off, three Black Panthers driving across the country had the bad luck of stopping at the small fireworks store owned by the Simmons. As fate would have it, they'd pulled out a shotgun and tried to rob Paul and Tunch. The Simmons brothers had reached under the counter and come up blasting away. All three Panthers were dead in seconds."

Lou was still looking at me in disbelief. Then he said, "Cracker, there can't be more!"

"I think that's it. Let's see, during a ten-year span the Simmons killed fourteen people, beat Lt. Billy Fields half to death, and destroyed about thirty police units. I would say that this was a crime spree of epic proportions. And none of them are in prison as we speak."

Lou, seemingly astonished at my last revelation, said, "You mean none of them served time?"

"No, Lou. I said that none of them is in prison at the moment. I believe that Mickey got a couple of years for the chase and was found not guilty of the Garden City murder. Tunch entered a temporary insanity plea in South Carolina for the murder of the marine, and after tests showed that he was mentally challenged in a lot of areas, he did a few months in a mental institution. Paul was not charged with killing the nine black people in Hardeeville.

"As for the Black Panthers, the town of Hardeeville wanted to give Paul and Tunch keys to the city for killing the California robbers."

Still boasting a large, incredulous grin on his face, Lou told me he'd just been kidding before about Savannah being the crime center of America. "But, Cracker, now I'm convinced. Are the Simmons still around?"

"Yep. In fact, every time we go over to Hilton Head to play golf, we pass one of them on the side of the road selling peaches from an old truck. Next time we go, I'm going to stop and introduce you to them. You may want to get some tips from them on how to stay out of jail, and the peaches are good," I said as I laughed at the dumbfounded look on his wide Sicilian face.

Whether or not Lou believed me, only he knew. However, Lou often mentioned the Simmons family to his buddies from Chicago and Miami when we were relaxing at Dino's. In a way, they became folk heroes to him. The Simmons stayed in my mind for a long time because they bought me a fleet of Chevys.

32. The Death Penalty Crisis

In the seventies, the death penalty issue was front and center in the state of Georgia. Opposition to the death penalty mainly came from the black population, because they believed that only blacks got the penalty and rich white people did not. Hence, black voters supported only those statewide politicians who were against the death penalty.

In 1974, George Busbee got elected governor of Georgia with the strong support of the black voting population. At the time he began seeking the governor's office in 1972, he had campaigned in the black communities against implementing the death penalty. That was easy and safe since the Georgia death penalty statute had been held to be unconstitutional by the Supreme Court of the United States in 1972.

Unfortunately for Busbee, the Georgia legislature passed a new death penalty statute that the Supreme Court held to be constitutional in 1976. Hence, as each death penalty sentence was imposed against defendants in the various superior courts throughout the state, criminal lawyers appealing the death cases sought suspensions of the sentence while the appeals were pending.

Since the average appeal time in death cases generally lasted a minimum of ten years, Governor Busbee thought he would be able to keep his campaign commitment to the black voting bloc in Georgia for the length of his term of four years, and even for an additional four years of a second and last term of office. He could do this without offending the majority of voters in Georgia who supported the death penalty. In other words, he had the best of both arguments. Both voting blocs believed that he was on their side.

Over breakfast one morning, in November '75, I began reading an article in the newspaper about the arrest of a man who'd confessed to throwing a small child off the Talmadge Memorial Bridge in Savannah.

Like most people who read the article, I assumed that another crackpot had found his way into the police station and either wanted publicity or was looking for self-inflicted punishment for a fantasy crime. In any case, the article was given only a casual mention in the courthouse coffee shop by the gossiping trial lawyers, and only a casual remark by Louie the Tailor later that afternoon. Never in my wildest imagination did I suspect that the man was telling the truth.

That evening I had an appointment with Lou down on the Savannah Riverfront at a small bar that sold the best hamburgers and coldest beer in town. It was called The Exchange Tavern, and it was my getaway from the courthouse crowd. To Lou, it was his getaway from the inn and from the eyes of the undercover agents of various departments in our local, state, and federal governments. We both felt safe and 'out-of-reach' at The Exchange Tavern, a few blocks upstream of the Memorial Bridge.

As we sat there talking about everything but business and the Teamsters, I overheard the bartender's discussion with a customer concerning the river being dragged for a small child's body. Remembering the article, I motioned to Lou to pause the conversation and pointed at the bar where the conversation continued.

"Some of the police divers were here earlier. They really believe that man threw the baby off the bridge," the bartender said.

I moved my chair closer to the bar rail, and asked, "Did they give you any background info?"

"They said that the girlfriend of the man accused him of taking her baby girl and told her she'd never see the child again. They got him at the jail, but no one knows what happened to the little girl."

With that being said, Lou got involved. "Cracker, as deadly as this place is, no one would throw a baby off a bridge. We go over that bridge every time we go to Hilton Head. It must be two hundred feet high. Those big container ships go under it day and night. Nobody ever threw a baby off a bridge in Chicago. Ain't no way someone would do that."

We sat there until we'd finished the hamburgers, then asked for cups to put our drinks in, and left for Wilmington Island in our separate cars. We had lost our desire to hang out and get away. There was too much going on at The Exchange Tavern and an atmosphere of sadness was taking hold.

All our fears and questions were answered the next morning on an early local television news show. The body of a twenty-two-month-old girl was recovered from the Savannah River about two miles downstream from the Memorial Bridge. The unthinkable had happened. The telecast showed the divers bringing the limp body of the small child ashore from the police rescue boat. The pitiful sight made me turn off the television set, and I hurriedly set out for my office, hoping to get involved in something that would get my mind off what I'd just seen.

As I walked into my office, one of my secretaries gave me a note with a phone number for me to call. She said, "Judge Oliver wants you to call him right away. He said it's important. He got me to promise him that I'd make sure you called him before you got involved in something else."

She took it upon herself to start dialing the judge's office.

"Penny, this is not what I think it is, is it?" I asked as I began walking to my office to pick up the phone. I knew the answer by her not answering and looking away as if she didn't hear the question. Why me? Lord, why me? Not again!

"Good morning, Judge."

"Mr. Haupt, I'm appointing you to represent Joseph James Blake. He's in the Chatham County Jail. An arraignment is scheduled for tomorrow morning at 8:30."

My twenty or thirty minutes of pleading with the judge to let me skip this one fell on deaf ears. For the first time in my legal career, I didn't want to represent a client because of the nature of the crime. What this man did was so heartless and evil, I didn't think that I could assure him a fair trial because I had already judged him. That was something I had never done before and had hoped I would never do. As I've said before, a good defense attorney never judges his client. That task is for a jury.

That afternoon I met Blake. He was a slender black male in his mid-twenties, standing about six feet tall, and appeared to be very nervous.

"Mr. Blake, I'm Bubba Haupt. I've been appointed to represent you."

"Praise the Lord! Praise the Lord! I was scared they'd give me someone that didn't know what they was doing."

"Blake, I read the papers and saw the newscast that you called the police and told them that you had thrown the little girl off the Memorial Bridge. Is that right?"

"Yeah, but, she ain't dead."

"What? What do mean that she ain't dead? They pulled her out of the Savannah River early this morning. She's as dead as she can be."

"No sir! She's with God and being raised by Him and not a whoring mama. Don't ya see, attorney Haupt, if I hadn't given her to God, her mama would have raised her in a whorehouse, and that precious baby would've turned out like her mama," he said as tears rolled down his cheeks. "She ain't dead, she ain't dead. I loved her! I wouldn't harm her. I gave her to God by sending her through the water. So, don't say I killed her! No sir, I didn't kill that child. She's with God in heaven."

I stopped the interview because the answers I was getting made no sense. It was obvious that he was either a cold-blooded lying killer or crazy as a bedbug. He convinced me that I needed to have him undergo psychiatric tests, and I needed to prepare an insanity defense. I left, feeling no sympathy for him because I was haunted by the sight of the limp body of that little girl being brought to shore.

This case presented a paradox. Up until that time, I'd been popular among the blacks because they knew I aggressively defended those accused of major crimes, regardless of the color of their skin. They also knew that I couldn't be intimidated by the political powers and could care less about public opinion. They knew that my client, regardless of the color of his skin, or the victim's skin, would get a fair trial.

This all ended when a group of black ministers, whom I knew very well from my unsuccessful run for state senator, approached me as I walked out of the courthouse after attending a motion hearing in the Blake case. Their titular leader and pastor of the largest black church in Savannah was the first to speak.

"Mr. Haupt, can we bend your ear for a few moments?" he asked in his normal soft and friendly tone.

"Of course, Pastor. How are you today?"

"Not so well. We're very concerned that you're the lawyer for Blake. We're afraid you may get him off, and we don't want that to happen. He killed a baby, a black baby, and he deserves to die for it."

Stunned by his remarks, I found it hard to give him a reply he deserved. I really wanted to tell him to kiss my ass, but I held off and answered a little more civilly, "Pastor, I can't believe you just told me that Blake should get the death penalty, and I can't believe you're suggesting that I help him get it."

"No, sir, we don't mean that. We just want you to withdraw from the case. That's all. He killed a baby girl, and that was the work of the devil."

"Pastor, you sound like the Klan. What happened to your belief that the death penalty was not right? I've been in your church and the churches of the others here with you when all of you preached against the death penalty. Now, just because the victim is a black child, the man must die? How would you feel if the baby had been white?"

I backed away from him and looked sharply at the others. "You people are hypocrites, and I could care less how you feel about this." With that said, I turned to walk away but stopped and faced them again.

"You want to know something? I had made up my mind this morning before the hearing to withdraw from the case, because I was prejudiced against my client. But now I'm not going to, because you guys just convinced me to fight hard for him. Thank you for bringing me back to my senses. Good day, gentlemen." I walked away knowing that I had just alienated the black powerbase in Savannah.

Within just a few days, I discovered that black people, as well as rednecks, could make telephone death threats and that they could be just as cruel as the Klan. I learned this quickly the next Saturday morning when the Wilmington Island Pirates were playing for the county championship against the Frank Callen Boys Club from urban Savannah. This team was all black and was a dominant force in little league football.

However, we had a good team and knew that we could line up toe-to-toe and match them. As their coach, I was confident that we could beat them if we played our game the way we'd planned. Lou, with a towel wrapped around his neck, agreed. He was in charge of firing the boys up just like he maintained that the Chicago Bear coach, Papa Halas, had fired him up when he'd played football. I was hoping that he would temper the language a good bit, but I had my doubts.

While Lou was doing his job near the bench a few minutes before kickoff time, I was approached by a mother of one of the Callen boys, along with the wife of one of the Callen coaches. The two women looked very angry and said nothing to me as they approached. The coach's wife spit in my face. Stunned, I quickly turned away, not wishing to hit a woman. The second woman spit but missed. I kept walking away from them and saw Lou, with his towel in hand, coming towards me. He handed me the towel as he passed me heading towards the women. I grabbed his arm and said, "Lou, don't talk to them. I'm okay."

"I ain't gonna talk to them, I'm going over to the coaches and beat the hell out of them."

"No, Lou, let's tell the players and let them do it on the field."

"Okay, but after the game, I'm gonna beat the hell out of them."

As the final whistle sounded, I looked for Lou to make sure that he wasn't going to keep his promise. Thankfully, he was so jubilant with our victory that he was of a different frame of mind. I walked over to their coaches and offered a handshake in customary fashion. The Callen coaches, who in the years before had been good friends, turned away from me. They wanted nothing to do with me or my all-white team.

We withdrew from the county league the next month and formed an all-white football league. The racial tension had taken its toll and all because I was the lawyer for a black killer of a little black girl.

Perhaps my conversation with Lou weeks after the spitting event sums it up.

"Lou, I don't understand why people think I 'get' people off. It takes twelve citizens sitting on a jury to unanimously agree that a man—black or white—is innocent or guilty. It's the jury that walks them, not me. When someone walks because I made sure he had a fair trial, they blame only me, never their neighbors who voted to let him go free. It just makes no sense."

"Cracker, who are the first ones to come to you when they get in trouble?"

"What, do you mean?"

"Who do they come to get 'em off? You, and you know why? Because you ain't gonna listen to the blacks, whites, rednecks, or the Klan." Chuckling, he continued, "But you need to listen to Sicilians. These people trust you, even though they get mad at you when you are not on their side. It's as simple as that. So, forget about it. Keep beating the cops, black or white."

I will not recount the full trial, but there was one incident that occurred in the courtroom that some people found amusing. It gives you a vivid picture of the racial tension that existed during the trial.

Every morning before trial, the judge would caution the spectators, Louie the Tailor included, to keep quiet and not to interfere with the trial process. The first few days went by without an incident. However, on about the fifth day of trial, the lawyers were set to make their closing arguments before the jury.

Ryan went first and did a good job. After about an hour, it was my turn. The courtroom was packed, and everyone was expecting fireworks from my closing. I did not disappoint them. I approached the jury and opened with a simple statement as to why my client was insane. I offered them my opinion as to why this tragedy had happened. I told them that my opinion was based on what he told me from start to finish.

"Ladies and gentlemen, my client dropped this child off the Memorial Bridge and into heaven, because he did not want this child to become a whore. Blake believed that if the mother of this child was allowed to raise her, the child would grow up and be just like her mama and go to hell."

Before I could complete the word 'mama' out of my mouth, the mother of the child jumped up from where she had been sitting behind me and yelled, "Haupt, you are a son of a bitch!" The courtroom spectators were stunned and the judge quickly slammed his gavel on his bench.

"Bailiff, arrest that woman! I want her removed from this courtroom immediately."

As they were taking her out, he addressed the courtroom. "If there is anyone else that shares this woman's opinion of attorney Haupt and is going to interrupt this trial, then I want you to leave now before we reconvene."

An elderly black woman sitting in the back of the courtroom stood up and said, "Judge, Your Honor, I think that I oughta leave too because I feel the same way about lawyer Haupt. I think that he is a son of a bitch." She then left the room.

"If there is anyone else sharing this opinion, please don't announce it, just get up and leave the courtroom," he admonished.

That announcement brought a mass exodus of all the black spectators under the guidance of several deputies. When the exodus was completed, only the jury, deputies, lawyers, clerks, reporters, Blake, Louie the Tailor, and two unnamed white men from Miami sitting with Lou, remained in the courtroom.

"Mr. Haupt, Mr. Ryan, would both of you come up to the bench a moment before Mr. Haupt continues his closing argument."

When we huddled around the judge's bench, Judge Cheatham sheepishly looked at me with a slight smile on his face and said in a very low voice, "Mr. Haupt, I arrested the woman because she shouted obscenities in the courtroom. I did not arrest her for lying." He grinned and told me to resume my closing argument.

Blake was ultimately convicted and sentenced to the electric chair. The death penalty issue with Governor Busbee came into full focus. The days went by and I began to prepare an appeal for Blake. I received a call from the jail that Blake wanted to speak with me as soon as possible. I complied with his request and saw him the next day.

"Lawyer Haupt, I don't wanna appeal. I wanna die and go to heaven."

"Mr. Blake, I have to appeal your case. It's my duty."

"No. I don't want you to. I don't want to live on earth anymore or in prison."

After another fruitless thirty minutes or so of trying to convince him to allow me to file an appeal, I became convinced that it was hopeless. So, I pulled out a piece of paper and a pen and asked him to put it in writing and to date it. He did and I left. Blake was sent to death row at Reidsville State Prison the next day.

On the day set for the execution, I was in my office waiting to go to lunch with Lou. While we had a few moments, for some reason I do not recall, we decided to play a hand or two of gin. Shortly after the first hand was dealt, Lucy, one of my secretaries, came into my office and told me that the governor's office was on the phone.

"Mr. Haupt, the governor's executive secretary is on the phone and she wants to know when you're going to file an appeal and ask for a stay of the execution."

"Lucy, tell her that I don't intend to file an appeal or ask for a stay of the execution. Tell her to tell Governor Busbee that Blake wants to be executed and that I have it in writing."

Lou and Lucy looked at me as if I were crazy.

"Lucy, go tell her what I said. Blake wants him to use the death penalty. Blake doesn't want to live."

Lucy disappeared into the lobby and Lou and I continued the card game. A few minutes later, Lou broke the silence.

"Cracker, what are you doing? You gonna let the man die?" he asked as he laid his cards down and announced, "Gin."

"Lou, I have no control over that. If the man wants to die, he dies. He knows what he wants. So, I have to get out of his way."

"Are you serious?"

Before I could answer his question or look for my trusty bag of boiled peanuts, Lucy burst back into the room and announced that Governor Busbee was on the phone. Lou's eyes widened and I could tell that he was beginning to enjoy the intrigue and the standoff.

"Tell him I'm busy."

"What? I can't tell the governor that! He needs to hear that from you, not me," she replied in obvious distress.

I punched the button that was lit and spoke to the governor. "Governor, Mr. Blake doesn't want a stay of execution. He desires to die for what he did. I have it in writing, so I am not authorized to file an appeal or stay."

"Mr. Haupt, you can't trust his feelings at the moment. Without a stay, he dies tonight in the electric chair. When he changes his mind minutes before they pull the switch, where will that leave you?"

"What is more important, Governor, is where will that leave you? He's been sentenced to the electric chair by a jury of his peers and it's your duty to apply the law. So do it, and don't rely upon us defense lawyers to take you off the spot. We take enough abuse as it is in defending them. If you don't want to apply the death penalty, as you have told a lot of people, then grant him a stay on your own or commute his sentence to a life sentence," I responded as Louie the Tailor looked on in awe.

"I'd prefer you requested a stay," he replied.

"No sir. That is out of the question. I'm representing Blake and following his instructions. You represent the people of Georgia and you should follow their instructions."

There was a brief silence before he replied. "Thank you. I'll advise you of my decision in a few minutes." He hung up.

At four o'clock that afternoon, the governor's executive secretary called me and advised that the governor has granted Blake a stay of execution and that it would be confirmed by wire and a news conference at five. I then took a small piece of paper from my coat pocket that had a telephone number on it and reached for the phone.

At the other end was another one of my secretaries. "Joyce, you can come back. The governor has voluntarily granted a stay of execution and is confirming it with a wire and press conference. Tell the clerk I appreciate her allowing you to sit in her office all afternoon. You can come back to the office now. Don't tell anyone about any of this."

I looked at Lou and Lucy and informed them that I had already obtained an order from a superior court judge near Savannah that morning granting a stay of execution just in case my bluff hadn't worked. Joyce had been waiting to file it before 5:00 p.m. when the clerk's office closed in Savannah.

I won the bluff, and Governor Busbee had to announce that he had granted the stay on his own and that no one would be executed during his stay in office. He served two terms as governor and no one was executed during that time.

As far as Blake is concerned, I filed an appeal and the death penalty sentence was thrown out. After several years of appeals, Blake's sentence was eventually commuted to a life sentence.[37]

As for Louie the Tailor, he needed some early cocktails at The Exchange Tavern to relieve the stress caused by the crisis created by his cracker lawyer. I joined him within minutes of hearing the governor's news conference.

Memorial Bridge in Savannah

33. The Great Offender

Ron Pollock sat in my office in a state of semi-shock. Beside him was his attractive wife. In his hand was a wrinkled copy of the *Savannah Morning News*. With trembling hands, he handed me the paper and asked me to read the lead story. 'Local Businessman Charged with Child Molesting.' The facts of the article itself became unimportant. The name of the local businessman was Ron Pollock. I understood his shock and why he and his wife were waiting for me when I came in. I personally had never met the man, but I had seen his television commercials relentlessly advertising his home improvement company. Like everyone else in Savannah, I was aware of who he was. I told Pollock to relax and offered him and his wife some coffee. Nodding in the affirmative, I had Lucy bring in three cups of coffee and I continued the conversation.

"Mr. Pollock, I know who you are, but then I really don't. Tell me about yourself and your family and start when you were a child."

My statement puzzled him at first, for it sounded like a psychiatrist's opening line. I think he expected me to ask about the crime and his guilt or lack of guilt.

"Mr. Haupt, this is terrible! I'm ruined!"

I interrupted him, "Mr. Pollock, we'll have plenty of time to talk about everything, but right now I want to know all I can about you. I assure you that there will be a brighter side and the only way I can represent you properly is to know you first. Calm down and talk to me about your life. I already know you have a successful business, or you couldn't afford all those TV commercials nor my fee. Now, let's take first things first. Talk to me."

Seemingly calmer, Pollock began, "I was raised by my grandparents in North Carolina. They were poor and worked hard for everything they got. I don't remember being a child. All I can remember is being old enough to get up at 4:00 every morning and go to work in the field. Everything we ate, we grew, and everything we drank came from the cow or the ground. When I was fourteen, my grandfather and I had a fight. He had caught me smoking a pipe I had found and went after me with a broken handle of an old shovel. He scared me to death and I ran away. I never saw them again and I've been on my own ever since. I don't believe I ever was a child. When I got old enough, I joined the army and got my education. Until then I bagged groceries and pumped gas at every grocery store and gas station between here and the North Carolina state line.

"When I was discharged from the service, I used my small savings to open my own business. I met Linda, got married, and we have three children. We've got two boys in their teens and a little girl, she's eight years old and she's spoiled rotten. I've always been a churchgoer. Because of my grandparents, I had no choice but to be religious. When I got married, I chose to be a regular churchgoer. We attend Bible Baptist Church and I drive the Sunday school bus every Sunday picking up kids and taking them to and from church. I've been doing that for years. We have a nice home on Wilmington Island. My business is good and we have a pretty good bank account. I guess I'll lose that by the time you finish with me. Whatever it costs, I'll pay. I want to sue the newspaper for ruining me by printing nothing but lies. They even printed the name of my company in this article."

Pollock sat back in the chair and seemed rather proud of his accomplishments, which he should have been. His wife sat silently looking up, perhaps expecting me to ask her about her life. I didn't. But I did ask her if she and her husband were happily married. She answered with an affirmative nod. At this point, I read nothing into that type of an answer. After arranging my fee, I got the details from Pollock on the charge against him.

It appeared that an eight-year-old little girl, whose father was an FBI agent, complained to her mother that Pollock had fondled her in her privates and had taken off her clothes. It was supposed to have happened while she was at the Pollocks' house playing with the Pollock girl. They lived across the street, so she was a frequent playmate of the Pollock girl and was constantly in and out of their home. Pollock was unaware of any problem until they came to arrest him. He was upset that the girl's parents hadn't come to him first because he believed he could have cleared the matter up. It was the child's imagination. He was taken to jail and bonded out on a ten-thousand-dollar bond.

How the newspaper reporters found out so quickly was a mystery. Maybe the other child's parents had called the media. At any rate, Pollock believed that he and his family were embarrassed and ruined because of a child's fantasy. Why the newspaper would do this to him, a good hardworking Christian family man, was inconceivable. I sympathized with Pollock's plight. Whether he was found innocent or guilty wouldn't really matter to most newspaper readers, since many of them would never read or hear the outcome.

Sometimes the outcome of a trial goes unreported depending on other news activity that day. The very nature of this charge is ruinous and will follow the accused or the convicted for the rest of his life. A charge of murder is far more acceptable to society than the charge of child molestation. Truly, this charge is the 'great offense.'

Pollock had been ruined and destroyed by the article, and there was nothing he could do to the newspaper as long as they had printed the accusation on the warrant fairly. Accurate judicial reporting was exempt from the laws of libel in Georgia. Why there wasn't a statute preventing such reporting until after a conviction was beyond my comprehension. Why this wasn't a self-imposed policy of the city's only newspaper, was even more reprehensible. Fairness demanded it. The certain destruction of an innocent defendant and his family required it.

That evening, I drove by the Pollock home and the home of the purported victim, since it was only about a mile from Dino's where I was going to meet up with Lou. Pollock's description of the neighborhood was accurate. The houses were large and well-maintained, occupied by well-established families. It was hard to picture a child molester living amongst them in that day and age. The prevailing ideology suggested child molesters lived in low-income areas.

When I arrived at Dino's, Lou was sitting in the VIP area of the bar having his usual vodka. He wasn't happy.

"Cracker, I heard the news this evening. The son-of-a-bitch down the street has hired my lawyer to get him off. That ain't gonna happen. We draw the line here."

I motioned to Ozella to bring my usual. I sat down and looked at Lou and said, "Can I defend myself?"

"There ain't no defense for this."

"Lou, I would hope by now that you understood who I was, because it's the very reason you came and got me."

My opening argument appeared to have no effect.

"Cracker, when a grown man attacks a little girl, he won't see the rise of the morning sun in Sicily. That's true in Chicago, as well."

"Lou, what if he's innocent?"

"He ain't."

Then I realized I had another card to play. "Lou, the victim's father is an FBI agent and I don't believe a word he says. When did you start believing FBI agents?"

He cocked his head and said, "An FBI agent?"

"Yep. That's why the accusation appeared in the paper the same day. Lou, I'm not going to take his word for it, and you shouldn't either."

Lou appeared conflicted. I had brought up a subject he'd believed his whole life: Never believe the feds.

"Lou, if you want to believe the agent, then go ahead. But you ain't going to make your lawyer believe him."

Lou sat silently, took another sip or two of his vodka, while he wrestled with conflicting emotions about child molesters and FBI agents. I broke the silence.

"Lou, I would expect you to be on my side going against an FBI agent."

Lou gave me a hard stare and said, "I can see your point. If he's innocent, then he should have a good lawyer, but not my lawyer."

"But he does have your lawyer."

The issue wasn't over between me and Lou. This case almost caused an irrevocable break in our relationship. For me, it became the catalyst for examining my motivations and the life I'd chosen.

I began my own investigation of the child's story. I went to Pollock's home and met his children. They represented the ideal Christian family, or what was considered the ideal family at the time. A picture of Christ in the family room told me a lot. Pollock neither smoked nor drank and never cursed in my presence. There was no question in my mind that the charge didn't fit this man, and that a figment of an eight-year-old child's imagination had cruelly destroyed a fine father and family. Showing Pollock in this setting with his family was all I needed to show a jury to prove his innocence. My task was to present Pollock as he was, and let justice take its course. I urged the case to trial as quickly as I could to lessen the damage to him. I also talked to the editor of the newspaper and received his assurance that if Pollock were found not guilty, they would do a favorable story about him. The editor also agreed to reconsider the newspaper's policy on future cases. He seemed to understand the gravity of the effect of being charged and would, therefore, hold off publishing accusations against individuals until they were convicted.

My trial strategy was simple. Put his fine family in the courtroom and put his beautiful little girl against the story of the other child. His wife's appearance at the end would seal it. There was no way a jury would tear up this family on only the say-so of an eight-year-old girl with no supporting evidence.

The trial went as planned. I handled the FBI agent's little girl with kid gloves. I even broadened her fantasy by getting her to say that when all this happened, Mrs. Pollock and her playmate were in another part of the house and that she and Mr. Pollock were alone in his bedroom. When she admitted this, the district attorney slammed his file shut. I put the Pollock child on the stand and she contradicted the girl's testimony by saying that her daddy was never alone with the other child. Furthermore, she asserted that she went everywhere with her playmate on that morning. She was as cute as she could be in her fluffy white dress and ringlets. (She looked like Shirley Temple.) Her mother came last and backed up her child. I presented Pollock as a fine Christian family man that he was and the horror this had been in his life. Only the jury could vindicate him and save him and his family. When the jury went out, there was no doubt in my mind as to the outcome of this case.

I looked to see if Lou and his buddies from Miami were in the back of the courtroom seated in their usual location. They were not. This didn't worry me.

While the jury was out, the mother of the child I had questioned approached me while I was gathering my papers from the trial desk. She had a defiant look of anger that remained as she spoke to me. Her exact words I cannot remember, but her meaning I do. She resented my ability in the courtroom that would more than likely free a man she felt had molested her child. Her hatred of him was only exceeded by her resentment of me. She told me that his next attack on a helpless child would be on my conscience if I had one. Her words and feelings indicated to me that I had won Pollock's case already. I politely exited the courtroom to prevent any further confrontations with her. I had become accustomed to such verbal attacks by people who thought they are always in the right and that no one should ever question their belief or opinion or whether an individual should have a right to be defended or have an advocate. In her belief system, there would be no trials, just executions. Unfortunately, she was just one of many.

When the jury returned in thirty minutes, I knew the answer. Not guilty! What a feeling of joy and happiness for saving an innocent man. All the years of schooling and training were more than worth it at that moment. The little Pollock girl began to cry out of joy for her daddy. I shook hands with the jury, the judge, the clerk, and several unknowns, and congratulated Pollock. He then asked me if I would call the editor of the newspaper and start the ball rolling for a favorable article. I did.

The next morning the local page of the news bannered the headlines, 'Pollock Is Not Guilty.' The reporter was very kind to Pollock and gave his church background within the story. Both Pollock and I were satisfied and I had earned my fee. The jury had vindicated a good man and we had proven that the judicial system worked and that justice was served. Confident of my talents in the courtroom, I went on to another and far more difficult case. Pollock was where he belonged, with his fine little family.

That night I sat with Lou in the VIP room of Dino's Den. Lou appeared to be apologetic and made sure that I knew he was wrong without having to admit it. After a few drinks and casual conversation, Lou proposed a toast, lifted his glass and said, "Good job." I didn't ask him why he hadn't been in the courtroom during the trial. Perhaps I didn't want to know the answer.

Three months later, I answered a call from Linda Pollock. She told me something that broke my heart. Her husband had been arrested again on a child molesting charge; this time it was his own little girl. I told her I would try to get a bond set before the day was over. I hung up the phone and experienced an awful emptiness that would linger for a long time. Whether it was the sting of a victory gone sour or the realization that I had just taken part in a fraudulent masquerade of the American Dream, was immaterial, because it was both, and I just felt empty. I thought about his little girl and the agent's child. Thoughts of bewilderment. What have I done? How could I have been so wrong?

I left the office to go see Pollock, but not before I told Lucy that I wouldn't be back until Monday. I would need the weekend to gather my thoughts and to make something out of this tragedy. I couldn't get his little girl off my mind, and neither could I forget the other mother's resentment and her warning that the next child would be on my conscience.

Meeting with Pollock was different this time. I met with him alone in a dismal conference room at the county jail. I had already been told by the detective in charge of the investigation that Pollock's daughter had gone to her schoolteacher and had asked for help. Her father had been molesting her for the past two years and she didn't want to go home. She had asked her mother to help her, but her mother hadn't believed her. The detective also told me that the other two children had been removed from the house. Needless to say, Pollock and I had a lot to talk about.

"Ron, I want the truth this time or you can get another lawyer. Tell me the truth," I said sternly.

Pollock began to weep. He admitted that he was sick and that he wanted me to help him. He admitted fondling his little girl over the past two years and the other child.

"If I could help myself I would, but I can't. I've tried! I've been sick for a long time, but I was too embarrassed to get help."

Looking into Pollock's eyes, I asked, "Did your wife know what you were doing?"

"Yes."

Now I was angry. I was angry at Pollock and I was angry at his wife. While Pollock may have been sick, his wife wasn't. How could she have betrayed her little girl and not protected her? Why in the heck hadn't she taken her children and left? How could she have sat through the first trial knowing what she had known? How could she have protected a pervert? I knew of no law that could have been used against her and thought that was a shame.

"Ron, I'll defend you, but this time I want to help you."

For me, there was sometimes a distinction between defending someone and helping them. At this moment, I didn't want to defend him, but I felt I should try to help him.

"We're not going to deny the charges because I will not put your daughter through another trial. Let's confirm the illness and let the court help you. It will mean a prison term, but at least you'll receive the treatment you need. Do you agree?"

"Yes, but please get me out of here. I want to go home," Pollock responded.

"I'll get Judge Cheatham to set a bond this afternoon and your wife will come and get you." And then I left, wondering what 'home' he had in mind.

Sunday morning, my friend David Powell and I went fishing. It was a beautiful warm morning. Whenever I went fishing on the river that flowed past Mob Island, I would relax and the stress of my profession would seem to evaporate, whether I caught fish or not. For David, catching fish mattered. Since I often used David as a sounding board, I had to wait until the fish stopped biting.

"David, do you think a certified mentally ill person guilty of a non-violent crime should be in prison or in a hospital?"

"What kind of a crime?"

"Child molesting."

"Did he hurt the child?"

"No, not physically. Just fondled her."

"He didn't make her do nothing sick, did he?"

"No."

"It's better he get treated in a hospital than go to prison. That way he can get cured and we don't have to worry about him when he gets out."

"What if the child was his own daughter and he had been doing it for two years?"

"Huh!" David looked up from his ice chest. "Not his own daughter!"

"Yes."

"Then I don't know. He's really sick then, and I don't think sending him to a hospital is punishment enough. He's probably ruined her. That's a tough case. I wouldn't want to be on his jury."

My sounding board was true to form because I couldn't disagree with a lot of what he'd said. He echoed what society at that time felt; that when a mentally ill person commits a 'sick' crime, the person is not mentally ill and should go to prison, not to a hospital. The only conclusion I could determine was that our mental hospitals were full of only bad-check writers and forgers, the acceptable crimes. Insane or 'sick' crimes were only committed by sane people. In other words, if you committed shoplifting and they found you mentally ill, you'd go to a hospital, not prison. But if you committed a sick crime like rape, you'd go to prison, not a hospital. So, a mentally ill verdict was only applied to 'acceptable' crimes and not 'sick' crimes.

One thing for sure, I wouldn't put David on my jury and certainly not Louie the Tailor. I was content with David being my fishing partner and sounding board only. Now I had to figure out how to deal with Lou.

That night, I met Lou at Dino's, not because I wanted to, but he asked me to. Reluctantly, I arrived early enough to have a couple of drinks before our meeting. Lou came through the door with a scowl on his face. The real thing, a Sicilian scowl. I knew what was coming and I hoped I was ready. Lou waved at the server and pointed at his table. The drink arrived the same time Lou did. He sat down, looked at me, and said nothing. I shifted in my seat not knowing what to expect. I could tell he was mad. His face was red and the veins in his neck bulged.

"Cracker, you proud of yourself? You got that bastard off so he could molest his little girl some more. Sicilian justice is what he should've got. He could still get it."

"Lou, you know that I am hired to win. You hire me to win and I do win. You want to get another lawyer who may not win all your cases? I'm a hired gun and you know it."

"You gotta draw a line. Little girls should not be molested, and I don't want you to handle those cases."

With that said, I finished my drink and left. There was nothing I could say to change his mind, and I certainly wasn't going to change mine. If he wanted a new lawyer, then so be it.

On Monday, I was met by Lucy telling me that the newspaper hadn't reported the Pollock arrest. Apparently, the editor had changed his policy or some police reporter had been slack. I preferred to believe the former. Maybe the first Pollock case had some meaning after all. I told Lucy to get ahold of Mrs. Pollock because of a message she had left on the answering service. It was supposed to be important.

A few minutes later, Lucy told me Mrs. Pollock was on the phone. Linda's voice trembled as she told me that the Division of Family and Children Services had taken her children. I told her I already knew and until this problem was handled, they probably wouldn't return them. After all, what else could they do?

I didn't discuss my opinion of her because I could tell she was hurting. But I still couldn't understand how a loving mother could sacrifice her child to this man's illness. She had no reason to be angry at anyone but herself. I needed to end the conversation before I told her how I felt. I was perplexed. Something was wrong. I was feeling animosity towards my client and his wife. This was wrong! How could I be this man's defender if I'd already judged him? Didn't a mentally ill person deserve the best defense available under our system of 'blind' justice? I realized then that I was letting the crime judge the man. If I couldn't come out swinging on his behalf, then I was depriving him of his greatest right, the right to a fair trial.

This right separates our system from most legal systems in the world. It's the foundation upon which this country's greatness and strength are built. Lawyers don't judge, only judges and juries judge. It was my duty to speak on his behalf and to guarantee that he had his fair trial regardless of how people like David and Lou felt. In the past, I'd been proud of my position in this system, but I was

232

beginning to wonder. I pulled myself up short; I didn't want to become one of those hypocrites who celebrate the Constitution and the Fourth of July while hating defense lawyers at the same time. I was now ready to do what was required of me. I was ready to do battle. Bring it on.

I set up a series of examinations for Pollock with a prominent psychiatrist, Dr. Arnold Tillinger. He confirmed that Pollock had a mental disease known as 'pedophilia.' He defined it as a mental illness in which children are the preferred sexual object. Until shortly before that time it had only been defined as a 'sexual perversion' by *Webster's Dictionary*. In 1968, however, the American Psychiatric Association formally classified the condition as a mental disease. What's more, it was considered incurable.

People suffering from this disease almost always hide it rather than confess it. To admit to being a pedophile is to ostracize oneself from society. The doctor explained that pedophilia was truly as much of a curse as leprosy was in ancient days. Education and understanding conquered our horror of leprosy; perhaps pedophilia would meet the same fate. But not then. All of this was new to me. I had never had to defend a pedophile.

Dr. Tillinger told me some alarming information about Pollock's past. It seemed that the grandfather he spoke of had molested him constantly as a child. He had lied about the fight with his grandfather as the reason for running away from his home at age fourteen. He had run away because his mother had told him that his grandfather was really his father. She had been raped by her father at age thirteen and born his child. In a fit of anger against her father one day, she'd told her son of this crime. It was a confused and disturbed young boy who had fled his home and raised himself. He had never been an orphan. He had never really been a child. A poorer start in life I had never heard of, and I became deeply sympathetic to Pollock's plight. There was no question in my mind that Pollock needed treatment and not imprisonment. Society did owe him a break and it was my task to urge this. I finally believed in my cause.

The trial setting looked the same as the one before. The same judge, the same assistant district attorney, the same defendant, and the same parents of the other child sat in the front row. It appeared to be a flashback. Oh, how I wished that it had been, for we would have won again. This time the attitude of the defense was entirely different. I had never had a case where I was asking for mercy rather than justice. I felt like I was betraying him, nevertheless, I knew I was doing the right thing for him. I had never done this before, and I never did it again. I could not neutralize a young child's fantasy, and neither could I present the atmosphere of the All-American family. My defendant was a broken mentally ill father that society had no use or sympathy for. He was an admitted child molester.

Even the jury was hard to pick. I didn't want fathers, mothers, grandmothers, or grandfathers. That left very few. If there were such a creature as a highly educated single male who had a background of child abuse, he wasn't to be found near the courthouse that day.

When we concluded the jury selection, we had eight grandfathers, two mothers, and two single males to be sworn in. We recessed for lunch and prepared to open with what we had, which was only a plea for understanding and mercy. I had seen better days.

All afternoon we heard the sordid details of the charges and evidence against Pollock. The other little girl was called to the stand to tell the jury of her past experience with Pollock. This time it sounded real, without a suggestion of fantasy. This time she was very believable, so much so that I did not cross-examine her. I was afraid that I might say something that would make her cry. I couldn't risk that. As the prosecution called Pollock's little girl took the stand, Pollock began to tear up. This cute little child who looked like an angel in her white fluffy church dress was getting ready to condemn her father and send him to prison in the same dress she'd worn when she'd freed him the last time.

This was the most pitiful sight that I had ever seen in a courtroom. This was not courtroom drama as depicted on TV; it was just a pitifully sad picture of the destruction of a family, a child, and a father. Although I had not wanted the daughter to have to testify, it was out of my hands. The district attorney needed her testimony. Surely our judicial and penal system could have avoided this by some offer of treatment and some hope of putting this family back together. Instead, nothing was offered by the district attorney except twenty years of imprisonment; a plea deal my client and I would not accept. They wanted justice, punishment, and retribution. Never mind the fact that they wanted punishment for an illness and were making a little girl destroy her father—something that would follow her for the rest of her life, for the child loved him.

We went through the motions of an active defense. Dr. Tillinger presented an accurate and fair description of Mr. Pollock's disease. He also related the sad history of Pollock's childhood. As much as he tried to gain support for the need of treatment rather than imprisonment, his efforts were futile. He was appealing to the jury's conscience and sympathy, but they would have none of it. Within an hour, they returned a verdict of guilty and the judge sentenced him to nine years in the state penal system. There was no consideration given for treatment. Pollock was weeping as they led him away. I turned and saw the parents of the other child smiling at me. They had got their pound of flesh. They were vindicated.

At the time, I was deeply concerned about three aspects of this case. First, what did it benefit society to destroy the chance of reconciling the father/child relationship? With proper treatment and support by existing public agencies, these two people could have been reconciled with restrictions and control.

The second concern I had with this case was the failure of our judicial system to recognize the existence of a mental illness such as pedophilia. This has since changed with the passage of the Georgia Sexual Offenders Act. Now they combine incarceration with treatment and the implementation of strict control through local sexual offender registration.

My third and last concern had to do with Linda Pollock. What could have possessed a supposedly loving mother to sacrifice her child to an illness she knew her husband had? Why hadn't she heeded the pleas of her child? Regardless of her reasons for not coming forward earlier, why hadn't she been held accountable? Why hadn't she been held as an accessory under the same principle as we hold an accomplice to a bank robbery? These are questions that the legal system still has not addressed.

After the jury verdict was returned and the courtroom emptied, I gathered up my files and papers. It was then that I felt someone tap my shoulder. I turned to see Louie the Tailor standing there.

"Cracker, this is done. Let's get on with stuff that matters. You did a good job, but I'm glad you lost." We left the courthouse together and as we walked to my office nearby Lou invited Jean and me to join Dottie and him for dinner.

34. The Man They Threw Away

In 1980, the Gary Lively case provided an opportunity for the Georgia appellate courts to dismiss close to two thousand criminal cases pending in the state of Georgia. The case came to me as a surprise because I had long been an advocate of speedy trials, particularly in view of our state judges' attitudes towards not allowing bonds to indigent people accused of crimes. Namely, if you were charged with a serious crime and poor—regardless of color—you would not be extended a bail bond. So, forget the constitutional right of presumption of innocence, you rotted in jail until the prosecutor was ready to try the case. In most cases that was a year. In the Gary Lively case, it was eight years.

I received a telephone call from a jailer, Flapper Mahany, who told me that a man named Gary Lively wanted to see me. The name was familiar, but I couldn't recall why. At the jail, I met a nice looking, but very pale, young man about six foot two inches tall with black wavy hair. We shook hands and he told me he was charged with two counts of kidnapping, one count of aggravated rape, one count of aggravated sodomy, and two counts of sexual assault.

"Gary, that sounds like a lifetime of charges."

"Mr. Haupt, I didn't do those crimes. I wasn't anywhere near where these girls were raped, or whatever."

"Have they served you with the indictments?"

"Yeah, here they are." And he handed me a handful of old wrinkled papers. Sorting through the papers, I located what looked like indictments. I found the aggravated rape charge and read it.

"Gary, these charges refer to crimes in 1975. Where are the ones you are charged with now?"

"They're them."

"You mean you've been re-indicted or charged again with the same crimes?"

"No, they're the same ones."

"Gary, they are dated 1975. That's five years ago. Either I don't understand or you don't understand what I'm asking."

"Mr. Haupt, I was arrested in '75 and then they gave me these papers. I been waitin' here for trial ever since."

"Gary, that's hard to believe. You haven't been here for five years. You've been out on bond, haven't you?"

"No, sir."

I said nothing for a few minutes, trying to sort out the import of his revelation. I couldn't be hearing what I'd just heard. There was no possible way that a man could have been arrested and kept in jail for five years without being tried. No, there just had to be something else.

"Gary, did you have a lawyer?"

"They appointed me one at first, but I've only seen him one time."

"Was the case passed, or postponed, or put off by you?"

"No, I ain't heard nothing from nobody."

"Do you have a family?"

"Yes, my mother lives right down the road in Rincon. My wife divorced me three years ago and has my three children. I lost my family, my job, and our house," he responded with eyes that were tearing up.

Once again, I sat in silence. The reality of Lively's plight was just hitting me. This young man had lost everything and for what reason? Just because he had been accused of a crime? He'd already served five years! Had he been tried and found guilty of murder, he would have been eligible for parole in just two years, counting the time he had already served. I accepted his case without a fee and assured him of some quick results.

On leaving the jail, I was both happy and distressed: distressed, because of the unnecessary destruction of a young man and his family; happy, because I finally had a case that would prove once and for all the injustice of the bonding custom and hopefully, the end to it by a federal court order. This was to be a case that would wreak havoc with the criminal backlog of untried cases in Georgia. Justice would no longer be a fantasy. Or so I hoped. I notified the court of my representation and filed a motion to dismiss the indictments based upon grounds that the State had violated Lively's right to a speedy trial.

In researching the law, I found that 'time' alone was insufficient in having the indictments dismissed. In other words, the length of time between the arrest and trial had nothing to do with a speedy trial. How ridiculous! The law of

Georgia required that a defendant must go further and prove that he or she was prejudiced or harmed by the delay. Can one imagine that a person wasn't harmed by spending five years in prison waiting to be tried! But that is not the harm they were referring to. One had to prove that his defense or right to defense was harmed. This could happen if a witness died, evidence in a defendant's favor disappeared, or a witness had forgotten favorable testimony because of the passage of time.

After completing my research, I could understand, for the first time in my legal career, why prosecutors didn't particularly care about rushing to trial or a judge not worrying about extending a bond. They could do so without worrying about violating the defendant's rights. There was no time limit because there was no case in the history of Georgia jurisprudence that had dismissed charges against a defendant because he had been in jail too long or the prosecutor had waited too long to try the case. In fact, I found cases where the defendants had served more time than the maximum sentence for the crime they were accused of! Again, the passage of time had nothing to do with the right to a speedy trial.

It took another month to get a hearing on my motion to dismiss the indictments. Lively, still very pale, sat motionless as the judge opened the hearing.

"Mr. Haupt, I believe you have the burden of proving prejudice at this hearing," stated Judge Brannen.

"Judge, insofar as Georgia case law is concerned, yes. But I don't concede or admit for one moment that that is the law as we stand here today," I replied for the sake of a good appeal record.

"Let's don't get into the case law until after we hear the evidence," he responded.

"I call to the stand Detective Willis for the purpose of outlining the evidence that was presented to the Grand Jury at the time of the indictments against Mr. Lively."

Willis came forward with a very thin file folder and was given the oath by the clerk.

"Detective Willis, were you called by the district attorney to outline this case before the Grand Jury in 1975?"

"Yes, sir," replied a very courteous but nervous veteran police officer, who happened to be my first cousin.

"Do you have the same information in your file today that you had at that time?"

"Yes, sir."

"What information is that?"

"The written statements of the two girls involved."

"Would you please read those statements."

The written statements of each of the girls basically said that they had decided to walk to Rincon, Georgia, along a railroad track on this particular evening for no particular reason other than to have something to do. When they had arrived at their destination, they'd been too tired to walk back. A man driving a Dodge Charger had stopped and offered them a ride back to Savannah. On the way back, he'd pulled off onto a side road and taken a pistol from his glove compartment. He'd told the girls he wanted to have sex and had ordered them to undress. They had refused and he'd fired his pistol into the floorboard of his car. They'd gotten scared and acquiesced to his demand. When they'd had their chance to run, they had and then had called one of the girls' fathers. He'd come and picked them up.

"Then the automobile identification led to the arrest of Lively?" I asked.

"If you mean that the description of the car made Lively a suspect, yes."

"Where is the car?"

"I don't know."

"Where was the car the last time you saw it?"

"I never saw the car."

"You never saw the car?"

"That's right."

"Do you know who impounded the car?"

"I presume Effingham County did."

"Why? This is a Chatham County crime. There was no charge pending in Effingham against Lively." I was puzzled by the answers, and I was becoming agitated by my cousin's cavalier attitude.

"Mr. Haupt, it has been five years since this happened. How do you expect me to remember such details?" he responded, equally agitated.

"Maybe because you've kept a man in jail for five years based on charges from your 'details.' That doesn't matter to you, does it?"

"I object, Your Honor, to Mr. Haupt's badgering of this witness," the assistant district attorney intervened.

"I'm not badgering. I'm stating an obvious fact, and I think I deserve honest answers."

"Just a minute, gentlemen," interrupted the judge. "Mr. Haupt, this witness has said he never saw the car and doesn't know where it is. I believe he has answered your questions. Now, please continue with the witness or let him step down."

"Do you know if anyone in your department ever searched the car?"

"No."

"Then there was no examination of the interior of the vehicle to determine if these two girls were ever in the car?" I repeated.

"Not that I know of," he responded.

"Didn't you believe that a search of the car was necessary? After all, a pistol was fired into the floorboard and if a girl was raped inside the car, there would be pubic hair and other evidence available, wouldn't it? You didn't examine the car?" I asked in disbelief.

"Mr. Haupt, I'm only telling you what I recall. That's all I can do. I'm sure that somewhere down the line the car was examined and photographs and samples were taken."

"How would I find that information if it's not in your file? Was there some other agency involved?"

Willis paused and turned towards the prosecutor. "Do you know what he's asking for?" The prosecutor shook his head no and offered no help to the detective. After a few minutes of silence, I told the witness to step down and to leave his file on the prosecutor's desk.

"Your Honor, I believe it is obvious that the evidence in this case has not only eroded with the passage of time but has also disappeared. Had this case been tried within a reasonable period of time after Mr. Lively's arrest and indictment, then the defense would have had the benefit of the photographs, fingerprints, and any other evidence of innocence or guilt. On the other hand, if none of these obvious procedures of criminal investigations were done, then the defense would have had the opportunity to do so on behalf of the accused. If the girls were telling the truth, then there would be a bullet hole in the floorboard of the car. If there was none, then they had the wrong car and the wrong man. This car is no longer available. How much more harm or prejudice need I prove as a result of the prosecution not trying Mr. Lively for five years?" Having driven my point home, I sat down.

The judge looked at the prosecutor and awaited his reply.

"Your Honor, we do not believe that Mr. Haupt has proved any prejudice or harm by the delay. The loss of or the lack of evidence concerning the automobile would be in his favor, not to his detriment. Our failure to prove that Mr. Lively's car was the vehicle in which the crimes occurred would harm the State's case, not the defendant's. Now, if Mr. Haupt could prove that the automobile of Mr. Lively did not have a bullet hole in the floorboard, and that the disappearance of the car prevents him from proving this in front of a jury, then that would be a sufficient showing of prejudice or harm to the defendant as required by our appellate courts. But this he has not done. We, therefore, request that the court deny his motion and permit us to try the case and let a jury decide if Lively is guilty or not." With this, the prosecutor sat down confident of the law and the expected ruling of the Court.

"Mr. Haupt, do you wish to respond?" the judge asked.

"Yes, sir, but only to the prosecutor's conclusion of what I must prove before I can claim prejudice. There is no conceivable way that I could prove the absence of a bullet hole five years after the fact and after the destruction of the evidence by someone connected to the prosecution. That is absurd and borders on the ridiculous. I can't believe that such a learned prosecutor would make such a statement. That is tantamount to making a defendant prove that a pistol that is lost was not fired. That's amazing logic. No, that's amazing stupidity that I know the court will condemn. Thank you."

"Gentlemen, I will review your briefs and the testimony. I'll have a decision within the next few days. I'm somewhat alarmed that the DA's Office has offered no reasonable explanation as to why this defendant has not been tried and has been in jail for five years. On the other hand, I'm curious as to why a person who believes he is innocent of a crime would wait five years in jail before he obtained a lawyer to protect his rights. However, in either case, I'll make my decision and send each of you a copy of my order. Thank you."

He concluded and abruptly left the bench with a disgusted look and mannerism. He was certainly not satisfied with what he had heard from the prosecutor—at least that is what I hoped.

A week passed and I received a call from Judge Brannen's secretary to come to his office. I knew what it was for, and because I was to hear an explanation for his decision, I was not optimistic about a favorable ruling. I knew that it was an issue he had preferred not to confront. He was the youngest of our trial judges and had never been embroiled in a major public controversy. This issue would demand a lot of intestinal fortitude if the judge chose to rule fairly rather than politically. Personally, I believed deep down that Brannen was up to it. I believed that he would rule according to the evidence, even though his ruling may set free a man accused of very serious sex crimes against two innocent teenage girls. If he did, the public, the do-gooders, the guiltless, and his opponents would all condemn his actions, editorialize his liberal attitudes, and question his ability to serve as a judge.

"Mr. Haupt, I have issued an order dismissing the indictments against your client. In addition to finding that he was prejudiced by the delay, I have also concluded that five years in and of itself is too long," he advised as I was handed a copy of the order.

"Thank you, Judge, I understand fully the import of your decision and the abuse you're going to take. I'm impressed with your courage. Thanks."

"Don't thank me, just protect me in the court of appeals," he replied and strolled back into his office. I left and headed to the jail to inform Lively.

Gary Lively cried and it was extremely difficult for me to hold back my tears also. Knowing I could never feel his relief or gratitude, I told him that we were not home free.

"Gary, the district attorney will have to appeal Judge Brannen's decision and that means you must stay in jail until the appeal is decided."

"How long will that take?" he asked.

"About a year, if we're lucky."

"That long?"

"Yes. But you are on the way home, and that means a lot."

"Mr. Haupt, I'm countin' on you. I believe in you. Do whatever you think oughta be done." He placed his fate in my hands and was motioned out of the visitor's room by the jail guard. He turned towards me once again as he was being led through the door and in a loud voice, so everyone could hear, said, "You're the best dang lawyer in the world!"

As expected, the DA appealed Brannen's decision and relied upon the old cases that had held that passage of time was not sufficient to prove harm by the delay. I was confident that Brannen's opinion would prevail because he had made a finding of prejudice based on the evidence. In other words, he found that the long delay had prejudiced or harmed Lively's defense and that could not be overturned unless the court of appeals decided that there was absolutely no evidence of harm or prejudice and that Brannen was wrong in his factual finding. Such a ruling would be rare indeed because judges in Georgia have historically been omnipotent in factual findings. Only in errors of law are they reversed. Or so I thought.

During the interim of appeal, we had a change of district attorneys. My old friend and antagonist, Andrew Ryan, was defeated by an inexperienced trial lawyer named Spencer Lawton. Lawton had beaten him on the main issue of having a substantial backlog of cases awaiting trial. He used the Lively case as his main complaint, espousing the possibility that over a hundred criminals in Chatham County would be set free to run the streets to rape and kill once more. Needless to say, the voters were appalled at such a likelihood and believing that Lawton could correct the situation and overturn the Lively case, they voted Ryan out of office. Ryan did not deserve such blame because he was understaffed and overworked. I was saddened not only because he was my friend, but because he had ruined his health by overworking and worrying about a situation that he had no control over, and all for the sake of the fickle public. What's more, he had forgotten more about criminal trial work than Lawton would ever know. Ryan died not too long after his defeat.

It took four months for the court of appeals to prove me wrong. They overturned Brannen's decision by ruling that as a matter of law, not fact, Lively was not prejudiced by the delay. They had sidestepped Brannen in an unbelievable fashion by not addressing the judge's right to determine all issues of fact. They made no mention of Brannen's authority and alluded to the old doctrine that 'mere passage of time was insufficient.' Their decision convinced me of what I already believed; the appellate courts in Georgia determine first the result of the finding before they determine the reasoning. They make their decision before they consult the law, then they have their law clerks find a law that can support the outcome they desire.

In this case, the appellate court knew what a dismissal would mean and there was no way they could let several thousand untried criminals—notice I do not use the word 'accused'—back on the streets of Georgia. No, not these elected appellate judges, not by any stretch of the imagination. If any judge were going to turn the incarcerated criminals (or so they believed) loose without a trial, it would be a federal judge who would take the public abuse and ridicule and not the Georgia appellate judiciary; so the buck was passed.

Before telling Lively, I prepared a Writ for Habeas Corpus to be filed in the federal district court. I showed Lively a copy of the appellate court decision and the writ the next morning.

"Gary, I'm sorry that you can't leave jail today, but I want you to read what I am filing a few minutes after I leave here."

He slowly read the mumbo-jumbo language of legal words and sophisticated terms and looked up with a puzzled look. "I ain't got any idea what this is except where it says at the end that you demand my release. Does this mean we're winning?" I could only reply, "Yes." As I left, I turned around and watched the deputy lead Lively back to his cell. I was feeling depressed. I couldn't understand why everyone in the world wouldn't agree that keeping a man locked up for seven or eight years without a trial was just wrong, very wrong!

Two months later, the case was ordered to trial by Federal Judge Avant Edenfield, with the understanding that his hands were tied until there was a final outcome of the case in the state judicial system. He expressed shock with the handling of the case by the DA's office.

"Gentleman, I cannot comprehend how an accused can be jailed for five years without being tried. I can think of no excuse, nor has one been offered, and I can only surmise that this man has been thrown away for a few years without being tried. Had Mr. Haupt not appeared, I hate to think how much time this man would have had to serve. We've come further than this in our handling of criminal cases and in our protection of human rights. Notice I said 'human' not 'civil,' because this would have been unconscionable even before the Civil Rights Act. This man's treatment or lack of treatment ranks on the borders of gross negligence. As much as I would like to step in and mete justice, I have my hands tied by the very rules that the prosecution has ignored. Consequently, I can only issue an order requiring this case be tried by a jury in the state system within the next thirty days. If not, then I can consider contempt issues. Thank you."

Judge Edenfield looked sternly at the assistant DA and closed his file. He had not threatened them; he had promised them what he would do if his order was ignored. When we left, there was no question we would be trying the case within the next few weeks, or better yet, within the next few days.

Exactly eighteen days after Edenfield's order, the case was called to trial and a jury was impaneled. Lively sat silently with his hands covering each other on an alternating basis. His mother had brought him an old suit he used to wear when he was fifty pounds heavier. Now eight years later and living in a single cell eating jail food, time had taken its toll. Jail food means powdered eggs, one chicken leg, and two plain pieces of bread. When you are served a vegetable, it is exactly one tablespoon full, no salt and straight from the can. Had he been convicted of a crime, he would have been transferred to a state prison where the food is home-grown and served in healthy portions with plenty of exercise and activities to keep your mind from getting lazy. Lively seemed diminished both in mind and body. His pallid appearance and frailty made him look ten years older than his twenty-eight years. He was clearly depressed. If he were guilty, he would have been treated as a human being in a state prison and would have had the opportunity to better himself through education or trade skills. Keeping him in a small cell in a county jail was more punishment than he would have had if he had been convicted. Can you imagine? Lying on a bunk for eight years!

The trial was similar to the motion hearing with Detective Willis outlining the girls' statements at the time of the assault. Then each girl, both now married women, appeared on the stand and hesitantly identified Lively as their assailant. Each swore that their assailant had fired a pistol into the floorboard near the back seat.

The strangest part of the case came when one of the women claimed that around 11:00 that night, they'd decided to walk from Savannah to Rincon, Georgia, a distance of nine miles. They'd been barefooted and had walked the entire distance along a railroad bed containing small rocks and gravel. They'd been picked up at one of the crossings by a man who'd offered them a ride to Savannah early the next morning. They more or less testified from their prior statements given eight years earlier. On cross-examination, they admitted they had been with a couple of older boys whom they'd been forbidden to see. In fact, they had been with the boys near the place where they had been found the next morning by one of the women's fathers.

Luckily, I traced the automobile to a deputy sheriff from Effingham County named Syfrett. He testified for Lively that the automobile had been returned to Effingham by the Chatham County Police Department. He recalled examining the car and testified that he had seen no bullet hole in the rear floorboard. He didn't recall what had eventually happened to the automobile other than the fact that it had not been returned to Lively or his family.

The trial progressed and the flaws in the women's testimonies were apparent, but we were dealt a blow when Lively's ex-wife refused to testify for him. She refused service of her subpoena and then when I insisted that she be brought to court, she'd angrily told me that she was happier with Lively in jail and that she didn't want her children to be able to know or be with Lively. She had remarried and the children believed her new husband to be their father. Being with Lively would only upset them. I told Lively that her testimony was not necessary and that a jury would expect her to alibi for him. I never told him of her reasoning or refusal.

In my closing argument, I harped on the State's inability to produce any evidence that the automobile the girls had ridden in was Lively's, and the victims' strange and unbelievable story of walking to Rincon. I pointed out the strange absence of any lineup identification of Lively and that the only evidence the prosecution had was the car connection to him. If this was not his car, then it wasn't him. I offered the jury a more plausible explanation. The young ladies stayed out all night with their boyfriends and when they were confronted by one of the girls' fathers, they'd made up the crimes to avoid punishment and family disgrace. Whether this was true, I did not know. I offered it as only a reasonable explanation.

Whether the jury accepted this theory or just made a decision that Lively was not their assailant is unknown. It didn't take them long, however, to acquit Lively of all charges, and they never knew that he had been locked up ever since his arrest eight years before. That fact was never told the jury because it was inadmissible on the grounds that his eight-year incarceration was immaterial to his innocence or guilt.

This case had a conclusion that was happy, sad, and indeterminate. Happy because Gary Lively was found innocent of serious crimes and was freed from jail that same day. Sad, because Lively had been ruined and lost everything from his family to his home, car, job, and future. Gary Lively disappeared that afternoon and to this day, his whereabouts are unknown. Indeterminate, because the other issue, the one that would have freed thousands of accused people deteriorating in county jails waiting years for trials, was not decided. The not-guilty verdict ended the case and Judge Edenfield was never allowed to make new rules in Georgia.

I was saddened for another reason. Lively had an opportunity to file a civil damage suit that could have rocked the very foundation of the local courthouse. Such a suit would have informed all prosecutors and judges that delays of trials can result in extreme punishment of the innocent as well as the guilty. But he didn't stay and I can understand why. He had already been thrown away once, and he didn't want to give them another chance to do it again. His lack of trust in our judicial system was clearly justified. Justice had been only a fantasy to him and thousands of others.

I met Lou later at The Exchange on River Street for our usual sit-down.

"Cracker, you must be feeling pretty good about helping this guy. What a shame. The cops don't give a shit."

"Lou, what I can't get out of my mind is why this case was ever brought. Who would even believe that two sixteen-year-old girls would walk from Savannah, nine miles to Rincon, barefooted on a rocky railroad bed at eleven at night? The girls were with two older boys all night in Rincon and then decided to walk back the same way they came. The DA should never have brought the case. Lou, how could these two women ruin a man's life to escape a day or two of punishment?"

Lou took a sip of his vodka, "I agree, but it's over. We gotta go to Chicago next week."

In a way, I was glad. At this point, Teamsters business was a relief. Most of the time I enjoyed Chicago. Lou and I went there at least once a month, where we would meet with Accardo and Dorfman. We were treated like celebrities. There was always a limo available to us. We dined at Tony Romo's and we never had to pay. Yes, a Chicago trip was just what I needed.

35. The Most Hated Lawyer in Town

In the summer of '74, the city was to experience one of the most horrendous crimes in its history. The local newspapers posted the headlines: "Local Nurses Shot, One Dead." Two nurses had been kidnapped, raped, and shot in the head. One survived to tell the sordid details and to give the police accurate descriptions of the two white assailants. The girl told how she and her friend, Suzanne Edenfield, had been stopped by two men in a car, abducted, and taken to a deserted wooded area. They'd been stripped and had their hands tied behind their backs. Both men had raped them and then put a pistol to Suzanne Edenfield's head and fired. She'd fallen dead. Moments later they'd put the same pistol to the survivor's head and fired. She'd fallen beside the dead girl and faked her death. The bullet had miraculously hit her in the face and gone through her mouth and out her cheek. To make sure there were no survivors, the men had fired another round into the chest of each girl and then they'd left, leaving two supposedly dead young nurses.

The surviving victim had run naked to the closest populated housing area. Dripping with blood, she'd pounded on doors until someone had finally called the police to investigate the disturbance. She'd been taken to a hospital and treated for two gunshot wounds after she had led the police to her dead companion.

A complete description of the assailants was broadcast and published for information on two white males using the names of Jerry and Johnny. A description of the automobile followed, and a massive search began that would end a week later with a telephone call from Beaufort, South Carolina. The caller gave the names of two Beaufort residents who fit the descriptions and one of them owned a car that matched the one reported by the survivor. Within days, the arrests of Jerry Sprouse and Johnny Johnson were announced and the district attorney indicated he would seek the death penalty against both men.

Within twenty-four hours of the arrest announcements, I received a call from Judge Oliver.

"Bubba, I would like for you to represent one of the men arrested in the Edenfield case."

"Judge, I just took a lot of bruises in the last case you assigned me. Isn't there someone else available?"

"I understand how you feel, but I want you to be involved on behalf of one of them. Which one do you want?"

"Does it matter?" I asked.

"I'll appoint you to Sprouse; he's supposed to be the trigger man."

"You know how much I appreciate this, Judge," I said sarcastically.

The rest of the afternoon was spent at the county jail interviewing Jerry Sprouse and wondering if there were any other attorneys practicing in Savannah. By this time, a number of cases had taken its toll on my popularity. This case would be worse because the city had been blanketed with the news articles of the brutality and senselessness of this crime, and Suzanne Edenfield had been a beautiful and popular young student nurse from a nice family. The defendants were pictured as two out-of-town drug freaks. I couldn't think of two more hated men accused of a crime in modern Savannah history. I was soon to find out just how much public sentiment was against them and their attorneys.

From my interview with Sprouse, I decided that he was either extremely psychotic or 'burnt out.' The latter term meant that his brain cells had been damaged by alcohol and/or drugs. Sprouse recalled nothing except the girls picking them up. *Dear God, please don't let him tell me that the girls had actually picked the* guys *up*, I thought to myself as he began telling me the only facts he remembered. There was no way I could defend by blaming the girls. Can you imagine the reaction of the public and the hurt to the family of the Edenfield girl? No way!

"Mr. Haupt, I remember driving down Victory Drive when two girls pulled alongside us at a stop light. One of the girls leaned out the window and asked if we wanted to smoke some good Columbian. Either Johnny Johnson or me said, 'Yeah,' and the girl said to follow them."

He looked bewildered as I placed my face in my hands on the interview table. I didn't want to believe he was saying this. He continued, "We followed them to this park near a high school. They got a blanket out of their VW and a bag of weed. We all sat down and got high."

"Then what?" I asked.

"I remember Johnny pulling a gun and telling the girls to get into his car. He owned the car. After that, I don't remember anything until the next morning when we woke up at some motel in Savannah. I saw the news and about the girl dying on the TV and told Johnny about it. He said that we must've killed the girl. He didn't remember much either. We left town in a hurry, back to South Carolina."

"Jerry, are you sure it was the girls who approached y'all and it was the girls who had the dope?"

"Yeah, I'm sure. We had nothin' but beer. And they drank some of it."

"All right. I'll get the statement of the girl who survived and we'll go from there. If we don't verify what you just told me about the girls picking y'all up and having the dope, then I'm not going to use it." I paused and then reluctantly said, "If the girl admits it, then we will."

"Whatever you say. I'll go along with whatever you say."

As I left, I had many impressions about Sprouse and the case. He was a slender wormy-looking man in his early twenties with a weak chin and small beady eyes set too close together. He was extremely pale and shifted nervously while rubbing his hands against his dirty jeans. He seemed to me to be a follower, someone who went along with anything and everything. He never indicated sorrow or remorse for what he and Johnson had done. He never mentioned the dead girl or what grief her family must have felt.

There was no question that he had to have a psychiatric evaluation and that our defense would depend on the results. In my opinion, the man was sick. Why? Because there was no sense of remorse or empathy in his cold beady eyes that were too close together.

Meanwhile, my phone was ringing off the hook with anonymous callers threatening me, my family, my property, and my car. The most sickening threat of all came on a Saturday night after my daughter had left for Bluffton, South Carolina, for one of her overnight stays with her classmates. I answered the phone.

"Mr. Haupt, we have your daughter. We're going to rape her and then shoot her in the head like they did Suzanne. Will you represent us?" said a gravelly voice.

I hung up immediately and called Lou as I had in the Crawford matter. "Lou, I got another situation like we had with Crawford."

Knowing immediately what I was referring to Lou responded, "Give me his name."

"Lou, I don't have a name and I don't know if he's serious, but I got to assume he is," I told Lou about the phone call and threat.

"Cracker, get the address in Bluffton and I'll send a couple of my guys over there."

"I'll call you right back with an address."

I asked my wife for the telephone number our daughter had left us without telling her my reason. I called the number but there was no answer. I kept calling over and over for the next thirty minutes. Finally, I went into the den and asked my wife for the address in Bluffton. She could sense my alarm and demanded to know the reason. I gave a false reason concerning the keys to my new little sports car I had purchased that my daughter drove around every chance she got. That satisfied my wife. I left and went to my office, called Lou and gave him the address.

My office phone rang. "Mr. Haupt, we raped her. Now we're gonna kill her. Can we retain you now or do we have to be arrested first?"

The man hung up, not waiting to hear my pleas for my daughter. My thoughts were flooded with pictures of my daughter like those I had seen of Suzanne Edenfield. I can't recall a moment in my life when I had been more frightened and totally helpless. I tried calling the number again but kept misdialing until the phone finally rang. I let it ring for at least twenty minutes, refusing to disconnect the only line I had to my daughter. Finally, someone answered!

"Hello, is Caron there?" I said frantically.

"Sure, wait a minute." The young girl's reply brought tears to my eyes. My heart was racing and I went limp when Caron came to the phone.

"Honey, are you all right?" I asked, trying not to let her know I was crying.

"Sure, we've been to an oyster roast and had a lot of fun. Is there anything wrong?"

"No, honey, everything is perfect. I just wanted to make sure y'all arrived without any problem."

We talked a couple more minutes and then hung up, but not without me confirming the address. I sat back in my office chair and cried with relief. When I pulled myself together, I called Lou to confirm the address I had given him. I wanted to know if his guys were in Bluffton.

With a shaky voice, I said, "Lou, keep your guys there and tell them to follow my daughter home tomorrow."

"Cracker, I know what to do. Leave this to me. I've made arrangements. Remember, I don't tell you how to do your job; don't tell me how to do mine," he said irritably.

From that night on, until Lou left the island in the early '80s, I would surreptitiously give Lou my daughter's activities schedule. There was always a silver Mercedes sedan coincidentally driving behind any car my daughter was in. I know this because I saw them several times, especially when she was on her way to Bluffton. My wife and daughter never knew about my arrangement with Lou. I didn't want them to be afraid. I wanted them to have a normal life. I was comforted by the thought that Lou would protect my family. He would not hesitate to neutralize any threat against my family, or for that matter, me.

For the next several weeks, I took my daughter to and from school, and she was not allowed away from home without my wife or me. Once again, I had my phone number at home changed. I thought the phone company might contact me to see why I kept changing my phone numbers, but they never did.

Several weeks later, I had a visit from Sprouse's father. He told me he had traveled a long way to see his son and wanted to talk with me before he returned home. In response to my inquiry concerning his son's background, the elder Sprouse related a strange event that would compel me to call a psychiatrist. He told of how he and Jerry's mother had split up when Jerry had been four years old. Because of anger and resentment towards his wife, the elder Sprouse had never returned or kept up any type of relationship with Jerry. When Jerry's mother had died five years later, Jerry hadn't cried. Rather, he'd spit on his mother lying in her coffin at the funeral. Because his father hadn't come to get him, Jerry had been raised by foster parents until he'd joined the military. His father knew that Jerry deeply resented him for not returning, but he couldn't understand Jerry's reaction to his mother's death because he had been very close to his mother.

"I want to help him as much as I can," he offered.

"Mr. Sprouse, Jerry needs a psychiatric examination. I don't want to have it done by the state. I want a psychiatrist hired by him so that whatever information we receive will be confidential and we won't have to reveal the report unless we choose to do so."

The elder Sprouse agreed to help with the psychiatrist's expense and he left wishing us well. I did not hear from him ever again. It was left to me to pay for the psychiatric assessment.

I took a copy of the survivor's statement to Dr. William Wolfe, a noted psychiatrist experienced in examinations of the criminally insane. The statement laid out the freaky details. Dr. Wolfe recommended that Sprouse be seen by a certain psychologist for a series of psychological tests. After the testing was completed, he would conduct his mental examination and then render a report along with the psychologist.

Several weeks later, Dr. Wolfe delivered the results. Sprouse was mentally ill. He was suffering from paranoid schizophrenia, acute type. He was an introvert, drug dependent, weak-minded, and possessed extreme hatred of his mother, and now, women in general. This is why he had spit on his mother at her funeral; he was angry because she had left him.

Because of the nature of the crimes, finding a jury that was totally impartial and would accept an insanity defense would be extremely difficult, if not impossible. We supposedly found such a jury on the third day of jurors' examination. Judge Oliver swore in twelve jurors and two alternates.

The trial started the next morning and the only thing going for Sprouse was his mental illness and a defense of insanity. For the first time in Savannah history, metal detectors were in place to confiscate any weapons spectators might have carried into the courthouse. A special deputy was assigned to accompany me while I was in the courthouse. They were not aware that Lou and his guys were there to protect me as well.

To my dismay, Suzanne Edenfield's parents sat directly behind me and within three feet of my chair during the entire trial. Seeing them every time I turned towards my counsel table was a constant reminder of my deep sympathy for them, and I was reminded of the threatening calls I was receiving concerning my daughter.

My usual aggressiveness and determination to win at all costs were at odds with this feeling I had. How easy it would have been for me to have been in their place watching some unfeeling silver-tongued Southern trial lawyer make a desperate attempt to seek justice for his client and ask for leniency. Not an eye-for-an-eye, but mercy. This feeling of heightened sympathy for the victim was foreign to me in a courtroom setting. I had to remind myself that I was there to represent my client to the best of my ability. I quickly regained my balance in the face of my enemies and the trial began. After all, I had a Constitution to defend and a life to save, and this was my arena. I was ready!

District Attorney Ryan offered the investigating officer, Lt. Billy Fields, as his first witness. Lt. Fields outlined the disturbing facts and each detail leading to the arrests of Sprouse and Johnson. His photographs of Suzanne lying nude in the tall grass with her hands tied behind her back with a bullet hole in her forehead presented a strong case for the death penalty. Who could argue with such a horrific picture of such a once-beautiful young lady? Her father sat in a daze with hurting eyes while the pictures were being displayed to the jury. Tears formed in the eyes of several jurors, and it was hard for me to sit seemingly undisturbed.

On cross-examining Lt. Fields, I noticed that he kept referring to a three-page written statement of May Howard (I'm using a pseudonym to protect the anonymity of the surviving victim). That was unusual because the copy of her statement they had supplied to me had contained only two pages.

"Lt. Fields, have you supplied me with a copy of the statement you are reading from as required by the court's order?"

"Yes," he answered.

"That's strange; my copy only has two pages. May I look at yours?"

After looking at Ryan as if to get his permission, Fields handed me his copy. I noticed that the last page had not been supplied to me and was an entirely different statement dated after her initial one and after Sprouse's arrest.

"Your Honor, I have been supplied for the first time a statement by Miss Howard that I was unaware of. May I have a few minutes to read it and then cross-examine Lt. Fields?"

"Yes. Take a five-minute recess."

I sat at my counsel table and read the statement. My fear of Sprouse's statement concerning the drugs had become a reality. In the statement, she admitted that what Sprouse had said about the marijuana was true and that she had lied in the first one. How I would handle this without inflaming the minds of the jurors was a good question. I decided to 'soft shoe' it for the time being and see what happened. The trial was reconvened and Fields came back to the stand.

"Lt. Fields, why wasn't I given a copy of this statement with the other one?"

"I don't know. I guess it was an unintentional error. I'm sorry."

"Would you read it to the jury?"

"Yes." He proceeded to read the statement taken several days after Sprouse had been arrested.

I resumed my questions. "Then what this means is that she did not tell you about the dope being theirs?"

"Right."

"Thank you, you may come down."

The next witness was May Howard. She was a nice-looking young blonde woman of twenty years. She wore a metal brace on her right wrist that extended to her fingers. She also had a scar on the side of each cheek. She was thin and understandably very nervous. I knew that there was no way I should further punish this girl in front of this jury by accusing her of lying and misleading the police. Further, to suggest or try to prove that she and Suzanne had picked up two strange men to dope out with was unthinkable, but I knew that it had to be done if the entire truth was to be revealed. That is supposed to be the purpose of a judicial trial, seeking the truth. I knew the truth would hurt, not necessarily Ms. Howard, but the Edenfields. I deeply regretted that necessity.

When May Howard told her story, she avoided the issue of where the drugs had come from or who had asked whom to smoke dope. Rather, she went immediately to Johnny Johnson pulling a gun on them and ordering them into his car. She testified Sprouse had said nothing and done nothing. She said that Johnson had raped Suzanne, but Sprouse had never touched her. Sprouse had sat emotionless in the car and expressed nothing. She admitted that Sprouse had seemed strange and distant, but she didn't know for certain who had shot her and her friend or who had driven the car away. She'd escaped death by faking it and couldn't understand why she'd survived. The first shot had passed through one cheek and out the other. The second had hit her wrist. Both shots had been fired at point-blank range. She then demonstrated how her hand and fingers couldn't move without the metal brace and appendages. She cried as she described the horror and the pain and trying to wake Suzanne up as she had lain beside her. All in all, she made a good witness for the prosecution.

The biggest issue of the trial came when Ryan produced the man who'd made the telephone call that had led to the arrests of Sprouse and Johnson. His name was Tom Marlowe. He had been at the apartment of Johnson and Sprouse in Beaufort two days before the killing. While he'd been there, Johnson had boasted to him of how he and Sprouse were going to Savannah and rape some girls. He'd asked Marlowe to come with them.

I objected strongly to what the witness had just said. "Your Honor, Mr. Ryan has laid no foundation for the admission of this evidence. Johnson is not on trial here and this statement was not made by Sprouse. It was made by someone else."

"Mr. Ryan, shouldn't you show that Sprouse was present when the statement was made before you can introduce it?" the trial judge inquired.

"Yes, Your Honor, I'm sorry. Mr. Marlowe, at the time Johnson made this statement to you, was Sprouse present?"

"No, he was in the back room sleeping."

Ryan was surprised by his answer and asked to approach the bench. I refused to go with him to the judge's bench and demanded that all conversation between judge and counsel be recorded by the court reporter. This made Judge Oliver extremely mad because he hated controversy when it came to requiring a ruling that was important to a case. He preferred, in all of his cases, that lawyers agree on all issues, especially those that could result in a reversible error. He knew that Ryan had just made one. He wanted my cooperation but I wouldn't give it to him. Instead, I went on the attack.

"Your Honor, I move for a mistrial on the grounds that the statement made by the co-defendant out of the presence of the defendant is inadmissible and considering the magnitude of the statement of there being a plan to go to Savannah and rape some girls, I can't see how this court could erase the damage from the minds of this jury. Had Mr. Ryan laid the proper groundwork or foundation for this type of testimony, then the court would have excluded the statement before it was made to the jury."

"Mr. Ryan, you need to show me some law that would persuade me from granting a mistrial," Judge Oliver angrily advised. "Until then, I'm going to declare a recess until the morning. I'll see both counsels in my office at 9:00 tomorrow morning to argue the motion." He stormed off the bench, angry at both Ryan and me.

The next morning, the judge had cooled off and was business as usual. After greeting us, he advised us of his opinion.

"Gentlemen, we've gone too far to mis-try this case. I believe you have a serious error in this trial, Mr. Ryan, but I'm not going to stop the trial. I am going to tell this jury to disregard this fellow's statement because Sprouse wasn't present and had nothing to do with it. That's all I can do."

"Judge, the rest of this trial and all of the time and money involved in this case will be a waste," I countered as we were being ushered out of his office, but that didn't seem to bother him. The judge instructed the jury as he'd advised and the trial resumed.

When Ryan closed his evidence on the fifth day of trial, I was ready to proceed with the only issue I had, Sprouse's insanity. Of course, I knew that when a conviction came, it would mean nothing. There was a reversible error that would void any outcome except an acquittal. I presented Dr. Wolfe and the psychologist to prove that Sprouse was insane and suffering from paranoid schizophrenia, acute type. They revealed his background, his hatred for his mother, and his being deserted.

The psychological test showed that he was an introvert, weak-minded, and not violent. Indeed, the picture they painted of Sprouse was accurate and consistent with the testimony of May Howard. She had painted the picture of an emotionless introvert who had done no violence or harm to her that she knew of. I went against my rule and offered Sprouse as his own witness. I knew that we would run the risk of Ryan being able to upset Sprouse to the point he could become violent and that could throw out our defense based on the psychiatrist's testimony, but I believed the medical opinion and took the risk. I believed that Sprouse would come across as insane.

Sprouse remembered only the details before Johnson had pulled the gun and after they'd woken up the next morning. As much as Ryan tried, he could not excite, anger, or agitate Sprouse; neither did Sprouse show any remorse or sorrow for Suzanne, and Ryan realized this at the end. Ryan then very wisely highlighted the greatest symptom of this mental illness.

"Mr. Sprouse, you don't shed one tear for Suzanne Edenfield, do you?" Sprouse sat emotionless and the silence was convincing. When Sprouse was unable to reply for a minute or two, I interrupted the atmosphere and objected to the question as being immaterial. The judge sustained and the evidence ended.

After closing arguments the next morning, the jury retired to consider its verdict. After almost a full day of deliberation, the jury returned with a verdict of guilty on all counts. Then they were returned to the jury room to consider the death penalty on the murder conviction. After several hours, they returned and gave Jerry Sprouse the death penalty.

Many of the court spectators applauded the verdict and the sentence. I watched people approach Suzanne's parents, who were crying. Everyone in the courtroom was supportive of the victims and their families. I was supportive as well, but I did not agree with the verdict. First, there was no evidence that Jerry

Sprouse had shot anyone, or raped anyone, for that matter. The only evidence presented was that Sprouse had sat motionless and speechless in the car. To me, this was clear evidence of insanity. His crime was that he'd been there. They had given him the electric chair for being guilty by association. The electric chair is for shooters and rapists, and Sprouse was neither.

That night, I kept rehashing the trial and the truth of the case. Again, the insanity issue was misapplied. It was a myth. Same old story. Had Sprouse robbed a liquor store and hurt no one, the jury would have easily found him insane based on the opinion of a competent psychologist and a well-qualified psychiatrist. But since he'd been involved in such an insane and horrific crime, he must be sane! This jury was no different than other juries. An insane crime proves sanity!

I appealed this case to the Georgia Supreme Court. Unfortunately, Sprouse decided to escape from the Chatham County Jail. He was still on the lam when his death penalty was reversed on January 5, 1979. He was captured shortly after the reversal. Once again, this case was heard by a jury and Sprouse was given the death penalty again. Again, that penalty was reversed in 1982. Eventually, Sprouse's sentence was commuted to life in prison. I felt I had done the very best defense I could. Sprouse remains in prison to this day, but he is eligible for parole.

Although I won and fulfilled my responsibility to the law and my client, Savannah didn't see it that way. While they respected my skills and dedication, they never let me forget that I was on the wrong side. The irony is that many of my most difficult capital murder cases were court-appointed. I'd had no choice but to take them. Now, those same judges viewed me as an adversary in the courtroom. In their view, and the DA's office, I took my responsibilities to my clients too seriously.

Savannah elite could shun me, but Lou and the workers on Mob Island saw me as a hero. Lou could sense that I was tired and dismayed with the lack of understanding or recognition of my efforts to do the right thing. Lou offered to relocate me with the Teamsters in Washington, DC, but Savannah was my home and I declined.

36. 'My O My'

In spring 1976, the Honorable Alexander Lawrence ruled in the *Playboy* case that Louie the Tailor was a public figure and that we had the burden to prove that the article was written and published with malice before Lou could recover any award. To this ruling, we took exception and filed an appeal in the 5th Circuit Court of Appeals in New Orleans.

Lawrence was a legendary trial lawyer from Savannah. He was a small man in stature, completely bald, and had a silver tongue. In Southern lingo, that meant he could out-argue his opposition in such a convincing and demolishing way that those he defeated felt proud and actually thanked him.

I was told in law school that his legendary status came about from the famous Coca-Cola case in the late fifties. A man said that he'd swallowed a roach while drinking from a Coke bottle. Instead of this being the 'pause that refreshes,' he'd become seriously ill. He sued Coca-Cola for a large sum of money for making him ill and causing a mental condition. The condition manifested itself in his inability to drink anything from a bottle without suffering disabling panic attacks. This unfortunate incident of swallowing a roach had cost him his job and marriage. He claimed to be totally distraught and disabled by the time the case came to trial.

The publicity around this case brought Savannah to the federal courthouse where people lined the corridors so they could hear the hideous details. To the local citizenry, the thought of 'eating' a roach while drinking a Coke was mind-boggling. I should stop here and talk a bit about the most important character in this case, the roach.

If you live in Savannah's old historic section for more than a week, you will know what a cockroach is. It's a creature about an inch long with wings and thin prickly legs. The creatures are birthed in the great majestic oaks and pine trees found all over Savannah. These cockroach castles send millions of these creatures into the homes of innocent people to be seen at all times, but especially when you get up at 3:00 a.m. and turn on a light in any room in your home. What they eat, I have no idea, but they are healthy and fully nourished thanks to the accommodating people of Savannah. I venture to say that I've killed thousands of roaches in my lifetime only to realize that the more I kill, the more they reproduce.

Back to Judge Lawrence. You must understand that I was just a child and not present in the courtroom on the morning of closing arguments in the Coca-Cola case. So, I give you an accounting of what I heard all my life of the event that took place: While Lawrence had informed the jury that the man with all of his domestic and mental problems deserved sympathy, the problems were not the result of eating the unfortunate cockroach. With this understood, Lawrence had walked to his council table, picked up a small box, and removed a large, dark cockroach. He'd held the roach by its feet, lifting it up so that all of the jury could identify his prey. He'd walked up and down in front of the astonished jurors with the cockroach. They'd watched in anticipation and a little horror, sensing what might take place. And it had.

Lawrence had faced the jury, three feet in front of the jury rail, positioned himself in the middle, tilted his bald head back, opened his mouth wide, raised his hand dangling the spiny-ridged creature, dropped it into his mouth and crunched, chewing until it disappeared. He'd then turned to the jury, smiled, and said, "I've just eaten a cockroach, a live one, not one stored in carbonated liquid, and I want you to watch very carefully my every move until the end of this case. The judge will send you to lunch and when you return, he will give you his instructions. During this entire time, watch me closely. I am a man who is much older and smaller than the man who has filed this suit. If I get sick, bring back a big and fair verdict for him. If, on the other hand, I remain healthy and unaffected by the lunch I've just eaten, then award him nothing. Thank you for your indulgence and please forgive me for requiring you to witness such an unfortunate event to show you the truth."

Lawrence, like the triumphal warrior, had proudly returned to his seat and his grateful clients, the Coca-Cola executives. He'd smiled at the jury as they'd left for lunch. After the jury had filed out, the judge had admonished Lawrence for not warning him that he would perform such a dastardly act ahead of time. He'd told Lawrence that he would not be able to eat lunch and had gone directly to his office.

Legend has it that Lawrence had also left abruptly and gone to the men's restroom from which he was heard retching. Through the years that followed, Lawrence never confirmed what actually happened in the restroom. The jury? They returned a verdict in favor of Coca-Cola and the legend was born. So, this legendary cockroach-eater was now the trial judge in the *Playboy* case.

Lou and I flew to New Orleans to argue the appeal and were met by the distinguished John Roselli. I had met Roselli at the Savannah Inn when I'd played a round of golf with him, Lou, and another man from New Orleans (whose name I never knew). Roselli, unlike Lou, was not a good golfer, but he did have a quick and violent temper. On the third hole, he'd missed an easy putt. Passing a pine tree on the way to his cart, he'd whacked his club against the trunk and broken it in half. Lou had scowled and shook his head. Two holes later he'd whacked another tree with a driver. Lou had approached him with his own driver in hand and told Roselli that if he hit another one of Lou's pine trees, he would bury Roselli under the eighteenth green. Needless to say, Roselli didn't hit any more pine trees that day.

Roselli drove us to the Roosevelt Hotel close to Bourbon Street and suggested an Italian restaurant for our evening meal—Antoine's. After eating, we were presented with our large tab. Roselli looked at it and handed it back to the waiter and told him to give it to the manager. Afterwards, Roselli dropped Lou and me at the corner of Canal and Bourbon Street. We walked down Bourbon Street to a nightclub named 'My O My.'

"Cracker, this place has some broads better looking than the joints in Vegas. They dance better than the Rockettes. You're gonna like 'em."

He was right. The women were beautiful and stacked. They performed like the Rockettes. They sang, and to our delight, they partially stripped just enough to tantalize every man in the place. And the place was packed. On several occasions, I glanced over at Lou and noticed he had a silly smile on his face. These beautiful women ended the performance with a rousing Rockettes-like number with their legs kicking high in perfect unison. When they ended the dance, they bowed to the adoring crowd and then dropped their tights just enough to reveal...penises. I was shocked that I had been admiring 'men.' Lou was laughing out loud. My O My!

Lou laughed all the way back to the hotel and left me with a lasting remark, "Cracker, things aren't necessarily what they appear to be. Keep that in mind and you'll be all right."

I argued the *Playboy* case before the appellate court and flew back to Savannah. Lou stayed in New Orleans to handle a few matters with Roselli. On the flight back, I was laughing to myself about the My O My club and how Lou had enjoyed seeing my reaction to the revelation that I had been admiring men. I never forgot his statement that things aren't necessarily what they appear to be. That certainly was the case in the April affair.

It started with a call from a friend of mine who was a prominent attorney in Savannah. "Bubba, meet me for lunch at the Howard Johnson at noon. You'll never believe what I've come across."

When I arrived, he waved me over to his table. I could see he was excited about something. When I sat down, he began telling me about his good fortune. He told me about a beautiful model from England who had been arrested for shoplifting at the Greyhound Bus Station the afternoon before. When they'd booked her, she'd had no money for a bond but an alert police officer—seeing her beauty and peril—had seen a chance to make friends with some prominent lawyers. He'd made a call to the owner of the Howard Johnson's Motor Lodge next door to the bus station. The owner had agreed to bail her out and given her a room to stay in after arranging a date that evening. Thus began a most unusual and embarrassing incident involving many of the elite lawyers and aristocracy in Savannah.

It goes without saying that the motel owner saw an opportunity to do a few 'favors' for the Savannah lawyers, and he'd called my friend who'd called me. Well, I didn't bite, but my friend and about ten other lawyers did. So, for several months, each had an affair with the beautiful model from England. Some were even seen in public having dinner or dancing at popular nightspots with her. Believing themselves invisible, they disregarded the consequences of their behavior if their wives were to find out about it. And because these attorneys were all sharing in the delightful experience of having an affair with a beautiful woman, none worried about the others exposing him.

This went on for several months and their carefully kept secrets became the talk of the town. One of these Romeos was a close friend of mine and successfully engaged in the political circles of Savannah. He was single and owned a shrimping business on the island. One night, during the weekly Wednesday night meeting of Jaycees with two hundred members attending, he went to the microphone and announced that he had gotten engaged to the girl of his dreams, the beautiful April from England. Having had a few drinks, he made matters worse by confessing that she had satisfied him beyond his wildest dreams and they were deeply in love. We were all touched.

The next morning, I appeared in the state court for the criminal docket call. I noticed that April Ashley's name was on the docket for the shoplifting charge. I also noticed that while her newly announced fiancé was not in the courtroom, her numerous lovers were.

As each case was being called for a trial date, I noticed a deputy sheriff run into the courtroom through a side door with a big grin on his face. Something was up. It appeared that April had been caught shoplifting once again and had been locked up in the county jail overnight.

Brought to the courtroom to enter a plea, April had been put in a holding cell waiting for her case to be called. The holding cell was next to the room where most of her suitors were waiting to represent other clients. But something was going on and stoked my curiosity. I left the courtroom and went over to the sheriff's desk. He and two deputies were gathered near April's holding cell. The sheriff, laughing, walked over to me to explain what was happening. It wasn't hard for me to figure out that it involved the beautiful model from England.

"Bubba, she's a man."

"What!"

"She's got a dick."

"No way!"

"Yes! And she's mad. She's naming names and demanding money. She ain't holding back at all, and it's most of those guys in that courtroom over there."

While being strip-searched by a female deputy, it had been discovered that the beautiful model from England was not a woman, but a well-endowed man. I went back into the courtroom, and spotting my friend I said, "You're not going to believe this, but your girlfriend is a boyfriend and you've been sleeping with the guy for several months."

He went pale. Our conversation was overheard by another lawyer and quickly spread across the courtroom, causing a mass exodus of lawyers.

As the weeks went by, the legal community in Savannah pondered the question of how so many lawyers could have been fooled into thinking they were having an affair with a beautiful woman. The only answer I could come up with was that these lawyers were either pitiful lovers or incredible liars, or both.

April Ashley was sent back home to England the following morning with a lot of cash. The gay romantic scene in Savannah subsided for a good while. My

Jaycee friend left Savannah and moved to Atlanta. I have not seen him since. A year later I read in an Atlanta newspaper of a British Lord having to resign from Parliament because of an affair with a beautiful model named April Ashley. A picture of the two verified that she'd made it back to England. The April Affair was now an international matter thanks to my elite lawyer friends in Savannah. My O My!

37. Let Konter Get on Top of It

Lou and I were at Dino's discussing world affairs. I always enjoyed my discussions with him because he kept up to date on national and local news. He always told me to be aware of what was happening because you never knew how some obscure event across the country might affect you. But according to Lou, Savannah was an exception. Events that happened here just didn't happen anywhere else. His opinion about Savannah was never truer than what occurred within minutes of me sitting down there that day.

The bartender motioned for me to pick up the telephone that was always located on Lou's table. My daughter was calling to tell me to turn on the news. I turned to Lou and asked him to tell the bartender to turn on the television above the bar to the local news. The announcer was reporting the murder of a well-known real estate agent in Savannah. It seemed my daughter was warning me that I probably had a future client. I thanked her and told her that I'd be home within the hour.

Lou was watching the news report and began laughing.

"Cracker, y'all must have a murder every night somewhere and it ain't regular people." I looked up to catch the end of the news flash; too late. It was that annoying commercial where a dozen real estate agents stood on top of a roof shouting in unison: "Let Konter Get on Top of It!" I sighed and turned back to Lou, but before we could continue our conversation, the bartender, once again, motioned me to pick up the phone. It was my daughter telling me to write a number down because Mr. Kessler wanted me to call him right away. Wilbur Kessler was a close friend of mine, and his son was my daughter's classmate. So, I knew I had to call right away.

I told Lou I had to make an important call. Lou didn't move an inch. He was going to sit there with burning ears. I called Wilbur and he picked up on the first ring.

"Bubba, I'm in deep trouble. I shot a man and I'm here in a phone booth with my girlfriend. She's naked."

I was speechless. Here was a man who was an icon. Wilbur was a community leader in youth sports, active leader in the Chamber of Commerce, and an important railroad executive.

Carl Griffin, the local sheriff was his best friend, followed by the mayor. Clearly, he was one of the most popular citizens in our fair city. He belonged to the Savannah aristocracy.

I was not going to ask too many questions with Lou sitting there. If he heard me mention a naked woman in a phone booth, he would have picked up an extension phone to hear the conversation. While listening to Wilbur, I was still watching the news about the man found murdered. I put two-and-two together.

"Wilbur, was the man a real estate agent?"

"Yeah, come get me. I need to turn myself in."

"Okay, Wilbur, I'm calling Carl and I'm coming to you. What phone booth are y'all in?"

"The Bull Street side of the Hilton. Hurry, she's getting cold."

By the time I got there, he and the woman had already been spotted due to the screams coming from the booth. Police officers, thinking that Wilbur had kidnapped a naked lady, had taken them to the county jail. I went on down to the jail. While there, I noticed a disheveled woman wrapped in a blanket waiting for someone to bring her some clothes. I found out later that it had taken the officers about twenty minutes to find her a blanket.

One of the officers recognized me and asked if I was representing Kessler. I told him I was and I wanted to see the sheriff. After a few minutes, Carl Griffin appeared. Carl was a popular man in Savannah who was active in youth sports. Standing only five foot four and weighing 230 pounds, he was known as the 'Short Arms of the Law.' Everyone respected him, and I considered him a friend.

Carl motioned me to follow him into his office. Entering, he quickly shut the door. "Bubba, Wilbur has shot a man. He caught him screwing his girlfriend. I'm glad you're representing him, but I don't see how you can get him out of this. I'll do all I can to help him."

"Where's he now?"

"He's in a holding cell wait'in on the detectives to question him."

"Carl, I don't want anybody questioning him. Could you buzz them and tell them I'm representing him?"

Carl picked up the phone and did what I asked. Hesitating, he turned to me and said, "He's already confessed."

"Carl, that's the quickest confession I ever heard of. I need to see Wilbur now." A deputy led me to Wilbur where he was sitting at a desk facing two detectives and a recording device on the table. "Wilbur, don't say another word." I turned to the two detectives and said, "I want a copy of your tape. He didn't tell you I'm representing him?"

"No. We read him his Miranda Rights and that's on the tape." They got up, secured their recording device, and told me I could pick up a copy the next morning. As soon as they left, I looked at Wilbur in bewilderment.

"Wilbur, I'm here to help. You shouldn't have talked to them."

"Bubba, I ain't got nothing to hide. I did it. I hope the man didn't die."

"Wilbur, he's dead, and they're charging you with murder and kidnapping." Wilbur began crying. If ever there was a man so remorseful for what he had done, it was Wilbur Kessler.

"Wilbur, I'll file a motion for bond in the morning, and I think I can get you out of jail." I hugged him and left.

The following morning, I obtained the tape and filed a motion for a bond. Back in my office, I listened to the tape: The night before, Wilbur had had a date with a local real estate agent with Konter Realty. He considered her his fiancée. Wilbur explained to the officers that he had picked Sally up at her apartment and on the way to dinner, she'd said she wasn't feeling well and to drop her off at her sister's house for the evening. He had dropped Sally off. Later he decided to go back to the sister's house to check on her, but she had left. He'd proceeded to drive to the apartment of another real estate agent where he had noticed his girlfriend's car. Becoming suspicious, he had walked around to the rear of the apartment and peered through the window of the agent's bedroom. He had seen a naked man on top of his naked fiancée engaged in the throes of unrestrained sex.

He had run back to his car and pulled out a double-barreled twelve-gauge shotgun and a cooler from his trunk. He'd loaded the shotgun, grabbed the cooler, and gone back to the rear window. The real estate agent had still been on top of her, pumping frantically, as Wilbur had placed the cooler under the window, climbed on top of it, and placed the shotgun barrel through a tear in the screen. The gun had suddenly fired, knocking Wilbur off the top of the cooler.

Wilbur had then crashed through the back door and found his fiancée lying in shock underneath the bloody real estate agent—clearly, a climatic end to their evening. Pushing the guy aside, he'd forced Sally out the door and into his car where he'd driven to the nearest phone booth to summon help for the wounded man. He'd then driven to another phone booth near the De Soto Hilton and called me.

This was front-page coverage in the papers and on the morning and evening news for days. It was pitched as a love-triangle gone horribly wrong. According to the media, it was an open-and-shut case since Wilbur had confessed to premeditated murder. This was going to be one of my most difficult cases because of Wilbur's voluntary confession.

There were significant problems with the case. First, had Wilbur shot the man in the act of sex with his fiancée when he'd first seen them, then he would have had a chance to plead temporary insanity. But he'd gone to his car, loaded a shotgun, grabbed a cooler, and then gone back. According to Georgia law, he had had sufficient time to cool-off. Second, Wilbur wasn't married to her, so he wasn't an outraged husband. He legally had no claim on her. She could sleep with anyone she pleased, anywhere she pleased. Third, the dead man had a wife and three children. He'd been close to a local judge and active in the Savannah community. Even so, I was able to obtain a bond for Wilbur and he was released from jail.

During the weeks prior to trial, this case was a common topic when Lou and I would meet. Initially, Lou's curiosity focused on the naked lady in the phone booth. He wanted to know how she looked, particularly how she looked naked. I told him he would have to ask the officers at the county jail for a detailed assessment. But since Lou had banned the county police from the inn and Dino's, I was his only source of information on the woman.

Soon Lou's interest shifted to the case at hand. As we sipped our drinks at Dino's, he shook his head and said, "You're gonna lose this one, Cracker. I don't see a way out."

"You remember all those times you told me there was no way and I found one? Well, I'm gonna find one."

We toasted to the success of the past cases Lou and I had worked on together and to the new case that was seemingly impossible for me to win. A month later, the trial began. The only thing I had going was community sympathy for

Wilbur's plight and the recognition that he had contributed greatly to Savannah through his civic duties.

For several days, I listened as the DA proved a case of premeditated murder just as Wilbur had described to the detectives. On the morning of the third day, I saw the DA enter a photograph of the scene outside the rear window. The photo was taken at the crime scene and the officer swore that nothing had been changed. The photo showed the tear in the screen and the cooler sitting below the window in an upright position. I saw what I needed to win the case.

After the officer testified, the DA rested his case. I approached Judge Cheatham and announced: "Judge, I have no evidence. I rest my case."

"Mr. Haupt, I'm sending the jury out and then we'll discuss your announcement."

I watched the jury leave and then turned my attention to the DA. I knew what the DA was thinking. This was a high-profile trial and I was offering no defense to a kidnapping and premeditated murder charge. If Wilbur was found guilty, it was mandatory life on the murder charge and twenty years for the kidnapping. The DA was worried; what kind of trick was I planning to pull in this case? I smiled. I was planning to pull the mother of all tricks. The judge interrupted my thoughts.

"Mr. Haupt, I can't imagine you not offering any evidence in this case. Surely Mr. Kessler has some sort of defense."

"Judge, he does have a defense. It's in his confession and I can add no more to what he's already confessed to."

The judge had a bewildered look on his face as he asked the bailiff to bring the jury back into the courtroom. He announced that closing arguments would start the next morning. The DA would argue first and the defense would argue last. He excused the jury and sent them home. After the last juror left the courtroom, Wilbur patted me on the shoulder and said, "Bubba, are you sure we're okay?"

I looked at him, smiled, and said, "Wilbur, we got 'em." I turned to the back of the courtroom, where Lou and a couple of his buddies from Miami were sitting and gave him a thumbs-up. Lou walked up to me as I packed my files.

"Cracker, you must be crazy. Are you sure you know what you're doing in this one, 'cause I can't see it."

"Lou, you'll see it tomorrow."

Bright and early the next morning, the State gave its closing argument in the case: *The State of Georgia vs. Wilbur Kessler*. The DA eloquently argued for one hour, setting out an ironclad case of premeditated murder and forced kidnapping. I could sense that the jury was absolutely convinced beyond a reasonable doubt that Wilbur was guilty on all charges.

It came my time to argue Wilbur's case. Instead of approaching the jury, I approached the judge.

"Your Honor, I wish, as part of my closing, to demonstrate to the jury the innocence of Mr. Kessler."

"What kind of demonstration?"

I held up the last photograph the DA had presented that showed the scene outside the rear window. "I want to re-enact someone standing on top of the cooler and firing the shotgun. The officer has testified that Wilbur got up on the cooler, aimed, and shot the victim. We contend that's impossible. Had he done that, the cooler would have been knocked over and the photo shows that it was upright. So, I'd like to demonstrate the officer getting up on the cooler and firing the weapon."

"I'm gonna let you do the demonstration."

The jury was loaded into a van and taken to the police firing range. The cooler and shotgun were brought to the firing range along with Kessler and the officer who'd made the report. While newspaper photographers stood near the jury and Judge Cheatham, the cooler was placed on the ground in an upright position. The officer was asked to stand on top of the cooler where I handed him Kessler's loaded shotgun. They watched silently as the officer fired. The recoil of the shotgun blast knocked the officer off the cooler and the cooler tipped over. I asked him to set it up again and fire the second round to confirm the first round's result. He fired the second shot and he was knocked off the cooler and the cooler was knocked over again.

The jury was loaded back into the van and we all went back to the courtroom. When everyone was reassembled, I completed my argument.

"Ladies and gentlemen of the jury, I want you to compare the photographs of the scene after the shooting to what you have just witnessed at the firing range. This proves, beyond a reasonable doubt, that Mr. Kessler did not take aim because he never got on top of the cooler. Had he fired while standing on top of the cooler, the cooler would have been lying on its side, just like the cooler you saw at the firing range. So, it was not premeditated. I'll tell you what is the truth in this case. Remember your duty is to find the truth regardless of what it may look like to others who only read the newspapers about this case."

I turned and looked at Lou sitting in his usual spot in the rear of the courtroom with his friends from Miami. Lou rolled his eyes and then grinned at me. He knew I had something up my sleeve. There was a soft murmur in the courtroom as I turned back to the jury who appeared to be anxiously waiting for me to tell them the truth.

"Members of the jury, this is what actually happened: When the barrel of that shotgun appeared through the tear in the screen, the victim stopped what he was doing when he saw the barrel, grabbed it and the shotgun went off. So, the truth of the matter is that the victim accidently shot himself. Mr. Kessler did not intend to shoot him, but only to scare him and stop what they were doing. I rest my case."

The jury bought my argument. They came back with a verdict of not guilty of premeditated murder and kidnapping. They did find him guilty of manslaughter and he served thirty-six months in a 'camp' in the adjacent county of Effingham, nine miles from where he lived.

I was happy to win the case, and I considered this a big win. My client had confessed to premeditated murder and thanks to a photograph, I'd been able to sway the jury in my favor. Yet, this win was bittersweet because I couldn't help but remember how Frank Williams had been treated by our legal system. Unlike Wilbur, Williams had not been granted a bail when he'd been arrested for rape based on an eleven-year-old photograph and then arrested again for rape based on the same photograph. In both cases, he'd been found not guilty, but unlike Wilbur, Williams had lost everything.

That evening, I met Lou at The Exchange Tavern where we could enjoy discussing the case without curious onlookers. Lou was drinking a vodka and before I could settle in my seat, the waiter brought my usual—Johnny Walker on the rocks.

"Cracker, you're a tricky bastard. They knew you were comin', but never knew where you were coming from." He paused and then added, "Neither did I, you motherfucker."

Lou knew I didn't curse and sometimes took pleasure in shocking me with his language. In this case, I knew he was using 'motherfucker' as a compliment, so I nodded in appreciation. I looked up to check the score of the Braves game playing on the television behind the bar; too late. That stupid commercial had come back on: "Let Konter Get on Top of It."

Lou turned to me and said, "Is that the naked woman on top of that roof?"

I nodded my head and said, "Yep."

"How 'bout the guy who got whacked?"

"Yep. He's standing right next to her."

Lou laughed and raised his glass to the television and said, "Yeah, you real estate people really know how to get on top of it."

The Exchange Tavern in Savannah

38. A Plane Goes Down

Back in the seventies, gambling junkets were very popular in Savannah. Just about every weekend there was a chartered plane flying west to Las Vegas. I had a close attorney friend who organized a group to go at least once a month. The flight was free if you bought one thousand dollars in chips from one of the prominent casinos. The food was cheap and the room was below Savannah rates. You left on one day and flew back the next night, penniless.

I remember Lou calling me at the office during my preparation for a major murder case and asking me to ride with him out to the Savannah Airport. Needing the break, I told Lou I would be waiting for him when he got to my office. Thirty minutes later Lou and I drove to the airport. I asked him why we were heading to the airport, and his reply was, "To help out a friend." I expected him to tell me who it was, but he did not, so I left it alone.

We pulled into the private plane hangar area where I used to tie my twin-engine aero commander that I used frequently for trips to Atlanta, Florida, and the Bahamas. As Lou exited the car, I got out and walked over to check out the private planes for something to do while Lou did his business. After a few minutes, I looked over at Lou pointing his finger at a man standing beside a Lear Jet. The man had on a dark sport coat and underneath he wore a silk shirt unbuttoned halfway down his chest. He and Lou were arguing. I looked at the open door to the small jet and saw someone I recognized observing the argument.

The man was a friend of mine who owned several prosperous restaurants in the Savannah area. Cary Hilliard was very popular among his peers and was a frequent flyer in the gambling junkets. It was well known among Cary's friends that he was addicted to gambling and no one seemed to be concerned about it.

After a few minutes, I returned to the car. The discussion on the runway ceased, and Louie the Tailor motioned to Cary, who was standing on the stairwell, to come with him. Cary obeyed and they both walked together towards the car in which I was now sitting. Cary climbed in the back seat, and he and I had a cordial conversation. Lou drove and said nothing. When he dropped me off at my office, he told me to meet him for lunch the next day. I agreed, and the car with Lou in the front and Cary in the back drove away.

I stood on the curb in front of my office and wondered what had just happened. First, I'd been invited by my client to an argument that I'd not been allowed to hear. Second, I'd not been allowed to know any of the circumstances or why I'd needed to be there in the first place. It didn't make sense. And, an attorney's curiosity had just been ignited. No attorney likes to watch his client in an argument he can't hear or participate in. It's against our DNA, and it troubled me almost as much as rejecting a good case I didn't have the time to handle. The famous case of 'Midnight in the Garden of Good and Evil' (which I will explain) came to my mind and aggravated me once again.

Jim Williams was a well-known antique dealer in Savannah. He had some prominent clients throughout America such as Jackie Kennedy Onassis. He also was openly homosexual and well-connected to the 'Blue Bloods' (old money elite) of historic Savannah. I knew him casually and had visited his elegant old home/museum to buy a few items for my office.

I received a call from Jim sometime after midnight, asking me to meet him at the city jail. He was stuttering and I could hardly understand what he was saying. I thought he was drugged out and had been arrested on some sort of drug charge. Unfortunately, I had just completed a very difficult murder trial that had lasted two weeks and I was exhausted. So, instead of jumping in my car and going to the jail to see my friend, I told him to call Bob Duffy, another attorney in Savannah, and he would come immediately. I hung up and went to sleep.

The next morning, I headed to the coffee shop downstairs at the courthouse. I wanted to catch Duffy before he went upstairs for the docket calls. I was anxious to ask him how he'd come out with a drunk or drug-influenced Jim Williams. I was sure that Duffy would be hot to have been woken at such an hour to talk to Williams. I was wrong.

I saw Duffy, got myself a cup of coffee, and sat down next to him to wait for his 'I'll pay you back' quote. But that didn't happen. Instead, Duffy took a check from inside the pocket of his suit coat and held it up so that I could read it. I almost threw up. It was a $50,000 check made out to Duffy. He smiled at me and thanked me. "I owe you a cup of coffee." He got up and left. To a lawyer, this was a stab in the heart. Fifty thousand would have bought ten Chevys, and I had given it to another lawyer as a joke.

I left and went to the DA's office to see what Williams had been charged with. He had killed a young live-in companion during an argument at his mansion. The murder became the subject of the best-selling book and popular movie *In the Garden of Good and Evil*. I was sick for months, especially when Duffy told me that Williams paid him more the following month. Now back to Cary and the visit to the airport.

I met Lou the next day for lunch at the club. After we ordered, he began to explain what had happened the day before.

"Cracker, Hilliard took one of those junkets Judge Herndon puts together every other week. That motherfucker did it again. He got in to 'em for fifty grand." I watched Lou clench his fists as he continued, "And he used my name to get back here. The guys in Vegas weren't gonna let him leave. That motherfucker said he was one of my guys."

I knew Lou needed to let off steam, so I remained silent as he continued: "Cracker, he ain't one of my guys. He ain't even a member of my club. When he used my name, the guys in Vegas let him go. They should've called me before they brought him back."

"Lou, if they had called you, wouldn't you have okayed him?"

"Yeah, but only after I'd called his wife and gotten a guarantee on the money. This guy doesn't understand what he's done. Now I'm on the hook."

"Lou, why did you cover his debt to the Vegas casino? You hardly know Hilliard."

"His family's got clout here. A lotta clout. If I said no, they could've brought a lotta heat on me and the Teamsters. That motherfucker put me in a box."

"What did you tell the casino? What if he goes back and gets in deeper?" Lou paused, "I told 'em I'm taking it on the hook this time, but it's the last time.

Whatever happens from now to doomsday he's yours, not mine. It ain't my business anymore." I understood the situation completely, but Carey Hilliard was a friend of mine, and I was hoping that everything would work out. I knew that Carey was addicted to gambling in Vegas and when there, he usually lost large sums of money. Although I seldom gambled while in Vegas, I did win enough to buy a new Chevy every now and then. I never lost; I was one of Lou's guys.

Later that week, Lou called me and told me that Cary had covered the debt and the problem was over. But Cary continued the junkets to Vegas. Then one morning I opened the *Savannah Morning News* and I read that Cary, his wife, and pilot had been killed in an airplane crash outside of Savannah. The article recounted that Cary had been coming back from Charleston, South Carolina, in his company plane and had run out of gas.[38] He had just opened a restaurant in Charleston that was only 120 miles from Savannah or a twenty-minute plane ride. I was saddened and shocked. I had lost a friend. As a pilot, a lot of thoughts raced through my mind.

I called Lou and asked him if he had seen the newspaper and he said that he had. He said nothing else and I didn't continue the conversation. I would wait for another day. And that day occurred a month later at Dino's; after Louie the Tailor had had a few drinks.

I was sitting at the bar with my close friend Grady. We were having a drink and planning a fishing trip for the next weekend when Lou came into the bar and invited us to join him in the restaurant. At that moment, Grady saw someone he knew and went over to speak to him. As Lou and I settled in with a couple of drinks, Lou looked at me for a long moment and then said, "It's a shame Hilliard and his wife got killed. Cracker, she didn't do nothing. I only saw her a few times, but she was a nice broad."

"Lou, they said that the plane ran out of gas."

"It's crazy. The guy ran up another debt for over a hundred grand."

After that comment, I waved the server over and asked her to refresh my drink. As the owner of a private plane, I *knew* that the plane had not run out of gas. I also knew that the experienced pilot flying Cary's plane that night, always and without exception, would have topped off the gas tanks before taking off to any destination regardless of how short it was. This was an unbreakable procedure in the private world of businessmen who owned planes. I was suspicious. In view of Cary's Vegas debts, they should have checked before leaving Charleston to see if sugar had been put in the gas tank. This suspicion was further fueled by an occurrence that happened to me when I flew some friends to Chicago for the Jaycee National Convention.

Before leaving for the three-day trip, I checked with Lou to see if there was anything he needed for me to do in Chicago while I was there. He said that he couldn't think of anything, but I needed to check with him before I came back.

The morning of the day I was planning to return, I called Lou. "Lou, I'm flying out this evening. Do you need anything from Chicago?"

"What time you takin' off?"

"Between six and six-thirty tonight."

276

"I got a friend who needs a ride. I'll have my guy there by five. Cracker, you're gonna leave a little earlier. I want you to land on the island runway. I'll have a car pick the guy up and take him to the inn. You can fly over to Savannah Airport after you deliver the guy."

I hung up the phone and sat down on the edge of the bed in my hotel room. I was worried. I didn't understand why Lou would have me landing on the island and not the Savannah Airport where it was much safer. I didn't know who this passenger was, but I was concerned. The island runway is dirt and grass. The only advantage in landing there is that one didn't have to file a flight plan for this runway, and no one would have a record of the flight or passengers. As far as the FAA was concerned, I was flying from Chicago directly to the Savannah Airport.

The more I thought about it though, the more I relaxed. The small dirt airfield on Mob Island was used extensively by Lou and his friends. They would come and go at will without any surveillance or record of the flight. This couldn't happen at the Savannah Airport terminal. I don't believe the feds ever knew how extensively this field was being used. It was perfect for a King Air, the luxury twin-engine passenger plane at that time. It seated seven and could fly to New York or Chicago without refueling. The Teamsters had a King Air.

My Jaycee friends and I left in plenty of time to meet Lou's passenger, Sal, at the runway for private planes adjacent to O'Hare. When he and his driver showed up, I called Lou and told him Sal was there and we were ready to take-off.

"Cracker, the guy with Sal is gonna test your gas tanks for sugar. Don't take off without him testing your tanks."

"Lou, I've never done that before, why now?"

"Just do it. Trust me."

When I hung up, I recalled how Lou had borrowed my car after I had agreed to represent him and the Teamsters. When he had returned it an hour later, he had given me a remote-control gadget that cranked the engine from a hundred feet away. He had said, "Cracker, don't ever crank your engine from inside the car. Always push this button when you're a hundred feet away and then get in." I'd followed his instructions religiously. Now he was instructing me to check the gas tanks.

I was waiting in the lobby of the plane depot when the driver came back. He motioned for me to follow him out to the plane. It was windy and cold. Standing there, I felt sick with apprehension.

"Mr. Haupt, your tanks are loaded with sugar. You could've taken off, but you wouldn't have cleared the airport before crashing."

I didn't know what to say. I was in shock. Why would somebody want to kill me? I turned and went back into the lobby to find a phone. Sal noticed that I was pale and visibly shaken. He asked what was wrong. I just told him it was too dad-gum cold out there. I don't think he believed me. He went outside. I called Lou.

"Lou, the tank is full of sugar. What's going on?"

"Listen to me. Leave Chicago as soon as the tanks are flushed."

"Is anyone trying to kill me?"

"You and your buddies get out of there tonight."

"Lou, does this involve Sal?"

Raising his voice, he said, "Just get out of Chicago, now!"

After the gas tanks were flushed and refilled, we set out for Mob Island. While my buddies were looking for something strong to drink, I kept my eyes on Sal. At the time, I didn't know who he was, but later I was told by one of Lou's buddies that our passenger was Salvatore Gravano, known as 'Sammy the Bull.' I learned later that Sammy the Bull was connected to the Gambino Family.

This incident convinced me to sell the plane, but not before it went down. A few weeks later, my buddies, Dana and David, went with me to the Savannah Airport to fly the plane a few miles offshore to look at the collision of two cargo ships near the mouth of the Savannah River. We intended to fly over the scene and get a good look at what was happening because we were curious. We went to the hangar to make sure that we had topped the fuel tanks and tested for sugar. To my surprise, the plane was not there. I checked the registry and found that Grumman Aircraft had leased my plane to fly a jet part to New York, which was allowed under my contract with the airport. It was due back any minute.

As I was looking up in the sky, I saw my plane. That's when I noticed the airport staff frantically running towards the runway. I stopped the supervisor and asked what was happening. "The tower informed us that an Aero Commander can't lock its landing gear." I knew it was my plane. My buddies and I became part of a large group of onlookers as my plane circled the airport to burn off fuel.

The plane was finally given clearance to land. I watched as it slowly descended. My attention was on my plane's landing gear. Was it going to lock down when it touched the tarmac? As it slowly approached the landing, I watched the wheels collapse. The plane went belly-up, ripping off the two props and the underbelly while spinning out of control and onto the grass.

After the sugar incident, this was the last straw. Whether or not it was just a coincidence or another attempt on my life, I can't say. However, I never flew the plane again. Once it was repaired, I sold it. I'm still alive.

Bubba's Plane

39. Overkill

In every lawyer's trial experience, some events loom so large that others are completely overshadowed. Some are humorous while others are extremely sad. The one I am about to relate was shocking because of the overkill.

The case began when a man from North Carolina was reported missing by his family. An investigation ensued, and it was determined that he had disappeared from his motel room leaving his clothes and briefcase. An all-points bulletin was dispatched giving a description of his car, along with the tag number on his automobile. Nine days later, his automobile was stopped and three suspects were arrested. From information received from one of the suspects, the victim's body was found in a wooded area with a nine-millimeter bullet in his head. Once again, I was told by the court that I was to represent the alleged trigger man. My client (along with his brother and another suspect) was charged with murder, armed robbery, kidnapping, and auto theft. I obtained a copy of the police investigation report before I talked to my client, Patrick Mack, who was in the county jail being held without bond. The report outlined a sad and gruesome killing.

The victim was a good family man on business in Savannah. The assailants had hidden near his motel room the night he'd arrived and attacked him as he'd been unloading his luggage from the trunk of his car. Putting him in the trunk, they had driven his car to an area called 'Big John's Pond.' On arrival, they had ordered the victim out of the trunk and made him get on his knees and beg for his life; then they had shot him in the head. They took his money and his car and left him at the scene.

Mack and his brother were no strangers to crime in Savannah for they both had records a mile long. Mack was a young black man in his early twenties with a bad attitude. Talking to him was useless because he never made sense or told me the truth. The latter didn't matter so long as he could give me a sensible and defensible explanation as to why he'd been caught in the victim's car along with a nine-millimeter pistol, but he couldn't. He merely blamed one of the other suspects who had confessed to being there but said that Mack had shot the guy.

"Mack, what reason would he have to lie?"

"I dunno, but he's a liar," was his repeated response.

"How did you get the gun that killed the man?"

"I bought it for five dollars from a dude."

"What dude?"

"A dude I know."

"What's his name?" I persisted.

"Cornbread."

"Where does he live?"

"Somewhere in East Savannah. Hey man, I ain't gonna cause no heat on my buddy."

"Mack, I'm only asking you what the DA is going to ask you. Your buddy told the cops that you shot the guy."

"That dude, he lying. He lying."

"He's not lying unless we can prove it, and if you can't prove it, you're going to get the electric chair. It's as simple as that. So don't tie my hands by not telling me the truth. If I know the truth, then maybe I can figure a way out for you," I tried to explain without much success.

When I left the jail that day after my first interview, I knew nothing more than I had known after reading the police report. In fact, I knew less. A denial of the suspect's statement and the refusal to tell me the truth gave me an absolute blank. I had nothing left but my imagination and a bad client who would not, under any circumstance, impress or draw sympathy from a jury. As I went to my office, I could only think of another long-drawn-out death penalty appeal that could take ten years or more. Somehow, I had to come up with a defense I could run with.

I went back to the drawing board. I took the police report and the statement of the co-conspirator and read them over and over, hoping for a defense to jump out. There was no way to get around the facts that Mack had helped abduct the man from the motel, put him in the trunk of the man's own car, taken him to an isolated area, robbed him, and had been present when the victim had been shot in the head while on his knees begging for his life. In fact, Mack had been holding the gun on the man most of the time, and the only thing in Mack's favor was he had refused to shoot the man and had handed the pistol to one of his partners who'd promptly stepped up and shot him. This was a death penalty case if I ever saw one and I had seen quite a few. To make matters worse, since Mack denied he'd even been present, I couldn't attack any of the informer's story. I had to accept the whole statement as true without any contradiction, except that Mack wasn't there.

After several months of pre-trial sparring, the case was called to trial before Judge Oliver. Nothing had happened to change my mind as to the probable outcome because Mack was still refusing to tell me the truth. When we selected the jury that morning, I was resolved to put as much error into the record as I could so that Mack could get a new trial and hopefully wear down the DA's office with appeals. I can assure you that when you start a major murder trial relying solely on those tactics, your defense of the accused is weak, at best. However, that was my situation, like it or not.

Bill Searcy was the assistant DA trying the case. Bill and I had clashed on many occasions, one time when I had run against him a second time in the primary for state senator. The campaign had been very heated with Bill accusing me of being influenced by the Mafia because I had represented Lou in his suit against *Playboy* magazine. While I had represented Lou, and eventually, settled both suits under a confidentiality agreement, I had not been under the influence of the Mafia. Lou had been my client at the time. But to down-home Southern voters, the connection had placed a lot of doubts in their minds. The vote had been close; I lost by slightly more than a hundred votes. I took the loss hard and for a while, I was extremely bitter towards Searcy, but as the years passed Bill and I became good friends.

Searcy was beaten by a Republican two years later in the Nixon landslide and joined the district attorney's office as a trial lawyer. He became perhaps their best, except for Ryan, and was one of the few you could count on to keep their word in plea negotiating. I had a lot of fun trying cases against him and knew that he would eat me alive in this one. So when he entered the courtroom the first morning of the Mack trial, his sly wink came as no surprise. All I could do was shake my head, knowing what was coming.

For two days, I had to sit and listen to a tragic story of a merciless killing for no reason at all. I tried to object to anything and everything that even hinted of an error, either past, present, or future in an attempt to create law where there was none. How successful I would be, I'd never know because of the surprising outcome of this case. I'm rapidly approaching the shocking moment.

After the lunch recess on the third day of trial, Searcy was winding down the State's case after proving all the essentials of the crime charged against Mack. Over many objections, he had gotten in the damaging statement of the co-conspirator and had his way on virtually all issues, what few there were. I had made a valiant attempt to discount the statement concerning the man being shot on his knees begging for mercy by proving that the autopsy report indicated that the man had been standing up at the time of the bullet's entry into his head. I thought that if I could prove the co-conspirator was lying on that major point, then perhaps the jury would discount his entire statement and believe Mack when he told them that he hadn't been present.

However, I knew this was wishful thinking and the autopsy could easily have supported the 'on the knees' theory if explained to the jury properly in Searcy's closing argument. He knew what I was attempting to do and knew that I would make an eloquent argument on the believability of the co-conspirator. My attack on the autopsy report had been made earlier that morning and I had hoped it would knock Searcy off stride a little, at least enough to ruffle his feathers.

I noticed that Searcy had placed a box under his counsel table when we had returned from lunch. I thought it strange since I knew of no other evidence not already presented and accepted by the judge, so I forgot about the box once Searcy began questioning his last witness. When he was through with the witness, he turned and said, "Judge, I need a few minutes so I can review my notes and make sure I can rest at this time."

Judge Oliver looked up from reading his jury instruction book and replied, "I'll give you as much time as you need. I'll recess the jury for fifteen minutes. Deputy, escort the jury to their room."

The judge motioned for me to come up to the bench.

"How many witnesses do you intend on calling?" he asked.

"None."

"None?"

"My client will probably get up on the stand and deny he was there, and that's all."

"You don't expect anyone to believe him after all the evidence I've heard, do you?"

"No," and I turned and walked back to my counsel table knowing full well of the many years I would be committed to this case. This day was to be a grain of sand on Savannah Beach compared to the many hours, days, and years I expected to spend on appeal. I sat down and waited for the conclusion.

My ole' buddy Searcy stooped under his table, picked up the box, and walked to the court reporter's desk. He very carefully placed the box in front of the lady court reporter and told the judge he was ready to resume his case.

"Your Honor, the State is ready to offer its final piece of evidence and then we will rest." The judge ordered the jury back into the courtroom. Searcy walked over to the box, opened it, and slowly lifted out a man's head. He placed the head on the desk of the court reporter for the purpose of having it marked as an exhibit by sticking a tab to it with a number. Of course, we didn't get that far. The court reporter immediately fainted, falling to the floor. The judge turned away from the sight. I couldn't believe my eyes! Searcy had brought the victim's head into the courtroom, and I'm not talking about merely a human skull. The head had hair and dried skin with deteriorated features! While the courtroom was in complete disarray, Searcy stood in amazement at the reaction he was receiving from his surprise evidence.

Judge Oliver turned his chair back around towards the courtroom. Slamming his gavel, he yelled at Searcy to cover the 'thing' up or put it back in the box. Searcy quickly obeyed and the courtroom settled down to a low murmur. I was still sitting and still stunned. The court reporter was still on the floor when Oliver ordered the bailiff to remove the jury to the jury room and told him to allow any of them as much time as they needed in the restrooms. They filed out of the courtroom staring at the box and Searcy. I waited patiently for the jury to leave in order that I might make my comments in the way of an objection that would have a lot of merit, but Oliver was to have his say first.

Meanwhile, everyone had forgotten that the court reporter had fainted and was still unconscious on the floor, except for a lady on the jury. As she was leaving, she asked the bailiff if she could help the court reporter. The juror asked for a cold wet towel and began wiping the court reporter's face. Once revived and off the floor, she gave Searcy a stare that could have shucked oysters fifty feet away and went over to the reporter's desk. Making sure that the DA got her message, she asked the judge to excuse her for the rest of the day. He agreed, and another court reporter took her place.

"Before we go back on the record, I want to know if I was dreaming or not? Mr. Searcy, was that the head of the victim in this case?" the judge demanded in a steely voice knowing full well what the answer would be.

"Yes, Your Honor, but I don't understand what all the furor and excitement was over. This is a valuable piece of evidence that will answer what Mr. Haupt is going to argue about. It's necessary."

"Mr. Searcy, whatever possessed you to believe that I would allow the man's head to be introduced as evidence? And tell me please, why you ever thought of bringing this head in the courtroom in the first place? I've been on the bench for forty years, and I thought I had seen everything, but obviously I hadn't. This takes the cake."

"But, Judge, I know what Mr. Haupt is going to argue to the jury and this is the only way I could counter it," replied Searcy.

Judge Oliver looked at Searcy still in bewilderment and disgust, as only he could do. "Mr. Searcy, what are you afraid of in this case? You have a confession by an eyewitness; the defendant is arrested with possession of the victim's automobile and murder weapon. How much stronger a case do you want? Is there any doubt that this man will be convicted? Why are you running in fear of Mr. Haupt's final argument? Tell me, please! Maybe I've missed the point altogether."

"Your Honor, I appreciate your observation concerning the strength of the State's case, but I know from past experience that Mr. Haupt can take one small loose end and untie the knot. I was only making sure it wasn't going to happen in this case. I'm sorry if I offended Your Honor, and I will remove the box from the courtroom."

Searcy walked over to the box sitting on the court reporter's table that now contained, once again, the victim's head and gave it to one of his assistants to carry away.

While Searcy had been trying to appease the judge, I'd been making notes on how to make this incident aid my case. The word 'overkill' kept flashing in my mind. He had overkilled his case and given me something to hang my hat on. Now, let me explain to you what overkill means in a criminal trial. In the normal prosecution of a criminal case, a jury is pre-conditioned to hear the evidence presented by the State that tends to prove a defendant's guilt. They expect the State to prove the normal prerequisites for establishing guilt, such as motive, opportunity, and the ability to commit the crime. Then comes hard evidence like possession of the murder weapon and the fruits of the crime, like the theft of the victim's automobile. These factors alone were sufficient in this case to convict. But there was more. The State had introduced the testimony and statement of an accomplice and had expected the jury to believe him. Normally, and without more, a jury wouldn't hesitate to have believed this accomplice because his statement matched the evidence.

Now, this is where the overkill factor comes in. When the State goes further and tries through some unusual or desperate moves to bolster or back up a piece of evidence, such as the testimony of an accomplice, the end result is they actually place doubt in the jurors' minds where there previously had been none. In other words, they have shown insecurity or doubt in their own witness. Instead of displaying confidence and belief in their own case against the defendant, their attempt to back up the witness, as if in desperation, is a subconscious signal to the jury that their evidence, or witness in this case, may not be worthy of belief. The result is that the State actually places the reasonable doubt of guilt in the jurors' minds themselves without the defendant having to deny the witness's testimony.

The degree of desperation is also in direct proportion to the degree of doubt in the jury's mind. Slight overkill brings only slight doubt and means very little to the outcome of a case. On the other hand, a very desperate move such as Searcy's could be fatal to the State's case if handled properly by the defendant's lawyer. By this I mean, the defense has to take advantage of the overkill. Remember, the jury was out when Searcy had explained his problem and the judge had admonished him. The head of the victim was now removed from the courtroom and when the jury came back, Searcy would close his case and try to act as if nothing had ever happened, but a good defense attorney wouldn't let that happen. Needless to say, I didn't.

When the jury returned to the jury box and before Searcy had the opportunity to close his case, I stood up and really made the judge angry: "Your Honor, I want the record to show that Mr. Searcy attempted to place the victim's head into evidence for the purpose of trying to prove that the victim was shot while kneeling. For some reason, he didn't believe his own witness." Searcy started screaming, "Objection! Objection! Objection!" over and over and over and was obviously shaken. Oliver quickly ordered the jury removed from the jury box once again. When the last juror was out of the courtroom, there was stone silence. Oliver was glaring at me and was obviously shaken. He knew full well what I had done and why I had done it. He knew that I was going to hammer overkill home and he knew that a conviction in a gruesome murder case was now in doubt. He also knew that Searcy's error in judgment was to be the theme of the trial for the remainder of the case and no one, in his time on the bench, had a more effective closing statement in a criminal case than the one I was about to present.

"Mr. Haupt, I have no intention of letting you re-hash the incident of the evidence that I have ruled out. I know what you have in mind and I can assure you I am not going to aid you in your endeavor or let you take control of my courtroom. So listen to me very carefully. I have made a ruling that the victim's head is not admissible and that is the end of it. Do you understand?"

"Your Honor, I understand your sentiment, but I disagree with your instructions not to mention the matter again. I am going to argue to this jury that Mr. Searcy didn't believe his own witness and went to the vulgar extreme to try to save his case. I can assure this court they will hear all manner of possible reasons why Mr. Searcy chose to do this. I was appointed to defend Mr. Mack to the best of my ability, and I can assure this court that I will assert every legal right and use every legal means at my disposal in my efforts. If you restrict these efforts, then you'll be committing an intentional error. I'm sorry, Judge, but I've got my job to do just like you do. If you don't like the way I'm doing it, then fire me. Remember, you hired me for this case."

The courtroom was again filled with dead silence, as if waiting for a volcano to erupt. But the eruption never came. Oliver knew I was right, although he wasn't overjoyed by it. His anger or frustration was now directed towards Searcy for creating the monster.

"Mr. Searcy, did you want to place your objection on the record for whatever purpose you can think of?" he asked.

"Your Honor, I want the record to show that I never formally made the introduction of the evidence in question and that Mr. Haupt is out of order in his remarks."

"What do you say to that, Mr. Haupt?"

"He's wrong. The only reason the exhibit was not marked with a number was the court reporter fainted. Searcy did everything in his power to have it identified as evidence."

"Well, I'm going to try and finish this trial today. Mr. Searcy, you attempted to offer it and I am going to leave it at that." Turning to the bailiff, the judge said, "Get the jury back in here and let's finish the trial. Mr. Searcy, I believe you were going to rest your case."

"Yes, Your Honor. The State has nothing further."

Judge Oliver murmured, "Thank God."

The bailiff led the jury back in, and Searcy repeated his announcement concerning resting his case.

"Mr. Haupt, you may proceed for the defendant," Oliver advised, still obviously unhappy with the direction the case had taken.

"Your Honor, we have no evidence to offer and we close," I announced. Oliver and Searcy were surprised that I was not going to offer alibi witnesses or put the defendant on the stand. But they should have guessed that I would not have put a defendant on the stand who was belligerent and couldn't help his case with the best of his lies. I was content with my own ability to argue Searcy's overkill, and I didn't want Mack to take that advantage away from me.

There was another advantage that the law of Georgia gave me by making this decision. By not offering any evidence on behalf of the defendant, I would have the last argument. In other words, I would talk to the jury after Searcy and he would have no opportunity to reply, correct, or explain whatever argument I would make to the jury. To me, this right was worth far more than anything Mack could have told the jury. I also knew that Searcy would spend most of his closing argument trying to anticipate what I was going to say and offering an explanation before it was said. He had done this before in other trials where I had claimed the closing, rather than argue the strength of his own case.

It is a proven fact in the judicial scheme of things that the last words concerning a case before a jury are remembered over earlier statements. In other words, the last plea is the best plea, and far more effective than a plea made by a DA forty minutes before. That tactic and Searcy's response occurred as anticipated. Searcy used three-quarters of his time trying to overcome his overkill and apologizing for his error in judgment.

When it came time for my argument, I got up and walked over to the jury box. I quietly said, "Out of respect for the poor victim, who is lying in his grave without his head, I will not remind the jury of what happened today. Out of respect for his family seated in this courtroom, I will not mention it again."

Instead, I believed that overkill had already done my argument for me, and I spent the entire time telling the jury that Mack's mere presence at the time of the killing was not enough to convict him under the law. I urged them to believe the co-conspirator, even though Searcy hadn't when he'd said that Mack had refused to kill the man and had handed the gun to someone else who'd shot him. I told them that Mack had made the decision not to murder the man and such a decision should not be held against him. When the jury returned to the courtroom after four hours of deliberating, their decision came as no surprise to me. They found him not guilty of murder but guilty of armed robbery. Mack was sentenced to ten years in prison and five more on probation. Mack died seven months later of natural causes. Perhaps a greater force applied judgment in this case when the system could not.

40. The Final Issue

"Some things are not what they look and feel like."

—Louie the Tailor' Rosanova

By 1980, in my early forties, I was no longer the naive young lawyer who had set out to conquer the world. Although I still had the skills that had won many seemingly indefensible capital offense cases, I was tired. I was tired of having to defend clients accused of every despicable and senseless crime committed in South Georgia. I was tired of the pressure it placed on me and my family and the scorn of former friends and admirers who'd thought I would be governor someday. I began spending more time at the inn with Lou. The Teamsters' problems were easy to fix compared to fixing a man headed for the electric chair—or should I say, men who were headed to the chair.

By this time in my life, I had successfully created a reputation for being the best criminal trial lawyer in South Georgia. But that title had not come without collateral damage. I had lost my sense of direction and begun believing that truth had little to do with the trial of a case. Facts weren't as important as how good the lawyer was and how well he could confuse the jury and, in many cases, the judge. My motivation then had little to do with justice. I wanted to win.

Cases such as the baby being thrown off the bridge, the two nurses being raped and shot in the head, Floyd Brown's freedom taken away for thirty pieces of silver, a beautiful little girl being cruelly molested by her father, and so many similar cases began taking a heavy toll on me. I was getting tired of being the savior to the poor and the devil to the rich and elite of Savannah society. I was beginning to realize that being the lawyer for the Teamsters and the Mafia had lost its glitter. My encounters with Dean Martin, Buddy Hackett, and the guys from Vegas and Hollywood were not so special after all. It certainly wasn't worth the losses I had suffered and the hurt it had caused my family and friends.

By this time, I had learned that Fitzsimmons was an FBI informant along with many of the union officials that I had frequently played golf with. I had learned where Jimmy Hoffa was buried and that my friend Lou, and some of the men I was defending and socializing with, had been involved in the killing of the president of the United States—and many other crimes under investigation by the FBI. Finally, it was about this time that I learned that the Teamsters had put the inn up for sale due to the heat coming from the Carter Crime Commission. It had become obvious that they were moving on, and so was Lou. An era was coming to an end in Savannah and on this small coastal island. More importantly, an end was coming to me. I was no longer a warrior; I had become unmoored and set adrift. One of the last cases I tried was the Ronald Murray terroristic threats trial in early 1981. Because of its importance to me and my fate, I give this accounting.

I watched the movements of Ronald Murray's eyes. They never appeared to focus on any one object, and never on me. There was no eye contact at all. He reminded me of a gerbil and of my years—or should I say, my one year—of having gerbils as house pets. My daughter had seen a pair of gerbils in a pet shop and thought they were the cutest little animals she had ever seen. Of course, she loved all kinds of animals, including these gerbils that looked like rats, moved like rats, and acted like rats. And, they eat their young.

Ronald Murray was a small, thin man with a short, sharp nose, and pointy chin. With those beady eyes, constantly shifting from side-to-side, yes, he reminded me of a caged gerbil. He had called me to the jail to hire me in a case where he'd been charged with threatening the life of his wife. The formal charge was called 'terroristic threats' and was a misdemeanor. In other words, it was an offense of lesser gravity than a felony and the maximum penalty he could have received was a jail sentence of one year and a fine of one thousand dollars, either or both.

"Tell me about it," I said.

"I told her I'd kill her if she came home late again. That's all I said, Mr. Haupt. I was mad, and I didn't mean it all that much. I just wanted her to do right," Murray answered, still making gerbil-like movements with his head and beady eyes.

"How long have you been locked up?"

"Ten months."

"Ten months! You couldn't post a bond?"

"I ain't never been given no bond," he replied.

"The judge never set a bond?" I asked, knowing that something was drastically wrong or that Murray was ignorant and that was not apparent.

"No, I've written the judge five times," he replied.

"Which judge?"

"Judge Cook."

"He's the probate judge. He's got nothing to do with criminal cases. The state court judge is the one you should have written."

I made a fee arrangement with him and left the jail wondering why a man charged with a misdemeanor didn't have a bond set, and why he had been locked up for ten months without a trial for threatening his wife. I saw nothing difficult about the case and it should have had a quick conclusion, or so I thought.

I went straight to Judge Elmore's office hoping to shock him with the obvious oversight. I enjoyed surprising judges and listening to poor excuses from assistant district attorneys as to why cases were not called to trial. I was greeted warmly by Elmore with a firm handshake. "Bubba, how's it going? I keep up with the newspapers and some of the cases they hang around your neck."

I sat down in the chair across from his big oak desk. "Judge, can I bend your ear a short moment?" Elmore was always a good listener and courteous to lawyers. In my mind, he was the perfect judge for what I perceived to be a simple case with an obviously simple solution.

"I've been retained by a man named Ronald Murray, who's been in the county jail for ten months. He says there was no bond set. Judge, as you are well aware, if he was found guilty and got the maximum twelve months for a misdemeanor, he'd be out in six months because of earned time."

I was not prepared for the answer I was to receive from the always mild-mannered Elmore, who above all the other judges in the courthouse was most sensitive to human injustices.

"Bubba, I'm sorry, but I can't set a bond for Mr. Murray, and there isn't any way I will let him out of jail without a trial."

I was astonished by his answer. "Why?"

"I've heard too much about him, and I'm told he's extremely dangerous."

"But, Judge, he had a right to be treated like any other person, criminal or not. The man had an argument with his wife and threatened her. Good Lord, that's an everyday occurrence in some families. You don't have a big enough jail to prevent that crime if it is one."

"I'm sorry, but I've heard too much."

"From whom?"

"The police and DA's office."

"Judge, I can't believe you're not going to set a bond in a misdemeanor case on information given to you by the police. You don't work for them. You're supposed to be impartial."

That upset the judge. "Bubba, I'll set the trial for next week and we'll leave it up to a jury. That's the best I'm gonna do. That's all I'm going to say on the matter. I'll have the DA let you know what day. We already have a jury coming in."

He ended the conversation and walked into his secretary's office. I quietly left. I had never seen this side of Elmore and I felt a crusade coming on for Mr. Murray. If I won next week, I planned to recommend he sue the judge, the county, and the DA who'd put the 'dangerous' label on him. This was ridiculous.

I met with Murray a couple of times preparing for trial, trying to avoid any surprises. I asked him repeatedly if there was anything else, other than threatening his wife. Did he point a gun at her? Did he hit her? But the answer was always 'no.' He convinced me that he was telling the truth even though he was still unable to stay focused. He still made me think of those awful gerbils.

The morning before his trial I had coffee with Ryan.

"Bubsy, why is Elmore afraid of Ronald Murray?"

Ryan put his coffee down and looked me in the eyes without a hint of his usual humor. "Bubba, Murray is the most dangerous man in this county. He is as crazy as a bed bug. Compared to him, Matthew Washington is a priest."

"Bubsy, where are y'all getting this information? What's he done? He's only charged with a misdemeanor," I asked in bewilderment.

"Bubba, we can't prove it, but we're told he's killed several people and he burned his mother's house down. She's had him committed several times to mental hospitals, but they don't keep him long. Bubba, she's scared to death Murray is gonna kill her."

Ryan paused, took a sip of coffee and continued, "We have no doubt he's mentally insane and would kill his wife if we turned him loose."

"Then why don't you agree to an insanity plea and let's put him in a mental hospital and get him help?" I asked what seemed to be a logical question that offered a very logical solution.

"No! We couldn't do that. They'd let him out in a few days or certify him sane and there would be no telling what he'd do. He always gets mad at those who try to help him. No, we can't run the risk."

"Bubsy, what you're saying is the man is undoubtedly insane, but can't be trusted to be legally found insane for fear he'd be set free."

"That's right!"

"Then the system's wrong, not Murray. The law says a man who can't discern right from wrong is legally insane and is not criminally responsible for his acts."

"That sounds good, but we can't let it work that way. The public isn't safe unless people like Murray are in prison, not hospitals."

I could understand Ryan's sincerity but not his logic, and certainly not his method. Our laws concerning the mentally ill were based upon humane principles with a correct application of both justice and mercy. It made America unique in that our system of justice required that before a person could be punished and his liberty and constitutional rights taken away from him (or her), the person must first have been competent to have committed a crime. In other words, he must first be able to know right from wrong before he could be punished. That is why we don't put three-year-old children in prison. That is why the prosecutor must first prove that everyone he prosecutes or accuses of a crime must have the requisite mental intent and capacity to commit the particular crime.

Prior to Matthew Washington, when an accused person was found insane, he was transported to a state mental hospital and remained there until he was certified sane. In Matthew's case, as I pointed out previously, he was certifiably insane but had been certified sane and released within thirty days to kill again (or, as I sincerely believe, threaten to kill again). That system failed because of incompetence in the application of the law. Because of Matthew Washington, Georgia laws were changed.

The major change occurred in the procedure after a defendant was found 'not guilty by reason of insanity.' Instead of the state mental institution having the decision on release, the presiding superior court judge was burdened with this determination, and only after the accused had been hospitalized for a year. This provision showed the distrust that the state legislature had in its own mental health system. It took the decision away from incompetent professionals and placed it in the hands of an elected non-professional. What the State should have done was replace the incompetent psychiatrists with competent ones and required the system to function as it was designed. Instead, it had complicated the process and put the ultimate outcome in the hands of the legal experts rather than the medical professionals. It hadn't cured the system, as Ryan was admitting to me, because Murray would be out in a year.

What I couldn't get across to Ryan was that Murray was only charged with a misdemeanor and could only be sentenced to twelve months and didn't have to serve but six months. Had they offered him a 'not guilty plea by reason of insanity,' he would have gone to a mental hospital for the entire year. That would have been in everyone's interest, including Murray's.

"Bubsy, let me have a plea of insanity and that will get him to a hospital for at least ninety days. He's gotten no treatment in the county jail for the last ten months."

"I'm sorry, Bubba, but we can't deal on him. He's too risky."

I could understand his position because the Matthew Washington fiasco had hurt him politically even though none of it had been his fault.

"Then it looks like we try him tomorrow and you'll probably have to let him go."

"So long as a jury does it, there's nothing I can do about it."

The following morning, we selected a jury in the case of the *State of Georgia vs. Ronald Murray*. For the first time since meeting Murray, I could understand why he never focused and had gerbil-like head and eye movements; he was crazy, at least that's what everyone was saying. I couldn't permit their opinions to cloud my responsibilities to my client because I would be prejudging him, and that would violate his right to a fair and impartial trial. And, to be perfectly honest with you, I wasn't that much concerned about him because he had only threatened his wife and had only been charged with a misdemeanor.

The trial went along as expected and I made a fool of his wife. I accused her of bringing the charge so he'd be out of the way while she got a divorce and took everything away from him. By being in jail, fighting this charge, he was helpless to defend a divorce suit. The wife would never admit it, but the jury appeared to agree with me as indicated by their affirmative nods.

In my closing argument, I condemned everyone who had a hand in keeping a husband in jail almost ten months because his wife wanted to get an uncontested divorce and take his property and kids. I'll never forget the heyday I had with the unfairness of the system when they don't like you.

As I approached the jury box to begin my closing arguments, the jury became alert. They watched me with anticipation.

"Members of the jury, it is inconceivable that a husband and wife can have a quarrel in which the husband issues a threat and then he is thrown in jail with no bond and no trial for ten months. Under Moscow standards, this would have been harsh and unfair punishment. The district attorney's office has permitted this woman to use them and turn them into a Gestapo. You can't give him back the ten months he's served in jail, or his property he's lost in the divorce, but you can let him go free this afternoon and send a message to the perpetrators of this injustice that the public won't tolerate such tactics. If you don't, then God forbid that it will be you the next time."

I continued, "The only evidence they have is his wife telling you he threatened to kill her in the heat of an argument and that she believed he would because he's crazy. Why? He didn't harm her when he made the threat, and he was firing mad at her! Members of the jury, if that was a crime that required a husband to go to jail, then we need to build a new jail the size of Yankee Stadium just to accommodate the mad husbands in this county. And don't any of you feel confident that you wouldn't be one of them. Go to your jury room and write 'Not Guilty' and let it be your condemnation of the injustice done to Ronald Murray."

The jury retired and returned within ten minutes with a verdict of 'Not Guilty,' and that was the end of the case, or so I thought. Six weeks later I was to learn that this case, this easy victory, this eloquent defense and condemnation of gross injustice, would explode in my face and again change the mental health laws in Georgia, but it would do more than that to me. It would be, as my daddy would say, "the last button on Gabriel's drawers."

Approximately six weeks had gone by since the Murray verdict when a late-night movie on TV was interrupted with a special news bulletin. I was dozing and could hear the news reporter talking about a triple murder at a local bar located in the Howard Johnson's Motor Lodge. I became interested when they announced that they were switching to live coverage at the scene. The cameras focused on the entrance to the bar and then to the police car where they had the suspect in custody. I couldn't believe my eyes, and I really didn't want to either, but there was Ronald Murray smiling at the camera. The news reporter went on to say that one of the victims was his wife and that the other two were a young couple who had been sitting at the bar when they were shot in the back of the head. Their identities were not available at that time. The cameras showed the covered bodies as they were being carried out to awaiting ambulances. You can't imagine the opinion I had of myself that night while I anxiously awaited news of the names of the dead couple.

The following day was no better for me because I had still not learned the identities of the couple. I went to my office and refused to take all telephone calls. I was blaming myself for three deaths and my refusal to listen to Ryan, Elmore, and Murray's wife. She'd known! She'd known that he would kill her. I began imagining how she'd felt when she'd heard my jury argument and the jury's verdict. It must have been the same feeling when an accused hears the death penalty announced. How she must have hated me, and how she must have lived in fear until the night of the execution. I couldn't justify this one as merely doing my duty. After all, lawyers are supposed to have a conscience just as much as anyone when they enter the courtroom. I believed that I had been leaving mine outside, as though it were a wet raincoat and didn't belong inside where it was dry. I had come to the realization that I had put Murray on the streets and prevented the authorities from keeping him away from the public and away from killing his wife.

As I sat behind my elaborate dark oak desk, I looked at the picture of my family. It shared space on my desk with a picture of me and Bo Callaway. Bo's picture represented my first foray into state politics. Because of my association with Callaway, I had a pathway to Governor Lester Maddox about supporting changes to the criminal mental health policy. And while a mental health bill had been passed that mandated treatment for a year, it was not enough. I heard Lucy, in the reception area, greeting Lou. Lucy followed shortly with coffee.

"Cracker, don't blame yourself. You did your job. Keep your head up."

I was too weary to engage in any discussion of Murray. Lou saw my distress and changed the subject.

"Cracker, you ain't been on the golf course in a week or two. How about let's play this weekend. We've got a lot to talk about and I want to do it on the course."

I knew that Lou wanted to talk business and I knew not to question him at this moment. In fact, I was so tired, I didn't want to talk further. We finished our coffee and he got up to leave.

"Cracker, keep your head up. Call me when you get to the course this weekend."

The next few weeks were difficult for me. I couldn't forget the role I'd played in this tragedy of errors. I did reconcile with myself that I wasn't the only one to blame. First, no one trusted the ability of the mental health system to deal with serious offenders. Instead, they kept a man in jail until his conviction or release. If convicted, he would be shipped to the diagnostic center in Jackson, Georgia, where he would be locked down twenty-four hours a day, seven days a week, without any psychiatric treatment of any kind. Second, they would keep a man in jail with no bond for ten months with no psychiatric help. Not only was this against the law, but it also fueled his hatred and anger towards the system. Third, the prosecution should have accepted my offer of an insanity plea. This would have required Murray to be sent to the state mental hospital for a minimum of ninety days for evaluation. Medication could have been used to diffuse the situation.

This case, like the Washington case, changed the mental health laws again. Within a year's time, Georgia had adopted the 'Guilty but Insane' pleas. This meant that even though a person may be totally incompetent and unable to discern right from wrong, he or she would nevertheless be sent to a mental hospital and not released until the presiding judge held a hearing to determine whether he or she was no longer a danger to the public.

This was one of the last cases I tried, so it seems appropriate to name this chapter 'The Final Issue.' I was morally and spiritually bankrupt. The system had taken its toll on me. I no longer liked what I was doing, and I needed peace in my life. An era in Savannah and on this small island was coming to a close. More importantly, I was coming to a close. I was flaming out.

41. The FBI Informants

The entire time I was representing the Teamsters and Louie the Tailor—which was about ten years—the Savannah Inn and Country Club, its owners, management, and special guests were constantly under surveillance by the Justice Department, the FBI, and the Internal Revenue Service.

There were many reasons for this. First, the constant investigation taking place in Washington concerning the finances of the world's largest, richest, and most powerful union, made the Teamsters a political target for hungry politicians. Second, it was no secret that organized crime figures had a say in who received vast personal loans from the Teamsters. In other words, it was all about the money, except for the Hoffa issue.

When I say 'money,' I mean huge sums. Back in the seventies, 1.5 million Teamsters paid at least $20 a month in union dues. That's $30 million income a month. In today's currency market, that would be equivalent to at least $350–400 million a month, or $4.8 billion a year. That was only dues and had nothing to do with the premiums each member paid for the health care program run by Allen Dorfman. No other private corporations, foundations, banks, or hedge funds came close to matching their cash. As I discussed earlier, they even bailed out the C&S Bank (Bank of America) during my time.

Remember the 'Golden Rule.' Not the biblical one, the practical one: "He who has the gold, rules!" And no historian will disagree that the Teamsters—with the support of organized crime in the seventies—enjoyed almost unlimited power in Washington through its ability to fund state and national candidates. As proof of this, go on the internet and search for the hundreds of public officials who were eventually indicted and sent to prison in the eighties for various crimes, such as accepting bribes, embezzlement, and theft of campaign funds.

Also, understand that the Teamsters had the ability to shut down commerce at any time it saw fit. On the command of the president of the International

Brotherhood of Teamsters, trucking could stop at any moment. If it did, then planes wouldn't fly, trucks wouldn't haul, and produce markets would shut down from coast to coast. And more importantly, family cars and public transportation would cease for lack of gas, shutting down millions of jobs. Yes, that made the Teamsters the power that ruled.

Although Bobby Kennedy began the war on the Teamsters that ultimately brought them under the control of a federal trustee in 1989, it was the Hoffa issue that brought the heat on the Teamsters and the surveillance at the inn. I can recall vividly how Louie the Tailor pointed out to me a 'rat' standing or sitting in a golf cart somewhere on the golf course watching Lou. And he made no bones about it. He would usually call out to them.

"Hey, rat, come out in the sunshine and breathe the fresh air. The birds are going to shit on you if you stay under that tree much longer," he would yell at the undercover agent who looked out of place in his shiny street shoes on the golf course. No golfer would ever wear street shoes out on the course. Hence, this one fact made them stand out, and they never figured out how Louie the Tailor could uncover them so easily.

I recall, in particular, a justice department agent staying at the inn for six weeks, supposedly undercover. However, when Lou uncovered him the second day he was there, they eventually became friends, and Lou taught him how to hit a golf ball.

I guess what I'm trying to explain is that Louie the Tailor didn't mind the secret agents. What he did mind, was an informant; that was something that Lou had been raised to hate through the Sicilian culture. To him, an informant was a friend that betrayed him. And there were many, but not in the Mafia at that time, or so we thought.

Unlike the Mafia, the Teamster officials were not under the Omerta code. Hence, I don't recall a 'connected' friend of Lou's turning informant. If he did, then he would have been dealt with according to their code. However, a Teamster official was a different animal.

Lou's best friend in the hierarchy of the Teamsters organization was Frank Fitzsimmons. It was Lou who played a major role in rallying local union members in Chicago, Detroit, and New York to elect Fitzsimmons to succeed Hoffa as the union's president. Because of his loyalty to Fitzsimmons, Lou was given 'untouchable' status in union affairs and was the permanent CEO at the inn in Savannah. I know this because Lou made it no secret when we traveled, drank at Dino's Den, or when we played golf. This status also made him a favorite with the Dons of the Five Families, including Tony Accardo of the Chicago Outfit. Such connections proved to me how Louie the Tailor could call Sandy Miller of Delta and threaten to stop the Delta flights if Miller didn't add six more flights to Savannah for the golf tournaments as mentioned earlier.

In August 1981, I got a call from Lou to come down to Dino's. At that time, Dino's Den did not open until four o'clock in the afternoon. The call came at noon. That had me wondering. Lou wanted to talk with me in a closed nightclub with no one around. Something was up.

I drove straight to the entrance of Dino's. It was deserted, as it should have been at one o'clock in the afternoon. I approached the huge oak door and knocked. A few minutes later the door slowly opened and Lou motioned for me to follow him to the empty bar. He had a fifth of vodka on a table and a couple of glasses. One had ice in it and was half full.

As I sat down, I said, "What's up?"

"Cracker, someone's cut my heart out." He paused and asked me if I wanted a lemon in the drink he was pouring for me. I nodded in agreement.

"Cracker, Fitz is a rat. He's been one since '72."

"Lou, are you sure? How did you get the information? Is it credible?"

He went over to the bar and picked up the slender briefcase that he often carried with him when we met on business or traveled. He walked back to the table and opened it and removed a magazine. It was a *Time* magazine. He opened it and showed me the article.

Time was reporting that Fitzsimmons, Jackie Presser, and his father, Bill Presser, had been FBI informants since 1972. The article cited a declassified report filed by IRS agents that confirmed that the three Teamster officials had become informants to avoid secret indictments for bribery, embezzlement, and other charges.[39] Like Lou, I couldn't believe it. Maybe the Pressers, but not Fitzsimmons.

"I've heard rumors about Jackie Presser for years. That's one of the reasons I couldn't be around the jerk. But never in a thousand years would I have thought that Frank would rat on me and the people that put him in," Lou said, as he gulped another drink of his vodka on ice with a squeeze of lemon.

"I made some calls and my guys said the rats gave the feds evidence on Hoffa and some buddies. They did it to block Hoffa from taking out Frank. Then the

Presser rats went back to the feds and ratted on Frank. Frank turned and now he's a rat."

Lou squinted his eyes at me and said, "Cracker, we don't know what these motherfucking rats gave to the feds. Thank God I never told them what happened to Hoffa. I'm okay with union business and running this Inn. I'm okay except for the remodeling contracts. I've got to sweat that out."

Lou's feeling of betrayal reminded me of how Inman Averitt must have felt when his wife had wanted to betray him for a few pieces of silver. "Lou, I can't imagine how you feel. I've never had a close friend betray me like this." I wasn't sure how I could help him, so I just sat there drinking with him until the staff began showing up for work. Then we left.

Shortly after our conversation, Lou told me, while playing a round of golf, that he was going to retire and leave the inn and the Teamsters. He said he couldn't stand to see or meet any of the rats. Fitzsimmons had retired for health reasons early in 1981 and Lou didn't have to face him any longer at Teamster gatherings. However, Presser was still in office and was coming regularly to the inn for trustee meetings. Lou, squinting once more, growled, "The rumor is that Presser will be the next president of the union. I can't take that. I'm through."

In 1983, Jackie Presser was elected president of the International Brotherhood of Teamsters. By then, my friend Louie the Tailor had retired to his golf course in South Florida.

42. The Package

When I began my story, I described the delivery of a package to Mob Island. That package was meaningless to me until several years later when a friend of Lou's helped me put two and two together. Like most Americans, I had followed the news of the disappearance of Jimmy Hoffa. And like most Americans, I'd believed that he was dead and there was no shortage of suspects. Some suspected the Teamsters, because of his opposition to Fitzsimmons and several of the bosses of the Detroit local union where Hoffa began his rise to the presidency of the Teamsters. Others suspected the Mafia, who had given their word to the Nixon administration that Hoffa would not seek an office in the Teamsters if Nixon pardoned him.

The truth? All of the above. Let's go back and look at the historical facts as the news media has informed us, and what I know personally from my association with the members of both the Teamsters and the Chicago family of the Cosa Nostra.

Jimmy Hoffa served many years as president of the International Brotherhood of Teamsters. At that time in history, and probably so today, the Teamsters controlled the movement of all trucking on America's highways. In that position, as I have mentioned before, if the Teamsters refused to allow trucks to back up to Delta Airlines airplanes, then Delta could not fly. The same applied to all the other industries that depended on trucking, such as groceries, produce, steel, oil, automobile makers, etc. I would venture a guess that all major industries in this country would have stopped if the trucks had stopped. Hence, whoever controlled the trucks, controlled America.

When Hoffa was convicted of jury tampering by a federal court, he was sentenced to several years in prison, and he resigned as the Teamsters' boss. He went to prison, and five years later the Nixon administration was approached by a few loyalists of Hoffa who didn't want their old buddy to rot in prison. Somehow the issue arose in a meeting in San Diego between the new president of the Teamsters, Frank Fitzsimmons, and Louie the Tailor, and a few of his buddies.[40] Allegedly, as a result of that meeting, Nixon agreed to pardon Hoffa on the condition that he never return to authority in the Teamsters. According to my information and supported by news reports, the agreement with the Teamsters was backed up by the gentlemen of the Chicago Outfit. Not lost in this deal was the fact that Nixon received the union support and endorsement in Cook County (Chicago) in his next election.

As a result of this unholy alliance, Hoffa was pardoned and he returned to his home stomping grounds in the Detroit area. Unfortunately, he soon forgot his deal and those who'd made it happen. He began to campaign openly for the presidency of the Teamsters in opposition to Fitzsimmons. This angered my clients. Remember what I wrote earlier about how much their word mattered? Remember the Dean Martin feud? The Bay of Pigs? Well, multiply those by one thousand. Louie the Tailor and his confidants had given their word to President Nixon. Unlike most politicians of today, one's word meant everything then. It was sacred in their culture and was avenged with no limitations.

Eventually, Hoffa disappeared in 1975 after meeting a couple of union friends for lunch at a restaurant on the outskirts of Detroit. He was never seen alive again. No one was ever charged and no one officially knows anything. A few claim they were told that he was shot and cremated near the area where he was last seen. Others say he was buried in a few concrete pillars in New York and Chicago. But nothing has surfaced that comes close to the actual whereabouts of his remains. At least, not until now.

In 1975, I was well entrenched in the island lives of my clients from Chicago and their guests from Florida and the West Coast—more so, in their social lives than in my capacity as their attorney. My Southern 'drawl,' as they put it, was a novelty to them. However, their 'foreign' accent was amusing to me and my local friends and cohorts. But with all of that said, I did not know about the arrival of the package until sometime in 1976 when I heard Louie the Tailor describe the pickup at Saffold Field to a visiting friend from his hometown of Mount Pleasant, Illinois. I don't remember his name, but we enjoyed the evening at Dino's and a round of golf the next morning. To Lou's guest, being with a 'made' Chicago family member was a highlight moment in his life and one that he probably took to his grave with pride. Louie the Tailor was an icon in his neighborhood and any man who was invited to Mob Island to spend a weekend on the house with Lou gained untold respect back home.

After hearing of the delivery, I became inquisitive about the rest of the story. First, I wanted to ask Lou what was in the package and why its delivery was such an event that when he told it to his old friend, he described it in secrecy. In other words, he lowered his voice and looked around as to who could be hearing what he was about to say. Seeing that and hearing the low, cautious tone in which the story was told, I knew that the package contained something the other fellow would relate to, and I knew without a doubt, that it was not a drug delivery. As I said before, drugs were not tolerated on Mob Island. But for some unknown reason, this package was significant to Lou, his buddies, and eventually to me.

Weeks went by and my curiosity increased. In the world that I chose to live in, I knew that unbridled curiosity was neither healthy nor tolerated. However, being the young sprout from the South, I kept digging, believing that I would know when I had gone too far before I went too far. My narcissism allowed me to do this. Because of my training and education as a trial lawyer, I never doubted my ability to disappear in plain sight or believe that I was never there, or never heard what I knew I shouldn't have. All good trial lawyers have these attributes and proudly display them daily.

Law school at the University of Georgia was a breeding ground for young men (we had no women lawyers while I was there) who believed themselves to be future governors, legislators, and some like me, who believed that reaching the heights of a Clarence Darrow or an F. Lee Bailey was the ultimate success in life. Either way, we all were caught up in a narcissistic lifestyle, which defied truth and reality. But none of that mattered. We were all immortal, until the night we heard the news that Elvis had died. That woke a lot of us up, even me.

43. Irving

Irving Greenberg allegedly migrated from New York to Miami Beach during the late fifties. I first met him at Lou's cottage at the inn. Lou considered him a close friend; close enough that Irving could speak for Lou if Lou was unavailable. Irving was just the opposite of Lou. He was short, dumpy, wore glasses, was almost bald, and was a sloppy dresser. I understood that his wife had died a few years earlier and I never saw him with a woman. How Irving ended up at the Savannah Inn and Country Club, I do not know. He was a mystery. One I think I solved only recently.

I was always intrigued by Irving's presence at the inn and Lou's unwavering loyalty to him. At that time, the inn had three cottages. Lou resided in one cottage, the second cottage was the residence of the operational manager/director, and the third cottage belonged to Irving. The living arrangements made it clear that Irving was highly respected and an important member of Lou's inner circle.

Having Irving living at the inn was interesting. He was Jewish with a New York attitude living in a Baptist city. Club members did not like him and, with few exceptions, Irving didn't like them. He was a terrible golfer, a bad gin player, terrible sense of humor, and was somewhat reclusive, never leaving the island except to dine with Lou and me at Anna's Little Napoli. I was surprised Lou liked him. I was surprised I liked him.

Irving talked very little about his past. What information I had about Irving came from Lou. According to Lou, Irving had made some lucrative investments, acquiring condominium complexes located on Miami Beach. I knew Lou sometimes went to Irving when money issues came up. It was clear to me that Irving had a history with Lou, but neither would elaborate on the origins of their friendship. Only now can I surmise that their relationship was founded on mutual interests around gambling and other Mob-related activities.

While Irving Greenberg was by no means a prominent figure in the hearings of the *United States Senate: Special Committee to Investigate Organized Crime in Interstate Commerce* (better known as the Kefauver Hearings of 1950), he was referred to on a number of occasions. Irving was associated with the Sands Hotel in Miami Beach. According to the hearings, the Sands was run by a contingent of mobsters including Bennie Street, Dave Glass (both also were involved with the Grand Hotel in Miami Beach), 'Nig Rosen,' Max Weisberg, 'Big Al' Polizzi, and Herman Stark. Irving was listed as an associate, and he resided at the hotel. The Sands Hotel was used as a gathering spot for the Philadelphia Mob and other Mob families, as well as the headquarters for gambling operations located in neighboring hotels. In 1947, the Chicago Outfit boss, Tony Accardo, leased a home and moored his yacht in Miami Beach. It was in Miami Beach that Irving probably socialized with Accardo and other Outfit members who came to the Sands.[41]

While Irving wasn't particularly social, I quickly found out that he was the eyes and ears within the inn when he warned me to take care around the wife of one of the directors. The director's wife was an ex-Vegas dancer who enjoyed flirting with club members and, therefore, caused problems. I seemed to be her latest target, he said. I thanked him for the warning, but left a bit confused about why I'd been invited to Lou's cottage to meet Irving.

The confusion soon dissipated when I was invited to meet with the director to discuss a coming golf tournament while Lou was out of town. Arriving at the director's cottage, I knocked on the door and was surprised to hear his wife say it was unlocked and to come on in. I went in and found her standing at the bedroom door, topless. She was beautiful: tall, tanned, blonde, and stacked. Now I understood what Irving had been talking about. She told me to pour myself a drink and that her husband would be back shortly. She then dropped her miniskirt to the floor and as she turned her back to me, bent over and slowly picked up her skirt and tossed it into the bedroom. I stood there frozen, but my fear that her husband would return any moment made me realize that I needed to leave quickly. Irving had anticipated the scene and warned me. From that point on, I always took Irving's concerns seriously regarding women.

Shortly after my encounter with the beautiful Samantha, another incident took place, except this time it involved Lou. I walked into the golf club for my usual cup of coffee with Lou when I noticed Irving trying to get my attention. I waved to him and proceeded to Lou's table. As I sat down, I saw something I had never seen before. Lou's hand was shaking as he lifted his coffee cup. He looked like he hadn't slept the night before and he didn't respond to my morning greeting as I sat down across from him. I glanced over at Irving who quickly moved his hand across his throat in a gesture meant to silence me or tell me to leave Lou alone. This made me curious.

"Lou, what's wrong?"

"Nothin'," he replied while staring at his cup of coffee.

Now I was really worried. I nervously shifted in my seat and wondered what could be so serious that Lou, the unflappable mobster from Chicago, would be shaking in his boots. Wisely, I said nothing for a few minutes, waiting for Lou to tell his cracker lawyer what was wrong. By this time in our relationship, I had heard everything I shouldn't have heard. I was still under Omerta.

Lou looked over at me and said, "Cracker, somethin' happened that nobody can know about."

Now I wasn't just curious, but alarmed. "Lou, anything I can do?"

Lou stared at me for a few moments and then said, "You can keep quiet about what I'm gonna tell ya. If this gets out, I'm done here."

"Lou, I'm your lawyer and I'm under Omerta."

"Cracker, last night I left Dino's around 11:00. I was tired and planned to hit the sack. I was sleeping when I heard someone banging on my door. I got up ready for anything except this. I found a five-iron and opened the door. Maryann Right stood there naked. Her clothes were scattered around my porch."

"Lou, you're telling me Maryann was standing in your doorway naked as a jaybird?"

"Cracker, I tried to shut the door, but she pushed her way into the cottage."

"Did she say anything?"

"Yeah, plenty. She said I'm known for my big cock."

Now, my hand was shaking as I lifted my coffee cup. Maryann was a good-looking woman in her early forties. "Anything happen?"

"Yeah, she passed out on my couch."

"What! She passed out naked on your couch! Lou, what did you do?"

"Cracker, I wanted to get her out of my cottage as fast as I could. I thought about throwing her in the river, but I called one of my guys to get some blankets and get over here. We wrapped her up in a blanket, picked her clothes up, and the guy took her to one of the rooms."

"Lou, I know about her. Maryann has invited me over to her and Ted's house a couple of times. Lou, they wanted to do a threesome with me. Maryann said Ted likes to watch her have sex with other men."

Lou looked disgusted. "Cracker, I know you didn't go."

I figured this was not the time to joke with Lou, so I said, "Of course not."

"Cracker, there's a golden rule in this business. The owner don't fuck the wives of members. That destroys the whole club and we'd lose a helluva lot of money, and I'd lose the club."

"Lou, I understand. What do you want me to do?"

"Nothin' 'cause I'm gonna ban her."

"Lou, how do you ban the wife of a member without explaining it?"

"Cracker, I don't care. I don't want that whore coming here."

"Lou, let me talk to her and maybe no one will ever hear about this."

The next day I called her at her office and asked if I could come over there and chat with her for a few minutes. She misinterpreted my intent and gleefully said to come over anytime. Twenty minutes later I was sitting in her office drinking a cup of coffee.

"Maryann, I know what happened at Lou's cottage Saturday night."

She laughed and slid closer to me on the couch in her office. I got up and walked over to the window that overlooked one of Savannah's historic parks. Turning back to her, I frowned and said, "I hope you understand who Lou Rosanova is. The rumors are true about him. He makes people disappear. As your friend, I want you to understand that if anyone hears about what happened at his cottage, it will hurt Lou and you'll disappear. I'm telling you this as a friend. Don't play with him. You need to stay away from the club as much as you can and no matter what, stay away from Lou."

Maryann stopped smiling. I left hoping that this would be the end of it. I reported back to Lou and he thanked me. Irving later told me that Maryann and her husband were still soliciting men in the community, but not at the club. I guess Savannah's sex scene shifted to other venues.

I thought I knew Lou, but the Maryann episode taught me that a naked woman standing outside his door could frighten him more than a guy with a loaded gun. In Lou's conservative value system, another man's wife was off limits under any circumstances. He found the behavior of some of Savannah's most vaulted citizens to be disgraceful. Irving, on the other hand, found the behavior of Savannah's elite to be amusing.

Irving and I played golf once or twice a week, but only nine holes because we spent most of the afternoon looking for Irving's lost golf balls. It was during these afternoons riding in the golf cart, that I would ask Irving the things I could never ask Lou. It was through Irving that I came to understand more about the Kennedy assassination. He confirmed what I believed to be true: Roselli was involved in the actual assassination. When I told Irving that Lou and I had met recently with Roselli in New Orleans, he was concerned because Roselli was under investigation and Irving didn't want Lou or me to be casualties. After that conversation, I never saw Roselli again.

During this time, I became concerned that my discussions with Irving might be violating Omerta, so I went to ask Lou about it. Although I believed at the time that Irving was not a member of the Chicago Outfit, he was a trusted friend of Lou's, so there was some loosening of the rules regarding Omerta. Lou trusted both Irving and me and had no objections to my talking with Irving, although he forbade me from talking about any of my meetings with Accardo and Giancana. It was through Irving I'd learned about the Kennedy assassination and Lou's part-ownership in the Rancho La Costa Resort. His ownership in the resort was never made public that I was aware of.

While Lou and his buddies talked around Hoffa's demise, Irving gave me the whole story during a dinner at Anna's, but it started at Dino's. Through Lou, I was aware that a plane had landed at the airfield on the island. But that was all I knew at the time. Now, sitting at Dino's, I overheard Lefty and Charlie Greller discussing a package. Both had been drinking and I shouldn't have heard what I heard. Lou heard it as he walked up to the table. Clenching his fists and focusing his steely eyes on Lefty, he demanded Lefty shut up and get out of Dino's. Interestingly, I never saw Lefty again. Judging from Lou's reaction, I knew the package was special and something I shouldn't ask him about. It was through Irving that I knew just how special the package actually was.

As Irving and I ate our dinner and sipped our wine, I told him about what I had heard regarding the package.

"Bubba, tell me what you know."

"A plane flew into Saffold Field with a package and I know it wasn't dope. I also know that no one can speak about it. Now, what in the world could be in the package?"

"You're smart in not asking Lou about this. It's something Lou wouldn't want you to know. You would've figured it out, but I'll help you. It's between the two of us."

"It's something serious, isn't it, Irving? It's Hoffa, isn't it?"

"Yep. It was that son-of-a-bitch."

"Why bring him here?"

"Think about it, Bubba. This Inn belongs to the Teamsters and no one in their right mind would bring him to a Teamster property."

"Did Lefty and Charlie meet the plane and get the package?"

"Yep."

"Lou should never have used a van from the inn to pick up the package."

"He didn't. It was rented over in Beaufort and they dropped it off before dawn."

"So, you're telling me this package is actually Jimmy Hoffa?"

"Yep, what remains of him."

"What did they do with him?"

"Bubba, he's been planted under one of the holes and I think you know which one. Remember when you asked me why Lou and his buddies from Chicago pissed on that hole?"

"Yeah, I never understood that."

"Well, this was Lou and the Outfit's revenge. They liked being able to piss on Hoffa's grave whenever they played golf. He embarrassed them with the president. They'll never forget that."

I lifted my wine glass to drink, paused, and put it down. "Irving, that can't be all of it."

"Whadda' you mean?"

"He wasn't sent here just for revenge. I may look stupid, but I'm not dumb. What's the real reason?"

Irving slowly lifted his glass to drink, took a sip, and looked at me. "Bubba, you just won't let it go, will you?"

"No."

"Okay. Here's the story. It's for the same reason they chose this island. They can come and go as they please. They can control who comes and who leaves because of the airfield. No one takes a taxi and the inn doesn't always register guests. If the package is buried in New York or Chicago, you don't know how many eyes are watching or ears listening. The garbage man or taxi driver can be a fed. Hoffa's grave would have been known within weeks or months."

I thought about what Irving had just told me. "That makes sense. No one can come looking for Hoffa here without Lou knowing. So, pissing on Hoffa daily was just a benefit and not the reason."

"Bubba, it's a small island. Lou knows everyone who works at the inn. They're all born here. Think about it. That's why they got you for their mouthpiece and the face of the operation. They knew you weren't a fed and you're not with the Outfit. You know everyone here and they know you. That's why Lou put you under Omerta."

I finally understood why Lou was on the island. They could operate without any interference from the federal government or local law enforcement. I had to smile knowing that Lou had been able to banish the local police from the inn. "Irving, Lou out-tricked them all."

Irving laughed and nodded in agreement.

"Irving, who would've thought it; the most powerful mobster in the country, other than the Godfather, was operating on our little island along with the most powerful labor union in the world. And it was all under the nose of the FBI, Justice Department, and the aristocracy of Savannah, Georgia."

We raised our glasses and toasted Lou.

Epilogue
Pigeons

By 1983, it had become obvious, perhaps only to me, that my value to the Teamsters and Lou was diminishing. The Teamsters were trying to sell the property and Lou was making plans to retire to south Florida. He was tired of the island and tired of dealing with informants who used to be friends, like Fitzsimmons. Lou was smart enough to know that if he didn't retire from the Outfit now, his days were numbered. While he still trusted me and Irving, he was quietly removing himself from the Outfit.

Lou never said goodbye. One day, he just wasn't there. I heard he had retired to his golf course in south Miami. We never spoke again. I read that he passed away on March 29, 2003, in the La Costa area of California, leaving behind a wife, Dottie, and two children. I had to smile when I read his obituary in the *Savannah News*. They listed his occupation as an "investment consultant." Yes, that probably accurately described his occupation. But he was so much more than that.

The media called him an enforcer for the Mob. The Kefauver Crime Committee considered him one of three hundred members in organized crime. *Playboy* magazine insisted that he was a Chicago mobster. He was all of these, but more. Let's look at the undisputed facts.

Lou was present at La Costa when President Nixon made the deal with Accardo and Fitzsimmons in the pardoning of Hoffa. He had sit-downs regularly with Mafia dons on the island who flew to him. He was solely responsible f okaying the $92-million loan to the largest bank in Georgia. Consider the that Louie the Tailor got whatever he wanted done in Las Vegas. F' Hollywood entertainers deferred to Lou. If he wanted you to disapp disappeared.

Lou was a hybrid. He didn't have a traditional Mob title, such as 'Capo,' 'Enforcer,' or 'Soldier.' Maybe 'investment consultant' in his obituary was the most accurate label. His genius was that he stayed under the radar. I would guess that he may have been one of the most important and powerful figures in the Outfit, if not one of the most productive, during that era.

While everyone labeled him a mobster, he presented himself as a legitimate businessman, great golfer, and a recognized celebrity in Las Vegas, New Orleans, and Hollywood.

Although my relationship with Lou started as the classic attorney/client relationship, it changed over time; he became a good friend. Lou was a complex man. Yes, he could be ruthless, but he also was warm-hearted. He cared about his friends and their families. He funded youth programs on the island. He gave golf lessons to pros and free lessons to kids who came to the club. His contributions, both in money and support, to my defense of minorities and the poor in the Savannah community helped so many individuals and families. He personally funded the Matthew Washington, Gary Lively, Jerry Sprouse, and Robert Blake cases. Without his help, I may not have been successful in seeing justice served.

It was through my friendship with Lou that I discovered how much alike we all are when it comes down to it. Lou was Catholic and I was Baptist, but we both shared many of the same values. In fact, I would suggest that Lou was more conservative than most of the Baptists in Savannah. I was glad I had the opportunity to know him. I just wish I had been able to say goodbye.

As for me, I was running in the fast lane most of those years. By the time I crossed the finish line, I couldn't tell if I had won or lost; probably both. I won a lot of cases that mattered to me. Being able to free innocent individuals who were victims of an inept justice system was truly fulfilling. But it took its toll. These cases broke my heart.

Gary Lively sat in jail for eight years of his adult life waiting just for a trial. He was married with three children. By the time I found him and got him a trial, he had lost his family and every earthly possession he owned, even though he was found not guilty. Frank Williams was accused of raping a white woman and because he was black, he was denied a bond. After waiting several months, he was found not guilty. A month later he was arrested again for rape, denied a bond, and once again, found not guilty. Only this time he lost his job, his family, and home. He became one of Savannah's homeless alcoholics.

While winning unwinnable cases increased my reputation as one of the top criminal defense lawyers in Georgia, it came with a price. I lost my own family, my home, and friends who mattered to me. Savannahians could not understand how such a popular young lawyer, who was labeled a 'star on the rise,' would defend rapists, child molesters, murderers, and cop killers. My family and the community never understood that it was about the Constitution. It was about justice and due process. It was about making the police and court system accountable to all its citizens. I never asked to defend these cases. I begged judges to consider assigning the cases to other lawyers, but they wouldn't. Yet, when I used all available resources and my talents to represent my clients to the best of my ability, the judges, law enforcement, and community became angry with me. I realized that everyone hated good criminal defense attorneys until they needed one.

My life as a lawyer came crashing down. I did what every lawyer shouldn't do and co-mingled my practice's trust account with my personal account. While the amount was less than three hundred dollars, it was something I shouldn't have done, and I was disbarred in 1983. My problems increased in 1984 when a former client accused me of deducting too much in expenses from a settlement I'd worked on in 1983. I pled guilty and spent eight months in jail.

The downward spiral continued and in 1985, a former client of mine was indicted in Florida for grand theft involving an attempt to extort money in a business deal. While I wasn't directly involved in the extortion, the DA thought I should have done more to prevent the crime. I was put on probation. Florida and Georgia eventually granted me a full pardon. In 2006, I was accused of failing to disclose material facts in the sale of securities. I was sentenced to twenty-eight years in prison. On review, the sentence was deemed excessive and it was reduced to five years in prison. Now I could empathize with many of my former clients who had been incarcerated. I was on the wrong side of the law. Walking in their shoes gave me a new perspective on the toll incarceration takes on the individual, his family, and friends.

I left my law practice, but never left my need to see justice served. This time, I took my talents to the streets of Savannah. When I was practicing law, I came to realize that so many people who are incarcerated never have the opportunity to see their families because their loved ones have no transportation. I created 'Unto the Least of Mine,' a non-profit ministry that provided transportation to thousands of families in South Georgia so that they could visit their loved ones in state penitentiaries on Saturday mornings.

Through my interactions with the women using the prison visitation vans, I discovered that their children received few gifts at Christmas, so we created 'Inmates' Kids Christmas.' We received gift donations from the community and churches and over 1,800 children participated in the program. I then opened the Victory House near Forsyth Park and in Hilton Head, South Carolina. We housed over six hundred homeless men addicted to alcohol or drugs. It was eventually merged into the Savannah Gospel Mission.

Recently, I was in Savannah and took the opportunity to walk to the fountain in Forsyth Park. I recalled the last time I had been there; it seemed like a lifetime ago. I remembered feeding the pigeons and pondering how I had gone from president of the Savannah Jaycees, outstanding young man of the year, respected and successful attorney, to being spit on, my life threatened, and my reputation tarnished. I had been labeled a 'Mob lawyer' in an unforgiving Savannah society. I had agonized over the injustices I so often witnessed during that time. I remembered how tired and depressed I had been.

Dragging myself back to the present, I realized something was wrong, very wrong. I looked around and realized there were no pigeons to be seen in the park. They were gone, just like Lively, just like Williams, just like Louie the Tailor, and just like me. All gone, except for Hoffa, who is buried under a green on a private golf course on a Savannah Island.

Bubba and his daughter feeding pigeons on River Street

Good Luck Bubba

Big Lou

Notes

[1] For more information, see: O'Toole, Patricia (October 1998). "Dawn in the Garden of Good and Evil" in *Smithsonian*, 29(7); Colcock, Charles, O. F. Vedder, Frank Weldon. (2007). *History of Savannah GA: from its settlement to the close of the eighteenth century*. Athens, GA: Digital Library of Georgia.

[2] In 1972, Governor Jimmy Carter authorized an Executive Order establishing the creation of the Georgia Crime Information Center (GCIC). Georgia Department of Archives and History, Crime in Georgia, State Crime Commission, Dec. 1974.

[3] While Lou maintained that he had played for the Chicago Bears in the 1950s, we have not been able to verify this as factual.

[4] Raymond Floyd with Guy Yocom (2018). "Softening the Stare." Golf Digest. June, 69:6, 113–116. My wife and I stayed with the Ray and his late wife, Maria, on several occasions at their home in Miami.

[5] US Department of Labor, Form LM-2 Labor Organization Annual Report. File Number: 000-093. Dated 30 March 2012. For more information on the history of the Teamsters see: Witwer, David (2003). *Corruption and Reform in the Teamsters Union*. Urbana and Chicago: University of Illinois Press.

[6] Brill, Stephen (1978). *The Teamsters*. New York: Simon and Schuster.

[7] Molden, Dan (1992). *The Hoffa Wars: The Rise and Fall of Jimmy Hoffa*. New York. SPI Books.

[8] Lardner, George, Jr. and Kevin Klose (21 January 1983). "Gangland-style shooting in Chicago." *The Washington Post*.

[9] Roemer, William F. Jr. (1996). *Accardo: The Genuine Godfather*. New York: Random House Publishing Group.

[10] Brashler, William (1977). *The Don: The Life and Death of Sam Giancana*. New York: Harper and Row Publishers.

[11] Hammer, Richard (July 1974). "Playboy's History of Organized Crime: Part XII, the American Nightmare." *Playboy Magazine.*

[12] "Rosanova Sues ABC-TV, Quits Savannah Inn Post." *Savannah Morning News*, January 28, 1975, Section I, page 1.

[13] Gosch, Martin A., and Richard Hammer (1974). *The Last Testament of Lucky Luciano.* Boston: Little, Brown and Company.

[14] Marin, Carol (12 May 2004). "Requiem for a Chicago Mobster: William 'BJ' Jahoda." *Chicago Tribune.*

[15] Epperson, Wayne and Steve Crosby (27 June 1972). (123rd year issue 150, page 1A) Home edition. Headline: "Rosanova Denies Link with Crime." Staff photo by Walt Johnson. Original Caption: Rosanova discusses probe: "I'm not connected with organized crime." *Savannah Morning News.*

[16] Herbie was the main character (a VW Beetle) in the Walt Disney Production of *The Love Bug* released in December 1968.

[17] Godwin, John (1978). *Murder USA: The Ways We Kill Each Other.* New York: Ballantine Books.

[18] Sifakis, Carl, *The Mafia Encyclopedia*, 3ed., NY.

[19] Dale Eggeling Biography, Ladies Professional Golf Association. Retrieved from https://www.lpga.com/players/dale-eggeling/46284/bio.

[20] *Rosanova vs Playboy Magazine*, 411 F. Supp. 440 (1976); *Rosanova vs Playboy Magazine*, 580 F. 2d 859 (1978). July Issue, 1974 of *Playboy.* We also sued *Penthouse* for saying fundamentally the same thing *Playboy* had said about Lou.

[21] Molden, Dan (1992). *The Hoffa Wars: The Rise and Fall of Jimmy Hoffa.* New York. SPI Books.

[22] Barton, Tom (27 October 1999). "Hotel's Condo Plans Could Unearth an Old Mystery." *Savannah Morning News.* Editorial Page.

[23] Mayle, Mary Carr (16 November 2003). "Dowager Queen Reigns Again as Wilmington Plantation." *Savannah Morning News.* Accent Section Page: 1L.

[24] Maheu, Robert (1992). *Next to Hughes: Behind the Power and Tragic Downfall of Howard Hughes by His Closest Advisor.* New York: Harper Collins. See also: Rappleye, Charles and Ed Becker (1991). *All-American Mafioso: The Johnny Roselli Story.* New York: Doubleday.

[25] Bissell, Richard M., Jr. with Jonathan E. Lewis and Frances T. Pudlo (1996). *Reflections of a Cold War Warrior: From Yalta to the Bay of Pigs.* New Haven: Yale University Press.

[26] Kornbluh, Peter (1998). "Bay of Pigs Declassified: The Secret CIA Report on the Invasion of Cuba." New York: The New York Press.

[27] Bissell, Richard M., Jr. with Jonathan E. Lewis and Frances T. Pudlo (1996). *Reflections of a Cold War Warrior: From Yalta to the Bay of Pigs.* New Haven: Yale University Press.

[28] Schneider, Peter (2016). "Havana, Cuba: Contraband Capitalism and Criminal Organization in North America." *Italian American Review* 6:1 pp. 11–125.

[29] Rappleye, Charles and Ed Becker (1991). *All-American Mafioso: The Johnny Roselli Story.* New York: Doubleday.

[30] Heyman, C. David (1998). *RFK: A Candid Biography of Robert F. Kennedy.* New York: Dutton Adult.

[31] Neff, James (1989). "Mobbed Up: Jackie Presser's High-wire Life in the Teamsters, the Mafia, and the FBI." New York: *The Atlantic Monthly Press.*

[32] Turner, William and John Christian (2006). *The Assassination of Robert F. Kennedy.* 2nd edition. New York: Basic Books.

[33] O'Sullivan, Shane (2018). *Who Killed Bobby?: The Unsolved Murder of Robert F. Kennedy.* Reprint. New York: Skyhorse Publishing.

[34] Jackman, Tom (26 May 2018). "Who Killed Bobby Kennedy? His Son RFK, Jr. Doesn't Believe It was Sirhan Sirhan." *The Washington Post.*

[35] Ibid.

[36] *Floyd Brown vs State of Georgia*, 239 GA. 435, 238 S.E. 2d 21 (1977).

[37] *Joseph Blake vs State of Georgia*, 239 GA. 292, 236 S.E. 2d 637 (1977).

[38] *Savannah Morning News,* December 12, 1982, page 1A.

[39] "All the President's Teamsters." *Time Magazine.* 31 August 1981.

[40] Hammer, Richard (July 1974). "Playboy's History of Organized Crime: Part XII, the American Nightmare." *Playboy Magazine.*

[41] Investigation of Organized Crime in Interstate Commerce. Hearings before a Special Committee to Investigate Organized Crime in Interstate Commerce United States Senate, Eighty-First Congress, Second Session S. Res. 202, Part 1, Florida. 26 and 27 May; 13, 14 and 15 July; 9 and 10 August; 19, 22 and 26 September 1950.